AEROMODELLERS'
Handbook

AERO MODELLERS'
Handbook

<u>The</u> guide to the hobby
Second edition
LES NETHERTON

Patrick Stephens Limited

To Gran

First published under the title 'How to Go
Aeromodelling' in 1984
Paperback edition 1986
Second edition 1990

British Library Cataloguing in Publication Data

Netherton, Les
  Aero modellers' handbook.-2nd ed.
  1. Flying model aeroplanes
  I. Title
  629.133134

ISBN 1-85260-384-4

Patrick Stephens Limited, part of Thorsons, a division of the Collins Publishing Group,
has published authoritative, quality books for enthusiasts for more than twenty years.
During that time the company has established a reputation as one of the world's leading
publishers of books on aviation, maritime, military, model-making, motor cycling,
motoring, motor racing, railway and railway modelling subjects. Readers or authors
with suggestions for books they would like to see published are invited to write to: The
Editorial Director, Patrick Stephens Limited, Thorsons Publishing Group,
Wellingborough, Northants, NN8 2RQ.

Patrick Stephens is part of the
Thorsons Publishing Group, Wellingborough,
Northamptonshire, NN8 2RQ, England

Printed in Great Britain by The Bath Press, Bath, Avon

10 9 8 7 6 5 4 3 2 1

Contents

Introduction

It takes just a couple of seconds!

He is out somewhere with a brand new model. It could be a very expensive radio-controlled power model, or a very simple little balsa wood glider, or a rubber powered model. The first thing he does is hurl this model towards the sky! Up it goes for the first few seconds, then suddenly it turns and dives for the ground and *Wham*! Pieces fly, and it lies there a mangled heap. No model. No fun. It's all over. It took just a few seconds!

Oh, dear! Oh, dear! How often have you, or I, seen this sort of thing happen to the average kid, or his father trying to 'make it fly' for him. It's 'just a toy' so it *must* be easy! Of course he may get it to fly once, and then the next time out it simply will not, and then it ends as before. A wreck. So it goes on and on, they never get anything to fly, so 'all models are a stupid waste of time and money'. Then one day they see someone else flying a model, and really getting it to work properly. Now this is the 'right' model, and so they purchase one, vainly hoping that 'this one will work'. But this one too only takes a few seconds to turn it to 'matchsticks'. Then they really give up!

What is the answer? There simply is no answer, except to learn at least something about the whys and wherefores of model aircraft. With a little knowledge you get very indifferent flying out of a model. With a lot of knowledge you also need a certain amount of skill at building before you can hope to compete with the average good modeller. It really does take a lot of knowledge, and a good deal of practice with a few good models, before you can say that you are up to a standard high enough to enter international competitions, and this is a far cry from the poor fellow mentioned above, whose lack of ability stems only from his attitude towards all models; he will persist in thinking that they are 'just toys'. His futile, laughable efforts are the result.

Don't run away with the idea that that chap with the radio-controlled model knows everything. Some of them do, but the chap who has just purchased one, and has never flown any other model before, is usually hopeless at getting any other model to fly. So be careful how you regard these chaps, too many of them cannot help you with even a 'chuck' glider! Some of the model shop proprietors too, these days, haven't the vaguest idea of aeromodelling in any form either (some that I have come across do not even know how to keep rubber fresh).

So what do you do to learn about your favourite hobby? The first thing to do is to find the hobby shop which has people working there who really know quite a bit about all types of models, and who have flown them. Then there is your local library, which has a number of books on flight in general, and also has a supply of magazines on flying and modelling. Read all you can lay your hands on, but be very discerning, as there are quite a few books these days that are no more than picture books, that tell you just about nothing! The aeromodelling magazines from Britain and America have a lot of useful ideas, plans, and sound articles to help you. I recommend you buy the good books and magazines that suit your style of modelling. Later, when you know what you are doing, and do not need the books anymore, why not pass them on to the local chap who is just starting out in aeromodelling, and who is really keen.

Since forming a small club at the local school, I have found the average beginner woefully lacking in the knowledge needed to make even the simplest model, and how to fly it. Either they refuse to try to understand the books they *may* have read, or they never read any books or magazines, or what they have been told does not gel in their minds. Whatever the case may be, I just plunged ahead and tried to give them all the information they asked for, as they needed it, even though this may have started at the end, worked through the middle, and arrived at the beginning, or, as in some cases, more muddled than that. Somehow their minds put all this mixed-up information into a straightened-out form, starting at the beginning and working through to the end, so that now I have to remain on my mental toes when discussing anything. Naturally this is also more fun for me, because now I can talk to them as equals, we can get on with more advanced stuff, and I do have my fun heightened when one of them takes on a newcomer and goes ahead teaching *him* how to get it all right. There are always a few people from the club at my home, and the chat usually revolves around modelling and what we should try out next, and this brings out some knowledge that I thought I had completely forgotten. A bit of quiet thinking when they have gone brings to mind all the bits and pieces, and the next chat gets us moving along new lines.

Meanwhile I was trying to sort out all the little bits of information I had passed on during the day, and writing it all down, and sorting it all out in chronological order. Somehow the section on aerodynamics always came out as the last bit of information asked for. This has to be understood first, before the rest will follow, and so I have put it in at the beginning. As the starting and running of motors seems to be a perpetual headache for even quite experienced modellers, I have decided to place this section at the end of the book for easy reference. Let me say straight away that I have given you only the essence of the subject under any one heading, which is enough to get you well started. It is up to you to follow up this start by reading other books. For instance, the section on aerodynamics can be taken very much further: the aerofoils given are only a small fraction of what exists, and there is a vast amount of information covering this unfinished, fascinating subject. Propellers, too, have books covering their theory and construction, which will keep you busy for quite a while. There is virtually no end to what you can dig up to read about once you have started.

One thing I would like to point out is that what I have said about construction of the airframe should not be taken as the absolute gospel, and therefore unalterable. You can start wherever you like when building a model (provided that you have read the whole plan through carefully first), but what I have written should be regarded as a guide for someone starting his (or her) first model, of the particular type mentioned in each section. With experience, naturally, you will want to try out your own way of doing things.

You will not be able to digest everything in this book at one reading—there are too many facts to be absorbed. I therefore suggest that you read it through once and make a note of the things you can not remember clearly, then read these parts while you actually construct a model, or are trying to get your model to fly.

The section on aerodynamics (at the very beginning of the book), if properly understood, will be of tremendous help to you when you are on the flying field, and will eliminate any guessing, and wrong adjustments, thus saving you time and unnecessary repairs. You will find out, in time, that you are applying these principles throughout your entire modelling life, and are always looking out for new ways of understanding flight.

Acknowledgements

To my late dear Gran for her inspiration so many years ago and which is still as bright as ever; the Air Force and its instructors for the 'gen' they passed on; the many friends before and after the war, who shared so much of aeromodelling and its many facts (most of which are contained in this book), among whom Peter Cumming, Ian Stewart, and the late Derrick Copeland were outstanding aero-modellers and friends; the designers of many kit plans, their names long since forgotten, gave information which has stuck in my mind (one ten cent Japanese model of about 1935 taught me about warps in wings); my wife Lorna for 'holding the fort' while I got on with it all, and for all the photocopies she arranged that saved me hours of running around, and for her help with the photographs; my son Gordon, and daughter Janice for the loan of their very new cameras; Mom and Bill for their generous help when things got tough; and the young and not-so-young club members who 'make' Saturdays, and who helped with the photographs.

Chapter 1

Basic principles

'Learning the secret of flight from a bird is a good deal like learning the secret of magic from a magician. After you once know the trick and know what to look for, you see things that you did not notice when you did not know exactly what to look for!'—Orville Wright.

I am going to assume that you have looked at any number of pictures and can tell me quite a few things about each of the aircraft shown overleaf. When you look at each one, and think about it, there are innumerable legends conjured up by such names as Triplane, Supermarine, Bleriot, etc. Now, however, I want to ask you to look at them all together. Study them as a group. Think only of them as aircraft.

What do *you* think is the difference between any one aircraft and the rest?

Answer: there is no difference—they are all alike.

I agree with you, all aeroplanes look different, but that is because they were designed for specific purposes. For instance, the Handley Page Heracles was designed to carry passengers; the Supermarine S6B for racing, as was the Gee Bee; the Triplane for dogfighting; the Supermarine Stranraer for reconnaissance; the Hyperbipe and the two quaint aircraft with open framework, the Bristol Boxkite and Bleriot, came into existence to get their designer/pilots in the air to fly, fly, fly.

So what is it that they all have in common? Well, they all have a fuselage (body), wings, tailplane, rudder, and wheels. Where the balsa glider has no motor and propeller to pull it up in the air, it has a catapult to shoot it up, so they are all really equal, except for size, and this makes no difference at all, because each and every part, like the wings, and fuselage, serves exactly the same purpose, no matter what the size may be.

The most important things, though, that they all have in common, are the basic principles of flight, which cover all aircraft, including models. Make no mistake, a model aircraft is not a toy, it is the real thing in miniature in every respect. If you were to change *anything* on a flying model, to go against the principles of flight, the model would not fly. A full size aircraft would behave in exactly the same way. This becomes evident when you remember that a vast number of full-size aircraft, designed for many different purposes, have all, at some stage of their design, existed as models in wind tunnel tests.

The basic principles involved in designing the jetliner, the light aircraft, the glider, and your balsa glider, are identical. In fact these principles apply to all aircraft, of all sizes and shapes, old and new, that are subsonic.

Now besides those wings, fuselages, tailplanes, and rudders, what are the basic principles? These are not obvious like the shape of the wings, or fuselage, but are invisible. Their effects are only noticeable if we alter their built-in positions in the aircraft; it becomes unmanageable, or completely unflyable. These common basic principles are: the centre of gravity, the centre of pressure,

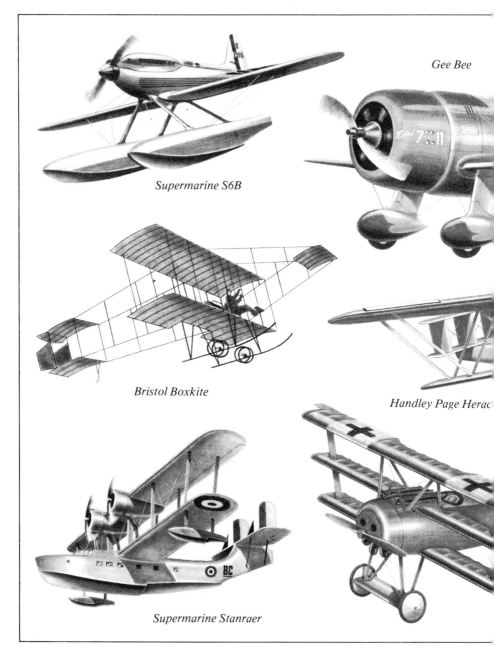

Gee Bee

Supermarine S6B

Bristol Boxkite

Handley Page Herac

Supermarine Stanraer

thrust, and drag—all unseen forces acting on all aircraft in flight. Here we will briefly see how they interact, and then explain each one in turn.

The centre of gravity, and the centre of pressure (or centre of lift), are arranged to fall on a vertical line through the wings. When an aircraft begins to move forward by the thrust, the drag starts at the same moment, air begins to flow over, and under, the wing, but this is insufficient to generate much lift, so

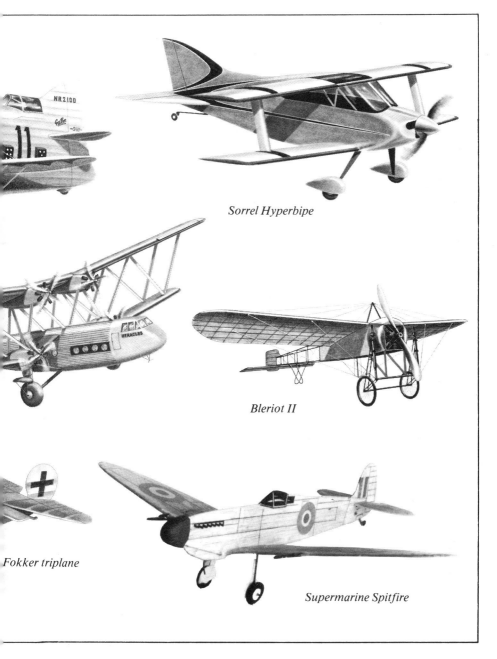

Sorrel Hyperbipe

Bleriot II

Fokker triplane

Supermarine Spitfire

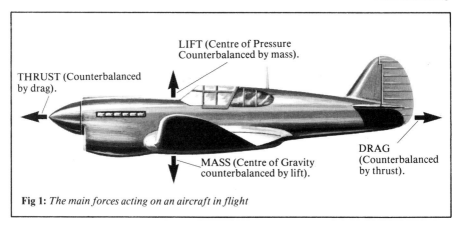

LIFT (Centre of Pressure
Counterbalanced by mass).

THRUST (Counterbalanced
by drag).

DRAG
(Counterbalanced
by thrust).

MASS (Centre of Gravity
counterbalanced by lift).

Fig 1: *The main forces acting on an aircraft in flight*

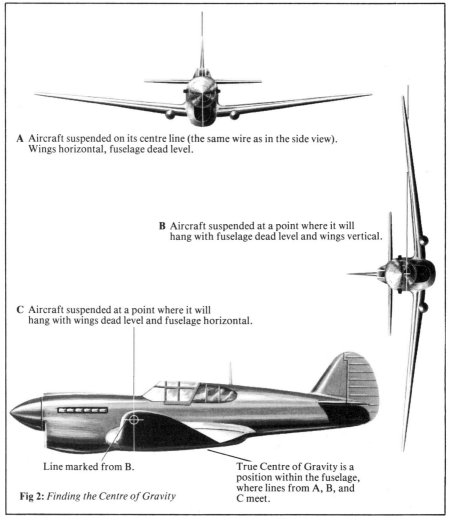

A Aircraft suspended on its centre line (the same wire as in the side view).
Wings horizontal, fuselage dead level.

B Aircraft suspended at a point where it will
hang with fuselage dead level and wings vertical.

C Aircraft suspended at a point where it will
hang with wings dead level and fuselage horizontal.

Line marked from B.

True Centre of Gravity is a
position within the fuselage,
where lines from A, B, and
C meet.

Fig 2: *Finding the Centre of Gravity*

the aircraft only runs along the ground with its tail down. Because the thrust is greater than the drag at this moment, the aircraft increases its speed, the airflow over the wing increases, drag increases, but at this point the lift is only enough to make the aircraft run with its tail up, but is still too weak to overcome the weight, or mass, to rise from the ground, and the aircraft will be at the point where it leaves the ground for a second, and then drops back again. As the thrust is further increased, the speed goes up, the airflow over the wing is increased, which increases the lift, and now the lift is greater than the mass, and the aircraft rises at a fixed rate, as drag is built up to the point where it is exactly counteracting the thrust. The aircraft is climbing into the sky. This is exactly what happens to the jetliner, the light aircraft, the glider being towed at an air display, and your balsa glider when you throw it. Yes, its thrust is the power you put into throwing, or catapulting, it.

Centre of gravity

Now let us take the centre of gravity and find it on an aircraft, and on the balsa glider. This simply means that all we have to do is find the point, in each of three axes, where the aircraft balances perfectly horizontally. If we mark each point on the aircraft, as we find it, we will see that it will show that this point, the centre of gravity, actually lies within the space in the fuselage, and cannot be seen; but its effect can be seen if its position is altered.

Centre of pressure

Centre of pressure is a point on the wing where the total lift generated in flight appears to be acting the strongest. This point should coincide with a line drawn vertically through the position of the centre of gravity. (Unfortunately this point does move backwards or forwards along the width of the wing, and causes problems.)

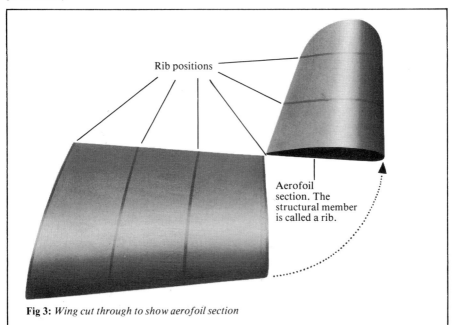

Rib positions

Aerofoil section. The structural member is called a rib.

Fig 3: *Wing cut through to show aerofoil section*

Let us stop here for a while, and take a closer look at what is happening to the air all around the wing. Now suppose we were to slice through the wing, we would find that it has a very special shape at this point. The shape of the cut edge is called an aerofoil section. First we will consider a flat sectioned wing. Because its front and back edge (called leading edge and trailing edge respectively) are blunt, the air does not flow smoothly, and this causes drag. It has been found, through experiment, that this shape does not give any lift until it is inclined to the airflow. Even then the lift is poor, and the drag, set up in the curled lines, is brought on rather soon. Simply rounding the edges only reduces drag slightly, but does nothing to improve the lift. If we add a curve to this flat wing section, the drag is increased slightly, but there is, at the same time, a definite increase in lift. Reducing the square leading edge to a curve, and tapering the trailing edge to a sharp edge, reduces the drag so that the wing can move slightly faster, and therefore produces slightly more lift. The drawback here is that no spars can be fitted, and so this type of wing can, usually, only be used on small models. It is quite adequate for this purpose. Most models, and all full size aircraft, need spars to strengthen the wing, and so we come to the section which can be fitted with spars, and because of its streamlined shape, produces very little drag. (All full size aircraft have this shape or variations of it.)

The highest point, on the top surface of the wing, is about $\frac{1}{3}$ back from the leading edge, and it is here that the point of greatest lift occurs. Briefly, this is what happens: the air meeting the leading edge splits into the top and bottom streams; the bottom stream simply adds a slight upwards pressure while the top stream has a longer route to follow, and so it speeds up to catch up with the bottom stream at the trailing edge. This speeding up causes a drop in pressure, all along the top surface, and because the air is moving at the greatest speed at the highest point, we find that the drop in pressure is greatest at this point—the centre of pressure. It is this drop in pressure that causes the wing to rise, in order to try to fill the low pressure area, and so produce its lift. This lift, from the top surface, is roughly twice as much as that generated by the lower surface.

Angle of incidence

There are two ways in which the same wing can be made to give more lift. The first is to increase the angle of incidence at the same speed, which simply means to raise the leading edge of the wing by a degree or two. The second method is to leave the wing at its original angle of incidence, and speed up its movement through the air. These methods can be used singly, or in combination. Of course the drag is also increased, but fortunately lift is always greater than drag, at low angles of incidence. At very high angles of attack we find a very different story. In this case there is still a certain amount of lift, but the drag has increased out of proportion. This condition is found in, or very near, what is known as the stall. It is essential that you understand exactly what the stall is, because any aircraft is prone to it, to a greater, or lesser, degree.

The stall

When the angle of attack reaches about 15 degrees relative to the airflow around the wing, and the wing begins to drop, it is said to be stalled. This means that the smooth airflow over the top surface has separated from the surface and broken up, causing eddies, or turbulence, that give rise to tremendous drag. The lift is

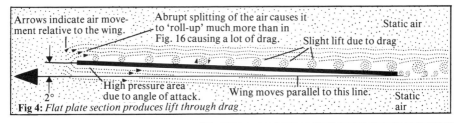

Arrows indicate air movement relative to the wing.

Abrupt splitting of the air causes it to 'roll-up' much more than in Fig. 16 causing a lot of drag.

Static air

Slight lift due to drag

High pressure area due to angle of attack.

Wing moves parallel to this line.

Static air

2°

Fig 4: *Flat plate section produces lift through drag*

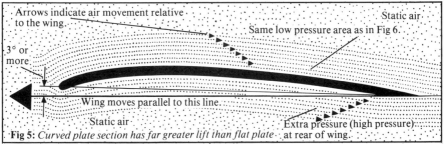

Arrows indicate air movement relative to the wing.

Static air

Same low pressure area as in Fig 6.

3° or more

Wing moves parallel to this line.

Static air

Extra pressure (high pressure) at rear of wing.

Fig 5: *Curved plate section has far greater lift than flat plate*

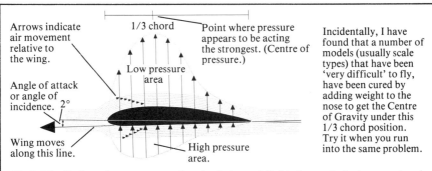

Arrows indicate air movement relative to the wing.

1/3 chord

Point where pressure appears to be acting the strongest. (Centre of pressure.)

Low pressure area

Angle of attack or angle of incidence. 2°

Wing moves along this line.

High pressure area.

Incidentally, I have found that a number of models (usually scale types) that have been 'very difficult' to fly, have been cured by adding weight to the nose to get the Centre of Gravity under this 1/3 chord position. Try it when you run into the same problem.

Fig 6: *Distribution of pressure around a wing in normal flight. Arrows indicate amount and position of pressure change.*

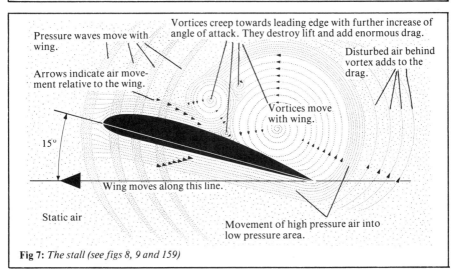

Vortices creep towards leading edge with further increase of angle of attack. They destroy lift and add enormous drag.

Pressure waves move with wing.

Disturbed air behind vortex adds to the drag.

Arrows indicate air movement relative to the wing.

Vortices move with wing.

15°

Wing moves along this line.

Static air

Movement of high pressure air into low pressure area.

Fig 7: *The stall (see figs 8, 9 and 159)*

still intact along the front portion of the wing, but its total is considerably reduced, and the wing drops. If the aircraft's nose is raised slowly, then the stall is usually gentle; should the nose be suddenly jerked up, then the stall can be vicious, and can easily lead to a spin. Incidentally, note that the line drawn through the centre of the leading edge, and trailing edge, is the line to use in order to measure the angle of incidence of the wing aerofoil, never the under-surface of the wing. Here are examples to show that the airflow relative to the wing is the thing to remember about the stall. The aircraft performing a loop is not stalling, even though its nose is pointing vertically up. The aircraft in a high speed dive is also not stalling, but if the aircraft is pulled out of the dive too suddenly, then it could stall at this point. The result, if very near the ground, could be that the aircraft would hit the ground dead flat. If the sharp pull-out is performed higher up, the aircraft would still stall, and then probably flip into a spin. If not high enough to recover from the spin, it would crash nose first while spinning. During level flight while cruising, or climbing with full power, if the motor should suddenly fail, and action is not taken immediately to get the nose down, to maintain the airflow over the wing, the wing will again stall.

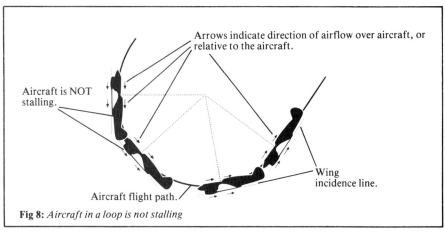

Fig 8: *Aircraft in a loop is not stalling*

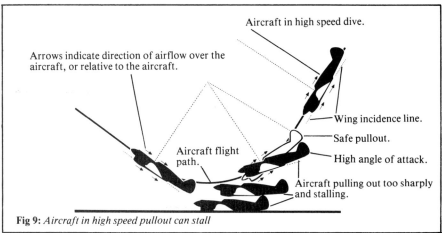

Fig 9: *Aircraft in high speed pullout can stall*

Thrust

This is the next force we should look at; and later on we will deal with its effects as far as models are concerned. In full size aircraft there are two sources of power, the internal combustion engine (petrol engine) and jet engines (turbofans and turbo-prop engines work on basically the same principles), and these use paraffin for fuel. Model aircraft use glowplug and 'diesel' motors, carbon dioxide motors, electric motors, rubber motors, rocket motors (known as Jetex which are now out of production, unfortunately), and pulse-jet motors. Now all of these power sources, except the jets and rockets, turn propellers to give the necessary thrust. The propeller can best be thought of as a rotating wing, set at a large angle of attack to its hub. It, too, has an aerofoil section exactly like a wing, and this produces lift in exactly the same manner, thereby adding to its screwing effect in the air, which is very much like a screw being turned into wood. The forward movement of the propeller traces out a spiral path at the tip, and one revolution on this path denotes the pitch, and this measurement, together with the diameter measurement, make up the necessary information we need to know about the propeller, when matching it to the motor, and aircraft. The thrust a propeller produces must be sufficient to overcome the weight of a particular aircraft, and size is relatively unimportant.

All propellers suffer from three important drawbacks, and these are *slip, torque,* and *gyroscopic force.*

Slip The propeller should travel forward a certain distance each time it revolves due to the angle of pitch of each blade. Because the air is a fluid, the propeller can not get sufficient 'grip' on it so it 'slips' slightly, and the distance it travels forward is less than it should be.

The **gyroscopic force** that a propeller produces is bound up with its mass, and the speed at which it revolves. The net result is that this force, if strong enough, affects the aircraft when it turns. For instance, looking at an aircraft from the front, and supposing the propeller is turning anti-clockwise, and the aircraft is banking to its **left**, or port, then the effect of this force is to keep the nose **up** during the turn. Conversely, when this same aircraft turns to its **right**, or starboard, this force will be pulling the nose **down**. If the propeller is turning clockwise the nose will tend to drop in the left turn, and rise in the right turn.

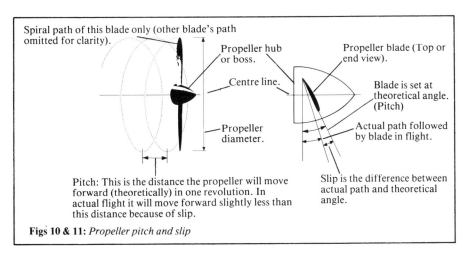

Spiral path of this blade only (other blade's path omitted for clarity).

Propeller hub or boss.

Propeller blade (Top or end view).

Centre line.

Blade is set at theoretical angle. (Pitch)

Propeller diameter.

Actual path followed by blade in flight.

Pitch: This is the distance the propeller will move forward (theoretically) in one revolution. In actual flight it will move forward slightly less than this distance because of slip.

Slip is the difference between actual path and theoretical angle.

Figs 10 & 11: *Propeller pitch and slip*

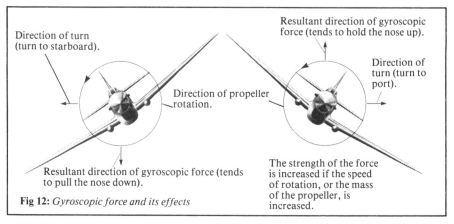

Fig 12: *Gyroscopic force and its effects*

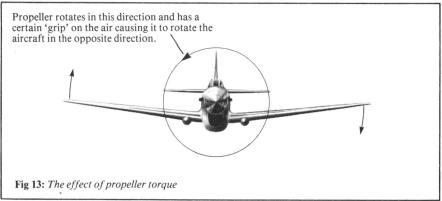

Fig 13: *The effect of propeller torque*

Torque is a reaction to the propeller's rotation, which affects the flight path, by rotating the aircraft about its longitudinal axis, in the opposite direction to the propeller's rotation.

Drag

The last unseen force is drag, which exists as induced, form, parasitic, and skin drag.

Induced drag is bound up with the wing, and lift, and this is by far the most important of the four types. The high pressure area under the wing slips around the wingtip, to try to fill the low pressure area on the top surface, and this turbulence becomes a vortex at the actual wingtip. All three actions produce a drag on the wing, and they all become more pronounced as the angle of attack is increased, to produce more lift.

Parasitic drag is brought on by such things as undercarriage struts, wheels, fuselage, bracing wires, external fittings, etc, which are all non-lifting structures. These should be cut down as far as possible.

Form drag is associated with the shape of a component, or fitting. For instance, undercarriage legs that are fixed are less drag-producing if the round strut has a streamlined outer shell covering it. Even bracing wires for the old time biplanes were of streamlined section, to reduce the drag that would have been caused by a round wire.

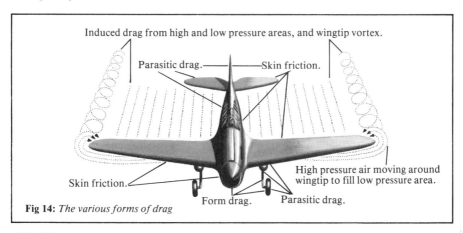

Fig 14: *The various forms of drag*

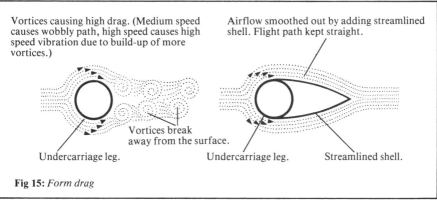

Fig 15: *Form drag*

Skin drag is brought about by the fact that the molecules of air adhere to the entire surface of the aircraft, and the next microscopic layers rub against each other. This rubbing diminishes the further out we get from the actual surface. Although this is the least offensive of all, it is still there to add to the total effect of drag. It is aggravated by a rough surface left on any part, and is reduced by a highly polished surface.

The total drag is, therefore, quite a considerable waste of power, and that is why it has to be cut down at every opportunity. Let me give you an example of how much power it takes to overcome drag. The Spitfire of the Second World War, at the beginning of its service career, had an engine of 1,030 hp which gave it a top speed of 365 mph with a maximum loaded weight of 6,317 lbs. This means that the drag it produced at that weight, or mass, allowed it to travel at 365 mph on 1,030 hp. By the end of the war its hp had risen to 2,050 and speed to 454 mph at 9,200 lbs. This was the Mk XIVe. Drag was virtually the same as the original, the nose had been slightly lengthened, the wing was as the original, fuselage was cut down, and the rudder was slightly altered, Practically the same aircraft as the original! Mass though had gone up by 2,183 lbs, or about $\frac{1}{3}$. So it had gained an extra 83 mph for nearly twice the hp. If the wing aerofoil section could have been altered at the same time, its speed would have been pushed up by quite a bit more than 83 mph!

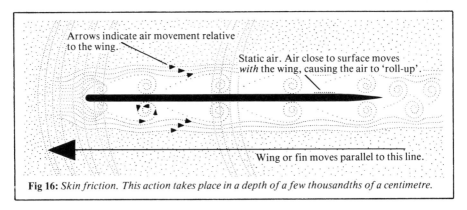

Fig 16: *Skin friction. This action takes place in a depth of a few thousandths of a centimetre.*

To return to our full size aircraft, and the balsa glider. These two have exactly the same problems with all the drag types we have discussed. In fact, there is no aircraft, model or full size, old or new, that does not have its performance affected by all the drag variations to a certain degree.

We have been talking in broad terms so far, and now we cannot see the whole picture of aircraft, and all the unseen forces, until we have gone quite a bit further into this fascinating subject. Don't forget that it all still covers the balsa glider, the light aircraft, and the full size glider; any full size aircraft and model in fact! Autogiros and helicopters use some of the principles of course, but have a completely different 'personality', so they will not be included from here on, and have purposely been left out.

The wing or mainplane

This is the most important part of all aircraft. All designing is started at this point, and the size, shape, and proportions of everything else, stem from the layout and design of the wing. Let's examine wings carefully, because the more we know, the better we can appreciate what is happening at any stage, and so we will be better able to sort out any problems we will come across later.

Aerofoils

The performance characteristics of any model you will build, are bound up inextricably with the type of aerofoil the designer has chosen for the model. This is a subject you should study very faithfully, if you wish to understand your models properly. As it is such a vast subject, I can only give you a very brief outline of it here.

The section used on the catapult gliders shown in this book is known as 'flat plate', and is quite adequate for the size of model. It could be improved by a slight curve to its present shape, by simply making the slot in the fuselage slightly curved, and gluing the wing to this curve. (In this case it would involve you in a tricky bit of construction for your first model, and has purposely been avoided.) The increase in performance, though, is quite dramatic, as the model has about twice the flying time of the flat plate section shown. Not unnaturally, this curved 'flat plate' is known as 'curved plate' section, provided the leading edge is rounded, and the trailing edge is brought to a point as shown. On a model of this size the curve can be made as the arc of a circle, and the effect on the flight will be very slightly less than a truly designed aerofoil, but it will help you to realise the tremendous increase in performance to be gained from even this alteration to the wing.

This aerofoil, though, has a big limitation if we try to use it on larger models, because we can not get spars into it that will be deep enough to give the wing the strength it will need. As spars are vital to the strength of a wing, designers have worked out aerofoil sections that will accept spars, and produce lift, with a minimum of drag. This means, too, that there are a variety of aerofoils to choose from, as each designer has worked out his own particular theory, and then these aerofoils are also altered by 'thinning' them. Each aerofoil is worked out very carefully and it is, therefore, wise to stick to the shape very accurately, rather than just sketch out what you *think* is an aerofoil. It is also best to use what is called a table of ordinates if you want to scale up a particular aerofoil. As all this needs a lot of explanation, I suggest you find a book devoted to this particular subject if you wish to go into it more deeply but I will give you some idea of the types of aerofoils you will come across in modelling. NACA 6712 is not used very much except, possibly, by some experimenters, and has to be exceptionally well made to work properly.

Of course, these are by no means all the aerofoils, but do serve to give you some idea of how much they vary, and the purpose they fulfil. It would be futile, for instance, to use, say, NACA 6512 on a control line stunter, or NACA 0015 on a thermal soaring glider. Generally, thicker aerofoils are used for slow flying models, and thin aerofoils are used for faster models. Undercambered aerofoils are usually considered to have more lift than flat undersurfaced aerofoils, and fly more slowly. Centre of pressure movement is greater on these aerofoils than on others, and is least on bi-convexed and reflexed trailing edge types. Incidentally, the bi-convexed type, shown above, will produce lift at 0 degrees incidence, and produces no lift at about –1 degree.

Aspect ratio

The outline shape, and its proportions, have a strong bearing on what we are looking for from a wing. The squat outline shape, as in the diagrams, is generally seen on aircraft designed for aerobatics, and the long narrow shapes are more generally used on gliders. As you can see, there is a relationship between length and width, and this is called its Aspect Ratio, which is abbreviated to AR. So if we take the length, or span, of a wing, in centimetres, and the chord (which is the width) also in centimetres, and *divide* the chord into the span, we get its aspect ratio. (On tapered, or eliptical wings, the mean, or average, chord is used.) If we *multiply* the span by the chord, we get the wing area.

Example Span: 35 cm. Chord: 7 cm. $\frac{35}{7} = \frac{5}{1}$ This is written 5:1, so the aspect ratio is 5:1. Wing area is $35 \times 7 = 245$ sq cm.

A wing of, say 5:1 is used in full size aircraft for fighters, because the span can be kept short and strong, for strenuous use in aerobatics. The area of the wing can also be more concentrated. The main snag to this, the lowest AR, is that the wingtips are broad, and this gives rise to a broad vortex at the tips. To make the vortex smaller, we taper the wing, or its tips. The Spitfire of the Second World War had a very broad wing that, because of its eliptical outline, had a very small tip, and consequently a tip vortex as small as possible. Generally, all the low AR wings on fighter aircraft of that war had a taper towards the tip, which not only cut down the vortex, but helped the rate of roll.

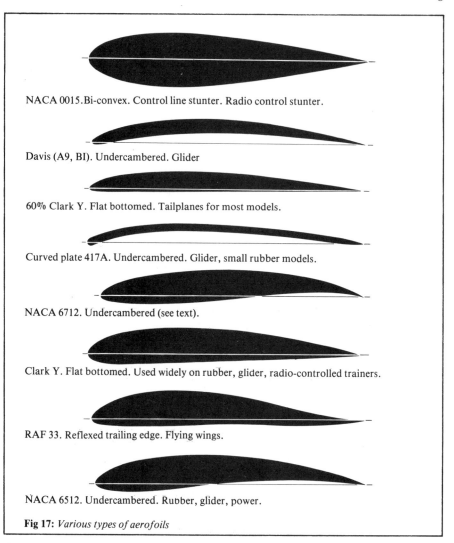

NACA 0015.Bi-convex. Control line stunter. Radio control stunter.

Davis (A9, BI). Undercambered. Glider

60% Clark Y. Flat bottomed. Tailplanes for most models.

Curved plate 417A. Undercambered. Glider, small rubber models.

NACA 6712. Undercambered (see text).

Clark Y. Flat bottomed. Used widely on rubber, glider, radio-controlled trainers.

RAF 33. Reflexed trailing edge. Flying wings.

NACA 6512. Undercambered. Rubber, glider, power.

Fig 17: *Various types of aerofoils*

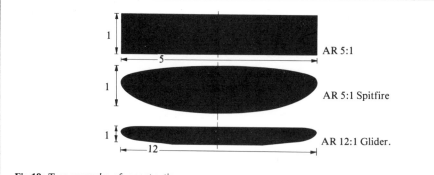

Fig 18: *Two examples of aspect ratio*

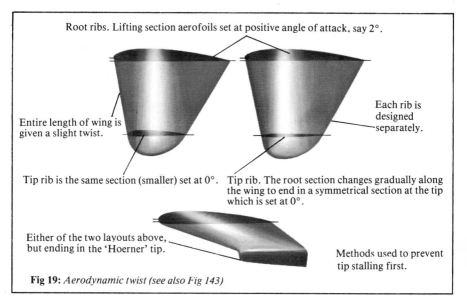

Root ribs. Lifting section aerofoils set at positive angle of attack, say 2°.

Entire length of wing is given a slight twist.

Each rib is designed separately.

Tip rib is the same section (smaller) set at 0°.

Tip rib. The root section changes gradually along the wing to end in a symmetrical section at the tip which is set at 0°.

Either of the two layouts above, but ending in the 'Hoerner' tip.

Methods used to prevent tip stalling first.

Fig 19: *Aerodynamic twist (see also Fig 143)*

Gliders, or sailplanes, have a high AR of about 12:1 or more, but seldom, if ever, much less. Aerodynamically, these are far more efficient proportions, but they suffer mechanically because the long spars can flex and twist more easily than short ones. Here, too, the wingtips are kept small, again because of the vortex, and nearly all gliders have tapered, or partly tapered wings.

Aerodynamic twist

This is a slight twist given to the length of the wing, from its root (where it joins the fuselage) to the tip. The root is set at, say, 2 degrees angle of incidence, and the tip is set at, say, 1 degree angle of incidence. Both wing halves are done this way, and this twist is called 'washout'. Other methods used are: a progressive change in the shape of the aerofoil, from a lifting section at the root, to a non-lifting section at the tip; or Hoerner tip to the wings, which is a specially curved down wingtip, that cuts through and blocks the high pressure from the lower surface curling around the tip, and entering the low pressure area on the top surface. All these ideas exist to break up that tip vortex, which gives no lift at the tip, and plenty of drag. When the wing is approaching the stall angle, it has been found that, on a wing without the twist, or other device, the tip vortex starts to grow from the tip, towards the root, on both wings. Sooner or later, with both wings losing more and more lift, one of them is going to lose too much, and that wing is going to drop. When that happens the aircraft stalls, and spins. When one, or other, of the above devices is used, and a wing nears the stall, the centre portion of the wing stalls, but the wingtip, and the outer portion, remain flying normally. The result is that the aircraft merely drops its nose back to a cruising, level position; the airflow, over the centre portion, rapidly returns to normal.

Dihedral

When viewed from the front or back, most aircraft will be seen to have their wings flat, or very slightly raised at the tips. This raising of the tips is known as dihedral. On a few aircraft the wingtips are lowered, and this is known as

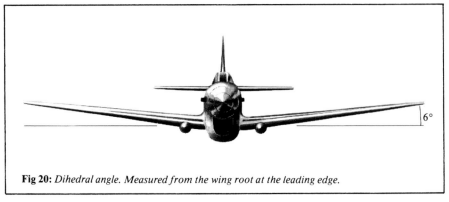

Fig 20: *Dihedral angle. Measured from the wing root at the leading edge.*

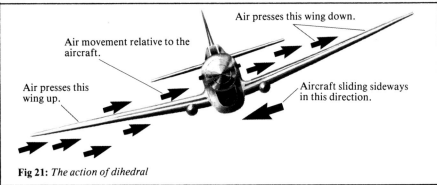

Fig 21: *The action of dihedral*

anhedral. We will not concern ourselves with this, because we have no use for it in modelling. Dihedral confers lateral stability to all aircraft in the rolling axis. Most full size aircraft utilise it, even if only a degree or two is used, but this is sufficient to make the aircraft less tiring to fly, because the pilot does not have to make all those tiny corrections to keep the wings level. It is done for him at the designing stage. In models, we find no dihedral necessary for control line, and in fully aerobatic radio-controlled models, dihedral makes rolling and inverted flight very difficult, so it is not used. Free flight models will not live out their first flight without it! In fact, models can use up to 20 degrees of dihedral on each wing half, but at this amount the loss of lift is very noticeable, and the stability in the rolling plane becomes poor. Anything from 5 degrees, up to about 10 degrees, on each wing half works well for most applications.

The action dihedral imparts is this: while in level flight, a gust of wind may strike the side of an aircraft, to tip it so that it is sliding sideways, and downwards. Now, because it is sliding to the side, the air will move over the aircraft towards the other side, and, in so doing, will strike the underside of the near wing, and the top side of the far wing, and this combined pressure rights the aircraft. A flat wing, under the same circumstances, would simply continue to slide sideways.

Tailplane or stabiliser
A wing, by itself, is very unstable in flight. If you take a piece of fairly stiff paper or thin card, and fold it flat, cut out half a wing shape, open it out, set it

at a slight dihedral angle, remove any twists, and carefully launch it to fly, you will find that it simple flutters around in a rotating motion until it lands. Any wing will do this because its centre of gravity is behind the centre of pressure; the centre of gravity pulling the back of the wing down, and the centre of pressure pulling the front of the wing up, so causing it to rotate.

If you were to take a wing from a model, and try to balance it with Plasticine to make it fly properly, you would find that it is still very tricky. It may glide well for a second or two, but then it will either rear up and stall, or it will tend to 'duck under' and fly upside down for a second or two—it is still very unstable. The problem is the forward and backward movement of the centre of pressure from its normal position. This movement will depend on the type of aerofoil the wing has; some aerofoils have a greater movement of the centre of pressure than others, and this movement is forward when the angle of attack is increased, and rearward when the angle is decreased.

The 'flying wing', as it is called, uses a number of design ideas to overcome this problem, but in so doing, it does lose a lot of the wing's efficiency, and so is seldom used. It is, however, always fascinating to see flying, and will always entice those of us who love to experiment.

So, in order to stabilise the wing we have to follow the birds, and add a small wing, at a set distance, behind the mainplane. Now, when the wing increases its angle of attack, so does the stabiliser, and this tends to keep the wing at a constant angle to the airflow. Similarly, if the wing decreases its angle of attack, so does the stabiliser, and brings the wing back to its usual angle.

The tailplane shape can be almost anything the designer wishes, but its area is usually calculated properly to suit the type of aircraft in mind. Its distance from the mainplane, and the angle it makes relative to the mainplane, are incorporated in the fuselage design, which, in turn, is based on the total concept of the mainplane.

Fuselage

All aircraft plans show (or should) a straight line running through the side view of the fuselage, this being the datum line, around which all designing is done. The wing is set either parallel to it, or at a positive angle, say 2 degrees, or slightly more, of incidence. The tailplane can be set at 0 degrees, or a positive, or negative angle, depending on the design. Whatever angles have been decided upon, there is never less than 2 degrees difference between the mainplane and tailplane, on any free flight model, because anything less leads to an unstable tendency, whereby the nose has a nasty habit of suddenly 'tucking under', as explained above. Aerobatic control line, and radio-controlled aerobatic models, because they are under direct control, are designed with the mainplane and tailplane set at 0 degrees, together with a symmetrical section aerofoil on both wings. This is to allow them to fly inverted, as well as upright. Nose, and tail moment arms, are also a factor in the type of model that is being designed. The chord of the mainplane is the measure used, and this is stepped off, from the centre of pressure point, towards the nose and tail.

Rudder

This is essential to steer the aircraft in a straight, or curved, path and, on full size aircraft, is used in conjunction with the ailerons, to bank correctly, to steer without skid or slip. Free flight models, with their generous dihedral, do this

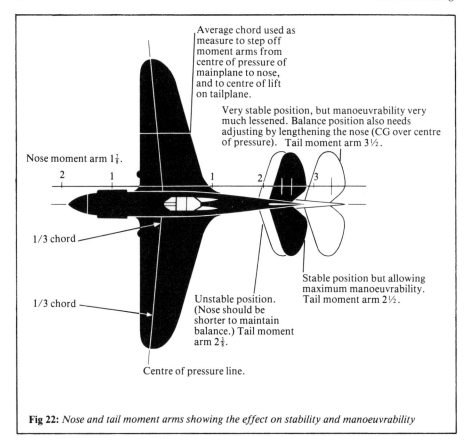

Average chord used as measure to step off moment arms from centre of pressure of mainplane to nose, and to centre of lift on tailplane.

Very stable position, but manoeuvrability very much lessened. Balance position also needs adjusting by lengthening the nose (CG over centre of pressure). Tail moment arm $3\frac{1}{2}$.

Nose moment arm $1\frac{7}{8}$.

1/3 chord

1/3 chord

Stable position but allowing maximum manoeuvrability. Tail moment arm $2\frac{1}{2}$.

Unstable position. (Nose should be shorter to maintain balance.) Tail moment arm $2\frac{1}{8}$.

Centre of pressure line.

Fig 22: *Nose and tail moment arms showing the effect on stability and manoeuvrability*

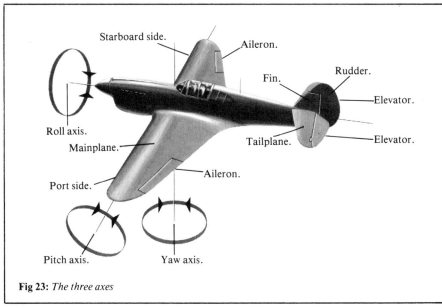

Starboard side.

Aileron.

Rudder.

Fin.

Elevator.

Roll axis.

Mainplane.

Tailplane.

Elevator.

Port side.

Aileron.

Pitch axis.   Yaw axis.

Fig 23: *The three axes*

automatically (if they are properly trimmed). The shape of the rudder is usually made to suit the style of the rest of the design, but the area is worked out from the side area of the fuselage, together with the amount of dihedral used.

Undercarriage
This is arranged in several ways, the commonest being the two main wheels and a tail wheel, or skid, and two main wheels and a nose wheel. In the former, the main wheels are situated (vertically) just ahead of the centre of gravity. In the latter, the main wheels are just behind the centre of gravity. In both cases, the legs of the undercarriage should, obviously, be long enough to allow the propeller to clear the ground with a reasonable margin, and should be spaced, in front view, to maintain lateral stability when landing or taking off.

Aircraft controls
Now let us look at the controls that are built into full size aircraft, and see how they are used. Basically these are: the rudder, elevators, ailerons, and flaps. We will take an aircraft, it does not matter what type, and imagine three lines passing through it at the same point. Taking one line at a time, imagine the aircraft being able to rotate about this line, in either of two directions, while it is in flight. The ailerons, working in opposite directions, control it in the roll axis; the elevators, working together in the same direction, the pitch; and the rudder, the yaw. Any one of these controls reacts exactly the same way as any other, to the effects of the air moving over it. Here, you should first imagine you are looking at it from the side, and then imagine you are looking at the same thing from above, as it makes no difference—the effect is always the same. When the movable surface is deflected to one side, the movement of the entire wing, or rudder, is in the opposite direction. Now it should be fairly easy to see how the ailerons, working in opposite directions, can tilt an aircraft to one side, or the other, depending on how they are used, and how the rudder yaws an aircraft, to one side, or the other, and how the elevators lower the tail to point the nose up, or raise the tail to point the nose down. There are two side effects that occur. One is that when the ailerons are used, the side on which an aileron goes down, tends to lag behind the other side, and the aircraft yaws slightly. The other is that when the rudder is applied, the aircraft yaws, and therefore one wing moves more slowly, and so drops slightly, while the other moves slightly faster, and so it rises slightly, and the aircraft banks gently.

The flaps are used to increase lift when taking off and landing. In both cases the drag is increased too. The take-off is affected by decreasing the length of the take-off run; and the final approach flight path is much steeper, and slower, than without flaps. The landing run is also decreased noticeably.

Two more controls are very interesting in their effect. The first is the slat, which is a very narrow auxiliary wing, attached within the wing leading edge, but is separated by a gap called the slot. Some slats are fixed, and some are automatic, but however they are worked their effect is to control the airflow over the wing slightly before the stall angle is reached, and during the stall, so that the portion of the wing directly behind the slat remains unstalled, and continues to provide lift. The aircraft can continue flying much more slowly, under complete control, with the nose up at a steep angle. This was used, for example, on the famous Fieseler Storch in the Second World War amongst others. The second is the drooped leading edge, combined with a lowered flap,

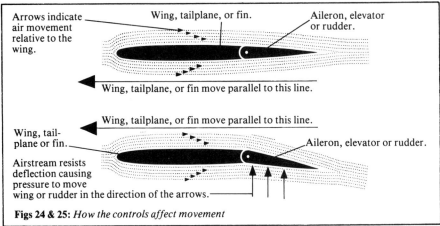

Arrows indicate air movement relative to the wing.

Wing, tailplane, or fin.

Aileron, elevator or rudder.

Wing, tailplane, or fin move parallel to this line.

Wing, tailplane, or fin move parallel to this line.

Wing, tail-plane or fin.

Aileron, elevator or rudder.

Airstream resists deflection causing pressure to move wing or rudder in the direction of the arrows.

Figs 24 & 25: *How the controls affect movement*

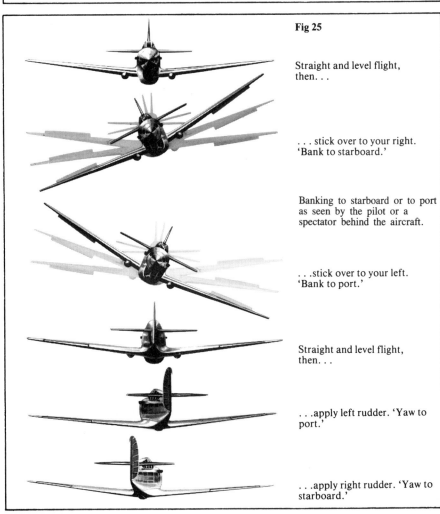

Fig 25

Straight and level flight, then. . .

. . . stick over to your right. 'Bank to starboard.'

Banking to starboard or to port as seen by the pilot or a spectator behind the aircraft.

. . .stick over to your left. 'Bank to port.'

Straight and level flight, then. . .

. . .apply left rudder. 'Yaw to port.'

. . .apply right rudder. 'Yaw to starboard.'

to help jet airliners to take off with a very heavy load. This is, virtually, the same type of wing as the curved balsa sheet mentioned earlier. These controls—rudder, elevators, ailerons, and flaps—used on full size aircraft, are carried over to radio-controlled models, together with retracting undercarriage and engine speed control. On control line models, the average model will have elevator control only. The rudder is permanently glued to point out of the circle, serves to keep the nose pointed out of the circle, and thereby keeps the lines taut. More sophisticated models have engine control (worked by an extra line, or radio control), as well as flaps combined with the elevators, and retractable undercarriage. International championship models have almost unbelievable realism built into the structure, as well as 'in flight' capabilities. Magazines highlight these models with photographs that show a dedication to the work that few of us can match, but are a terrific inspiration, and a never ending source of wonder and delight.

Fig 25

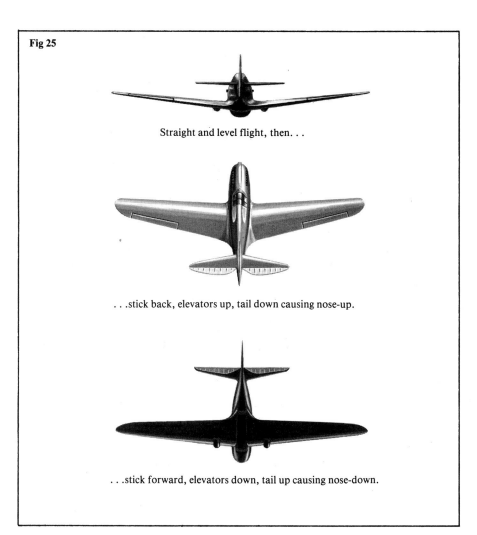

Straight and level flight, then. . .

. . .stick back, elevators up, tail down causing nose-up.

. . .stick forward, elevators down, tail up causing nose-down.

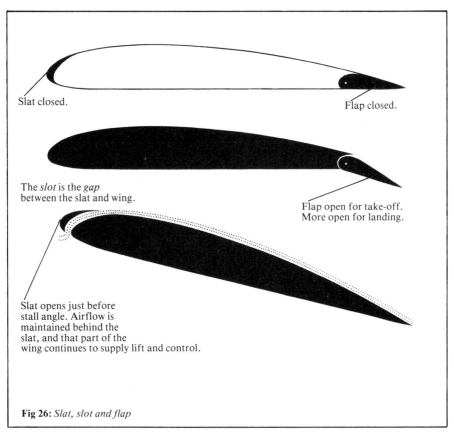

Slat closed.

Flap closed.

The *slot* is the *gap* between the slat and wing.

Flap open for take-off. More open for landing.

Slat opens just before stall angle. Airflow is maintained behind the slat, and that part of the wing continues to supply lift and control.

Fig 26: *Slat, slot and flap*

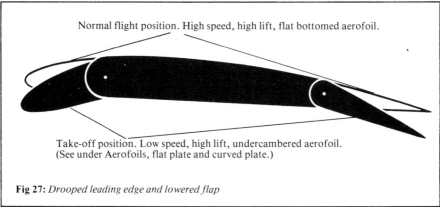

Normal flight position. High speed, high lift, flat bottomed aerofoil.

Take-off position. Low speed, high lift, undercambered aerofoil. (See under Aerofoils, flat plate and curved plate.)

Fig 27: *Drooped leading edge and lowered flap*

Now we can see that, although the balsa glider has been left behind a bit, we could only leave it out of this last section. But I hope you can now see that in this simple model lie all the hidden qualities that make the study of flight so tremendously fascinating, and that if you can imagine it to be very much larger, and more complicated, you'll be looking at the jetliner, or light aircraft, or whatever else you fancy.

Chapter 2

The models

Model aircraft have been shown to possess all the basic principles of full size aircraft. Now let us leave the full size, and have a look at the models. The really small ones can give just as much pleasure as the larger, more expensive, and more sophisticated types, and in their own way, can be equally, if not more, interesting (all adjustments become very much more delicate, and precise, and your workmanship must be very good to get them to fly well consistently). Radio-controlled models are, naturally, much more expensive, and complicated, than other models. They are not much more difficult to build, but need care, and patience, during construction, and initial flying training.

Here is a list of the range of models for you to see what is available at present.

Gliders
The smallest and simplest model is the glider, in profile fuselage or 'stick'

Above: Fig 28a *Profile fuselage, near scale, Spitfire catapult glider of 12-in (30.48cm) wingspan. An ideal first model that is very cheap, and easy to fly.*

Top: Fig 28b *Stick fuselage, high performance catapult glider of 13-in (33.02 cm) wingspan. Similar simple models exist as kits, and are also ideal first models.*
Above: Fig 29 *Built-up structure, tissue-covered towline glider of 36-in (91.44 cm) wingspan. Try one as your second or third model. They're easy to build, simple to adjust, and fascinating to watch with their graceful flight.*

fuselage. These can range from about 6 in (15.2 cm) wingspan, up to about 48 in (121.9 cm) wingspan, or more, and these large models are usually an adaptation of the 'stick', to a hollow tube, in round or square form. The wing, and tail assembly, are sometimes changed to a built-up system. Launching methods range from hand throwing, to catapults of various types, through to towline, and some even use a small motor to climb to altitude.

Rubber power

Next in order are the rubber driven models ranging from about 6 in (15.2 cm) span up to about 40 in (101.6 cm) span. For **indoor flying,** a special grade of balsa is hand cut to fractions of a millimetre to form strips for the entire construction of 'Microfilm'-covered models, which can only be flown indoors. Demanding less skill is the 'Manhattan' type of 20 in (50.8 cm) span which is covered in condenser paper. Even easier is the EZB (Easy B) model made from manageable sizes of balsa

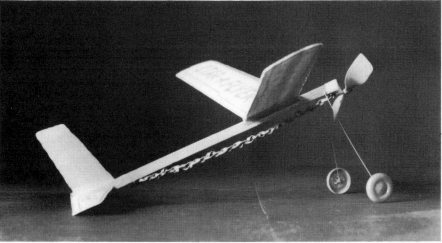

Top: Fig 30 *A microfilm covered model is capable of long flights, at walking speed, in large enclosed spaces such as school halls and large aircraft hangars. Small models can be made to fly around the home lounge on flights of several minutes' duration. Tackle one of these when you have had quite a bit of experience with other models.*

Above: Fig 31 *'Stick' fuselage rubber-powered model is inexpensive, easy to fly, and will highlight quite a lot of the knowledge needed to trim and fly rubber powered models.*

and tissue covered, enabling beginners to enjoy indoor flying. Peanut scale of 13 in (33.02 cm) span is demanding both in building and flying skills. Tiny 6 in (15.2 cm) to 10 in (25.4 cm) span 'Microfilm' models can be flown in the lounge and in school halls. Larger models are flown in Blimp, Zeppelin and aircraft hangars, and indoor sports arenas. (See model magazines for plans and dealers). Models for **outdoor flying** can be purchased as kits from hobby shops (see Yellow Pages). There are ready-made 'stick' fuselage models such as 'Sleek Streek', kits like 'Delta Dart' and 'Profile Scale' (as the Spitfire in this book, but with rubber power), and 'Nocals'. All these are about 16 in (41 cm) span, and very, very easy to build. 'Bostonian', 'Embryo', and 'P30' are simple built-up construction models under 30 in (76.2 cm) span with the rubber enclosed in a 'box' fuselage. Larger and more

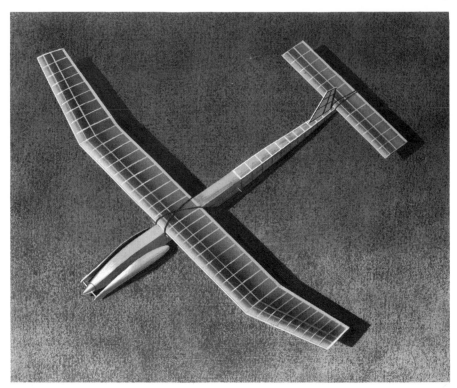

Above : Fig 32 *'Wakefield' and 'Coupe de Hiver' models, built-up structures and tissue-covered are top performers in rubber-powered flying. Either type can be tackled after you have successfully flown smaller rubber models.*

Below: Fig 33 *A smaller rubber-powered scale model of 18-in (45.72cm) wingspan is a difficult bird to get to fly well. Try one only when you really know ALL the tricks of building and trimming a model to fly consistently. Larger scale models are only slightly easier to cope with.*

complex are the 'Coupe de Hiver' and 'Wakefield' models with built-up construction, and tissue covered. The fuselage is a hollow tube of square or round section with the rubber enclosed. The propeller is hand made, and folds during the glide. The undercarriage is omitted which further improves the performance.

Scale rubber

Scale rubber models range from 6 in (15.24 cm), up to about 36 in (91.44 cm) wingspan, and include the 13 in (33.02 cm) wingspan 'peanut' scale. Flight performance of scale models in general is well below that of the former type, due to greater drag and weight, and in fact it is quite rare to see one of these models capable of good flight performance. They are always a distinct challenge to any modeller. These models can be greatly improved by removing the rubber motor, and installing a carbon dioxide motor, or they can be used as free flight or control line types, by the use of the smallest glow plug or diesel motors.

In the rubber powered scale model, the weight of the engine of the full size aircraft is missing, and the weight of the rubber motor, behind the centre of gravity, makes them, generally, 'nose-light', and too tail heavy. They therefore have the tailplane enlarged to help keep the tail up, or better supported, in the air, and the length of the rubber motor kept less than the fuselage length, in order to maintain the centre of gravity as close to the centre of lift of the wings as possible. The scale propeller is also far too small for a model, and would have to rev at high speed for a long time to fly the model adequately. As the rubber motor does not deliver power for more than about 25 seconds, it will be seen that a very much larger propeller is needed, to use the power available, in order to get the model as high up as possible. Even then, with the larger propeller, scale models seldom glide down with the rubber having fully unwound.

Powered models

Next come the powered models, and these use any of the following motors:

Below: Fig 34 *A semi-scale free flight model of 56-in (142.24 cm) span. Note the large tailplane, and shallow dihedral angle, together with a fairly spacious fuselage under the mainplane make this an ideal model to convert to a radio-controlled trainer using two or three functions.*

diesel (more correctly, these should be referred to as compression ignition motors), glow plug, electric, CO_2 (this is carbon dioxide), solid propellant, or rocket motors (now unfortunately out of production, they were known as Jetex, and were very good little motors), and pulse-jet motors.

These models are mostly of built-up construction, like rubber models, but are more heavily built to take the extra stresses brought about by the extra speed when the power is on. A rubber powered model can very often be converted to power by a few alterations, to take either a small glow plug, electric, CO_2, or diesel motor.

These models can be broken down to three main categories; free flight, control line, and radio control.

Free flight

Free flight can be regarded as an extension of the free flight rubber model, and is heavier because of the necessity of greater strength. Free flight means just that—the model is allowed to fly where it will, and consequently a very large field is required, as can generally only be found outside a city or town. Even then the model sometimes continues its flight for many miles over the countryside, and is sometimes lost. Generally, they are fitted with a timer, which stops the motor after a run of 20 seconds, or thereabouts, the model having reached a height of a couple of hundred feet during that time. When the engine stops, the model is virtually a glider, as with the rubber powered model. It is allowed to fly as it will for about 3 minutes, and then if it is still well up, the timer releases a hold-down gadget on the tailplane, which then 'kicks up', causing the model to enter a strong, controlled stall, which brings it down nearly vertically, thereby avoiding a fly-away and the possible loss of the model. These models range from about 25 in (63.5 cm) span, to about 72 in (182.8 cm) span, and some are even larger. CO_2 models range in size from 12 in (30.48 cm), up to 30 in (76.2 cm), because of the very small size of the motor. Electric power is usually for the larger models, from about 36 in (91.44 cm) span, to 100 in (254 cm) span.

Radio control of one, two, or three functions can, and is, applied to the larger free flight models to regulate the flight pattern, for limited aerobatics, to guide the model from obstructions like trees and buildings, for thermal soaring, and also to bring the model back almost to the feet of the modeller.

Radio control

The true radio-controlled model is more specialised, in that its construction is very robust (and therefore a bit heavy), and with full radio equipment is mainly used for aerobatics. Its initial and operating costs are very high when compared with other models, and consequently is beyond the means of the average modeller. Manufacturers in America, and Britain, have developed small, light,

Opposite above: Fig 35 *A free flight model of 72-in (182.88 cm) span meant solely for contest work. Lightly constructed, with a very powerful motor, these models can climb vertically, and are capable of extremely good flights. Try one for your third or fourth model, but fit it with a motor of about half the power required, and mount this on elongated engine bearers to maintain the correct Centre of Gravity.*
Opposite: Fig 36 *A CO2-powered free flight scale model of the World War 1 Bristol Scout of 18-in (45.72 cm) wingspan. CO2 power is an ideal substitute for rubber power in small scale models.*

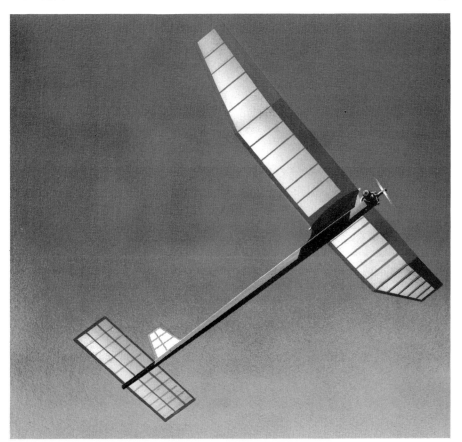

radio equipment for smaller models, which can be powered by the smallest glow plug motors, even CO_2 motors. These models utilise one, two, or three of the four functions but this is sufficient to keep the model under the will of the pilot, even allowing him a few aerobatics. This equipment is just as reliable as the larger type, and can be a terrific boon to a competent modeller who may be a bit pressed for cash, but is ready for radio in his models.

Opposite top: Fig 40 *This four-function scale radio-controlled model is, like the aerobatic model, beyond the capabilities of an inexperienced modeller.*
Opposite middle: Fig 41 *The two-function radio-controlled glider, treated carefully, can be used as a trainer in radio control.*
Opposite bottom: Fig 42 *A small semi-scale control line trainer of 19-in (48.26 cm) wingspan. The profile fuselage, wings and tail assembly are solid sheet balsa sanded to streamline shape. (The same type of construction as the Spitfire catapult glider.) Babe Bee .049 and 25-ft (762 cm) nylon control lines. An inexpensive way to start your flying.*

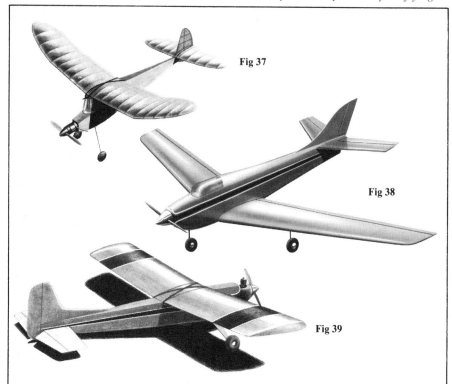

Fig 37
Fig 38
Fig 39

Fig 37: *This electric-powered free flight model has a Mabuchi A1 motor plugged into the nose. It is capable of very good flights, and is an excellent choice for your second or third model.*

Fig 38: *The four-function aerobatic radio-controlled model is definitely not for anyone with little experience in modelling or radio control. Work up to this bird with plenty of experience with three-function radio control first.*

Fig 39: *A radio-controlled trainer of 40-in (101.6 cm) span, using an .049 motor and two-function radio is an inexpensive way to start out in radio control, but it is wise to know something about how to build and fly free flight models before starting radio-controlled models.*

Control line

Control line models fall into various categories, such as speed, stunt, team race, rat race, and scale. Speed models come in small sizes with rather large motors, and vary in shape from usual to extreme. Stunt models range from not much more than a wing with a motor, to more recognisable models, but all in this category have very exaggerated wings to give better performance through manoeuvres. Scale models are usually highly detailed, and here, like radio models, they incorporate retracting undercarriages, motor control, and sometimes such exotic ideas as crop dusting, or bomb dropping, etc. These models use glow plug and diesel motors. Round-the-pole flying, which is very popular in Britain at the moment, uses electric power only. CO_2 powered models do not exist at the moment, because of the limited power run of these motors. All models, except stunt and combat, are very robustly constructed and are usually quite heavy, and the structures are similar to radio models in that they utilise a lot of sheet balsa, some hardwood, and plywood.

Below: Fig 43 *A more usual type of speed model with metal (aluminium) wings formed by carefully folded sheet. The enormous undercarriage is not fixed, but remains on the ground while the model lifts out of the cradle during take-off, and skids on its belly when landing. This necessitates the use of a metal pan (lower half of the fuselage) to obviate the damage that a wooden fuselage would suffer.*

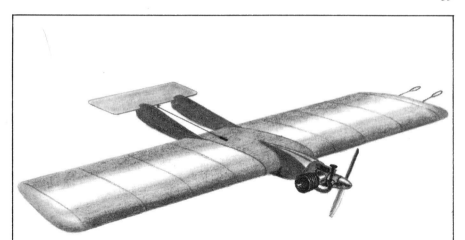

Fig 44: *The 'Combat' model's design considerations are typified by large wing area, light structure, and short tail moment arm (see Fig 22). Two models are flown in the circle, and the aim of each pilot is to 'chew off' as much of the crêpe paper streamer as possible from the opponent's model. The streamers are attached to the tail of each model by a simple wire hook. Terrifically exciting!*

Below: Fig 45 *The stunt or aerobatic model incorporates the same design principle as the Combat model, but this one must look more like a full-size aircraft.*

Above: Fig 46a *Scale model Sopwith Camel of 14¼-in (36.19 cm) wingspan. Electric powered, and with elevator control as in control line models, it flies well, and is just as sensitive to control as the full size aircraft was. The two fine copper wire leadouts are connected to fine copper wire control lines which are in turn connected to the centre pole.*

Below: Fig 46b *Electric flying. The pole, with revolving head, is placed in the centre of a large room (lounge), and the control lines are connected to the head. Power lines and the nylon control line are connected from the pole to the box which contains a transformer (12v, 1½ amp), hand controller and the control column sticking out of the top of the box. All those tubes simply hold the wires neatly wrapped around them. The pilot sits on the box and controls the model via the hand controller (throttle), and control column (elevator). A club-owned pole and box makes life easy for members and the whole set-up allows the unskilled newcomer to learn to fly very quickly.*

Chapter 3

The motors

Glow plugs

There is not a model shop today that does not have glow plug motors in profusion. They come in sizes ranging from the tiny 0.010, weighing about a $\frac{1}{2}$ oz complete with propeller, up to the large 0.60s and 0.80s, which weigh several ounces without the propeller. The Americans class their motors by cubic inches (ci), and the British by cubic centimetres (cc), which makes things a bit awkward when there are no handy tables to convert from one to the other. Overleaf is a rough guide to help you to find a motor of equal capacity, but be a bit

Below left: Fig 47a *The ubiquitous 'Babe Bee', capacity .819 cc (.049 cu in), and all its variations ('Black Widow', 'Golden Bee', etc) are inexpensive motors for small control line and free flight models. Ideal motors to learn to fly with, be careful to choose the correct propeller for free flight: 6-in diameter, 3-in pitch (and the fuel). Control line needs 5¼-in diameter, 4-in pitch (and the correct fuel). Let your hobby shop guide you when choosing the model to suit.*
Below right: Fig 47b *'Pee Wee' is half the capacity (.020 cu in) of the 'Babe Bee', but is quite happy pulling a 36-in (91.41 cm) span model around the sky.*

careful, as this does not mean that they are necessarily of the same power. While we are on the subject of power, the average model for 'fun' free flight is grossly overpowered, and this shows up in the plan where a large amount of downthrust is called for. You will later find that you can fit a motor of about half the capacity, and the resulting flight is much more realistic, and satisfying, than that screaming monster. Quite unnecessary in a lot of cases. The large powered gliders will show you what I mean, as these models need only a very small motor to make them fly.

Cu in	Cu cm	Cu in	Cu cm	Cu in	Cu cm
.010	.163	.19	3.1	.36	6.0
.020	.327	.21	3.5	.40	6.5
.030	.50	.23	3.8	.45	7.4
.045	.75	.25	4.1	.488	8.0
.049	.819	.27	4.5	.518	8.5
.061	1.0	.29	4.7	.549	9.0
.091	1.5	.30	5.0	.579	9.5
.099	1.62	.33	5.5	.61	10.0
.15	2.5	.35	5.7	.80	13.1
.183	3.0				

Diesel motors

Diesel motors are very neglected today, and this is a great pity as they are ideal motors for many applications, in free flight as well as control line. Too often have I seen the average modeller battle with a glow plug motor, even with the aid of a starter motor (that bit of equipment sets him back quite a sum of

Below: Fig 48 *Diesel and Glowplug motors compared for size. From the left; Mills .75 cc (.045 cu in) with 8-in diameter, 4-in pitch propeller; D.C. Dart .5 cc (.030 cu in) with 7-in diameter, 4-in pitch propeller; 'Babe Bee' .819 cc (.049 cu in) 6-in diameter, 3-in pitch propeller; 'Pee Wee' .327 cc (.020 cu in) 4½-in diameter, 2-in pitch propeller. The Mills and the Dart are diesel motors and the 'Babe Bee' and 'Pee Wee' are Glowplug motors. The diesels suit scale models better than the Glowplug motors do.*

money) and it still does not help him to get that wretched motor to run. The diesel motor does not need all that paraphernalia—no costly starter battery, no starter motor and its battery, and the fuel is far less expensive. Do not let anyone put you off the diesel; it will start very easily and anyone who says it will not has never tried, or is talking through his hat!

There is the case of the Mills 75, a small British-made motor that was tremendously popular throughout the world. Then suddenly it disappeared off the market for a long time. Now, thank goodness, its back again, being produced in India. It is exactly the same old Mills 75 we knew and loved. Let us hope the other motors come back again, and that the Dart 0.5 remains with us for ever. May the idiots that strut with T-shirts marked: 'I wouldn't be seen dead with a diesel', drop dead without the diesel to help them!

The diesel also does not make that hideous scream that the glow plug motors make, and that alone makes it very attractive in many places where the glow plugs spoil the flying site, and a diesel will always turn a larger propeller than a glow-plug motor of the same capacity, so making the model less difficult to trim, and better looking with a decent sized propeller. These motors, though, are definitely as good for your models as are the electric, the glow plug, and the CO_2. Just do not get me wrong; I love all motors, but I hate the prejudice that the diesel motor has suffered for so long, which has been brought on by people who should know better.

CO_2 motors (carbon dioxide)

One American and two British manufacturers make these motors at the moment, and they are all ideal power sources for small models from 12 in (30.5 cm) wingspan up to about 25 in (63.5 cm) wingspan scale models, and to about 36 in (91.44 cm) wingspan for light models. Their big attractions are their light weight, small size, clean operation, foolproof starting, and they are, above

Below: Fig 49 *The Mills .75 cc is shown set up for 'sidewinder' mounting for profile fuselage control line model. Note the very useful fuel cut-off arm just above the tank lid.*

Above: Fig 50 *The D.C. Dart .5cc, like the Mills a very good little motor for use in free flight scale models of about 35-in (88.9cm) wingspan. Both motors are also inexpensive and useful for small control line and free flight models.*

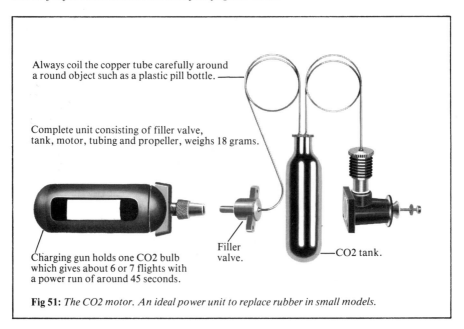

Always coil the copper tube carefully around a round object such as a plastic pill bottle.

Complete unit consisting of filler valve, tank, motor, tubing and propeller, weighs 18 grams.

Charging gun holds one CO_2 bulb which gives about 6 or 7 flights with a power run of around 45 seconds.

Filler valve.

CO_2 tank.

Fig 51: *The CO_2 motor. An ideal power unit to replace rubber in small models.*

all, nearly silent when running. The power run is variable, as is the power output, and so they can be made to run for various lengths of time, from about 20 seconds to about 75 seconds. No doubt about it, they are here to stay, and are an ideal source of power, unlike rubber which can be a nuisance when it snaps and tears out a good part of the fuselage. No such trouble here! A very old idea that has at last come to fruition through deep thought and skilful manu-facturing. Improvements will undoubtedly take place, and larger motors should be here soon.

Electric motors

There are quite a few different sizes and shapes of motor at the moment. These range from tiny (TO5, Mattel, etc), through the Mabuchi 26d for electric indoor round-the-pole flying (about 18 in, 45.7 cm span) and Mabuchi A1 for about 25 in (63.5 cm) span for free flight, the Hytork 48 also for free flight from 25 in (63.5 cm) to 50 in (127 cm) span, and the larger motors, Bullet 30, Cyclone 15, etc, for large models. All these motors are powered by rechargeable ni-cad batteries, and each motor has its individual battery charger. If given reasonable care, these motors last a very long time, and they, too, are practically silent, while recharging is very simple—in the case of the Mabuchi A1 for instance, you get about 10 seconds of flight power for every minute of charging. Maintenance is nearly non-existent, and when it is necessary, it takes no time at all, especially if you keep the bearings oiled and see that the brushes are always in good shape, and that you do not allow dust to get into the cooling apertures. These motors too, like the CO_2 motors, are instant starting, and there are no starter batteries, messy fuel, starter motors, and all the other junk to carry around. Fabulous in fact!

Glow plug fuels

There are several formulae for glow plug motors, and these will depend on the design of any particular motor. Some motors will run on just about any fuel make-up, while others are quite fussy as to what you give them. Methanol, castor oil, and nitromethane are the usual constituents. Nitromethane, nitrobenzine, and nitropropane are the additives in some fuels that give more

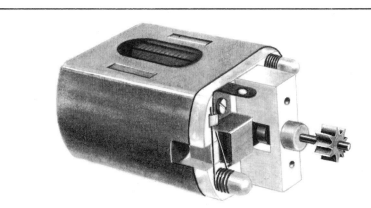

Fig 52: *A slot car motor with 2.6:1 gear ratio (10 teeth on the small gear attached to the motor, and 26 teeth on the large gear attached to the propeller shaft) can be used for round-the pole flying (see Fig 46).*

power and greater flexibility, and these are added in various proportions to commercial fuels. For average fun flying, make up your own fuel, which will be a lot cheaper than the ready-made fuel you can buy. This consists of 70 per cent methanol to 30 per cent castor oil. For better performance, replace some of the methanol with nitromethane, which should be from 5-60 per cent. A couple of drops of acetone will help to mix the nitromethane and castor oil. Never leave the lid off the methanol bottle, as it absorbs moisture from the air and soon spoils. Keep the lid on tight. Nitromethane should be kept in a dark place, as light affects it. Do not buy these chemicals from your chemist, as the price is too high, get them all from a chemical house that sells to the public, and explain what you are using them for, otherwise you may have difficulty in obtaining them. You may also get them from garages that cater for racing, and motor bike enthusiasts. If you can get nitrobenzine, then use only up to 10 per cent of it in place of some of the methanol.

Diesel fuels

These motors are a lot easier on the pocket than glow plug motors, and are ideal for free flight and control line models that are just for fun. The fuel constituents are also a lot easier to obtain and mix. Ether, castor oil, and paraffin are the basic materials; amyl nitrate and amyl nitrite are the additives which are needed in small quantities only, and are used at about 2 per cent of the total. Mix 20 per cent castor oil, 30 per cent ether, and 50 per cent paraffin, and add 20–30 drops of amyl nitrate per litre of fuel. Or you can use equal amounts of each, and add a few drops of amyl nitrate as above per litre. Any proportion of the ingredients between these two limits will also work, so you can try out any combination you like to suit your engine. When buying ether, just be sure you get water-free ether; you do not need anything of a higher quality that will cost you more.

Here, as with dope and fuelproofers, you must avoid inhaling the fumes of the fuel in the bottle or tin, and only run the motor outdoors, never, never run it indoors. Even with the windows wide open, a certain amount of the exhaust fumes will be inhaled, and this can lead to a chest complaint later on in life, so avoid all that trouble now from the very beginning.

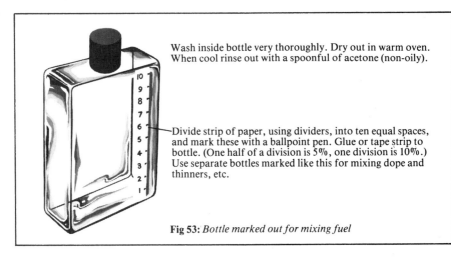

Wash inside bottle very thoroughly. Dry out in warm oven. When cool rinse out with a spoonful of acetone (non-oily).

Divide strip of paper, using dividers, into ten equal spaces, and mark these with a ballpoint pen. Glue or tape strip to bottle. (One half of a division is 5%, one division is 10%.) Use separate bottles marked like this for mixing dope and thinners, etc.

Fig 53: *Bottle marked out for mixing fuel*

Chapter 4

Tools and materials

Before you can start building models, you have to collect a few very simple and inexpensive tools. Some you may find lying around the house, and these can be stored in an old shoe box for a start. The most important tool you will have is the surface on which you construct the frames, as the alignment of wings will depend, almost entirely, on the untwisted and unbuckled surface of this. The best available is an ordinary cheap wooden surfaced table, about 4 ft 6 in by 3 ft 0 in (137.1 cm by 91.4 cm), the top surface of which should be veneered chipboard. Cover this with newspapers, and on top of these lay a piece of Masonite insulation board (also known as beaverboard or strawboard), size 50 in by 25 in (127 cm by 63 cm). This board is made of what appears to be small, fine, hair-like strands of wood or straw, which are glued very lightly into a solid board. Pins and tacks can be pushed quite easily into it, withdrawn, and leave no mark, but while the pins are in they are not easily pushed over sideways. You also need a box of dressmaker's pins, sharp scissors, large and small pliers, a good pair of wire cutters, 18 in (45.7 cm) steel ruler, one 'NT' design knife, and its blades (obtainable from art stores). These blades are extremely hard, and remain sharp for a very long time, there simply are no better on the market for modelling. A $\frac{1}{2}$ in (2.25 cm) red sable flat brush (also obtainable from the art store), balsa cement, clear dope (see below), and thinners, PVA 'Alcolin' glue, sandpaper P60 and P220, and sanding block, planed pine plank 12 in by 6 in (30.5 cm by 15.25 cm) for cutting balsa on, thumb tacks, carbon paper, some old match boxes, rubber bands (thin), clothes pegs, and an old shoe box to keep all the small tools in. Handy extras, if you can get them, are a hard drill and its stand, plus drill bits, a hand jigsaw, small vice, small hand grinder, and small round and triangular files, large and medium-sized soldering irons, soldering fluid such as 'Bakers', stick solder, and an old tin lid.

Soldering

This is a very simple operation, if you keep everything *clean*. By that I mean you *must* get rid of all grease and oil on all your equipment, and this includes your hands. First wash your hands with soap and water, then do not even scratch your head afterwards, as even the oil on your hair will get on your hands and then onto the job, and the solder will not stick. Got the message? OK! Then the next thing is to file off the black oxides on the tip of the soldering iron, and switch the iron on. (It should be quite a large iron for soldering wire for an undercarriage, and a medium size iron for soldering tinplate.) That tiny iron for radio work is hopeless for any of these jobs, as it does not hold enough heat for

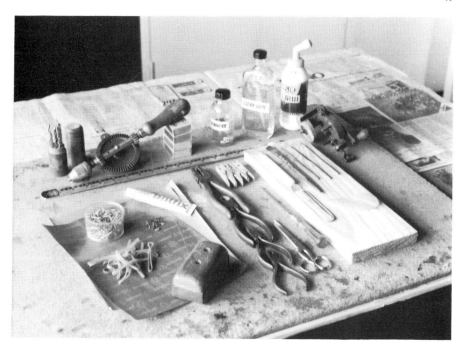

Opposite top: Fig 54 *The most important tool is the table and the insulation board laid on it.*

Above: Fig 55 *A few basic tools. Note matchboxes used for props, clothes pegs for clamping, and rubber bands for holding parts while the glue dries.*

Opposite bottom: Fig 56 *Handy extra tools. The jigsaw is best used for cutting plywood formers, etc. A fine tooth, hard back, dovetail saw (not shown) is ideal for cutting balsa blocks or thick strips of balsa.*

Below left: Fig 57 *Disc sander made from an old washing machine motor is ideal for sanding parts, including plywood pieces, to outline shape very quickly.*

Below right: Fig 58 *All set to solder a joint. That tiny iron in the foreground is hopeless for this job.*

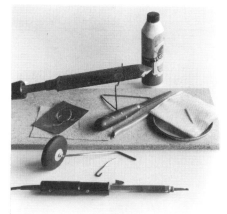

the job. Clean all the pieces to be joined, at the joint area, with fine 'wet-or-dry' paper used dry, and wipe off the dust with a piece of clean tissue. Put some flux, 'Bakers' soldering fluid or similar, in a small tin lid. Holding the solder stick in your left hand, and the iron in your right hand, put the iron in the fluid (it will splutter and fume so keep your face well back out of the way), and immediately rub the tip of the iron with the solder stick, and this will cover the tip of the iron with a coat of solder. This should be all around the tip.

Soldering an undercarriage

Bind the cleaned wire pieces with fine copper wire, or fuse wire, making sure that you have bound it tightly, and put some flux on the joint; it should wet the entire joint if you cleaned it properly. Lay the iron on the joint, and press the solder stick to the tip of the iron, then, as soon as it melts and runs, work it into the joint with the tip of the iron. If the solder will not 'run-in' on a spot, add some more flux to that point, reheat with the iron, and add a bit more solder. Allow the joint to cool *undisturbed*. The solder has set the moment it turns dull, and this is a good time to put the joint under the cold tap to get rid of the flux.

Below: Fig 59 *Cleaning one joint area. Be sure you clean right round the piece. Even if your fingers are clean, try to avoid touching the cleaned area.*

Bottom: Fig 60 *Cleaning the other joint area. This piece must be just as thoroughly cleaned as the first piece.*

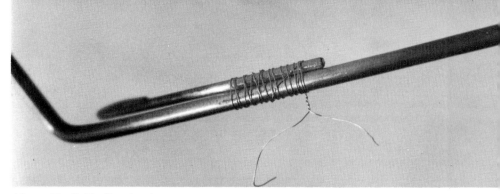

Above: Fig 61 *Binding the pieces.*

Below: Fig 62 *Making the joint. The iron will take several seconds to heat all the pieces before the solder will run into the joint.*

Bottom: Fig 63 *The completed joint. If properly done it will outlast the model.*

Soldering tinplate

The two pieces to be joined should have a drop of flux put on, and the iron and the solder stick brought together on the surface of one piece at a time. When each piece is coated on its surface, the coated surfaces are placed face to face, reheated with the iron, pressed firmly together, their positions adjusted, maintaining pressure with a stick or piece of metal, then the iron is removed, and the joint allowed to cool under the pressure. If the solder will not run, add more flux to help it, and if that does not work, the joint is dirty, and must be recleaned, or the iron is not hot enough, or big enough for the job. *Never* use solder with the flux in the core for this work, as it's meant only for making joints in electrical work, like radios, etc.

Tissue paste

Make your own tissue paste like this. Take an enamelled mug, and put one heaped teaspoonful of cake flour in it, and one level teaspoonful of white sugar. Mix this up first, and then add very little cold water, and mix to a smooth paste. There must be no lumps at all. Now fill the mug, to half full, with cold water and stir until all the paste is dissolved. Heat on the stove, and stir the mixture *all the time* (about two or three minutes), until it thickens. Turn off the heat, remove the mug, and stir a while longer. Add one teaspoonful of Dettol to the mix, and stir in thoroughly. If necessary, dilute the mixture with a little cold water *after the paste has cooled completely*. Do not add too much water. The paste should be thick, but not like a floppy jelly. Pour it into a stoppered wide-mouth bottle, and put the lid on. Keep this as long as you like, it will not go mouldy.

Dope

Make up your own dope this way: buy a litre of clear gloss lacquer, cellulose, not polyurethane, from a large hardware store, at the same time buy a 5-litre can of grade 'A' thinners (other grades are useless). Be careful not to spill any on furniture as it dissolves the surface finish; and keep it away from fire. Now take a glass jar, with a lid that fits well and, to this, tape, or glue, a piece of paper marked off in equal divisions (say 1 or 2 mm), so that you get ten divisions from the bottom to the neck of the jar. Pour the lacquer in up to the 4th division. Fill to the 10th division with thinners. Close the lid, and shake until all dope is dissolved. Now, to every cupful of this mix, add 1 teaspoonful of medicinal castor oil. You do not have to be too fussy about the amounts involved. Just place a mug, or coffee cup, next to your jar, and 'guesstimate' how much dope you have. Then work out roughly how much castor oil to add—rather have too little oil added than too much, as this will make the dope remain sticky, instead of drying. If it is too tacky when dried on a test surface, add a fresh mix of lacquer and thinners only, to the jar, to dilute the amount of castor oil that is in there. Test again. It should now be non tacky. Set aside until you need it. The castor oil keeps the dried lacquer pliable for a number of years, so that you do not have the covering on your models turning brittle. It also adds a gloss to the dried lacquer.

Types of wood
Balsa wood

This tree grows at a great rate in Ecuador, reaching as much as 40 ft high, with a girth equal to two men's outstretched arms, in only 8 years. Then it is mature and ready for felling, and when well seasoned, is the lightest wood known. Commercially it is used for life preservers, floats for life-lines, packing for expensive furniture, and as a lining for incubators and cold storage rooms. (You may find some for nothing when repairs are being carried out at these places.) This is our main material for aeromodelling, because of its light weight and strength. Balsa weighs between 5 lbs (soft and light), to 18 lbs (hard and heavy) per cubic foot, and comes in strip, sheet, block, and moulded form as, for example, shaped leading edge, and trailing edge. When the log is cut at the mill we get three types of cut—tangent, random, and quarter grain. Tangent cut is the usual balsa sheet, which has irregular, and deep, grain lines and this, when wetted, is the sheet that will curl. It is therefore, best used for sheet covering, if of the soft variety. The medium and hard sheets are generally used, in average models, for just about everything. The quarter grain wood is very much stronger, but will split if you try to bend it across the grain. Because it resists bending, it is best used, in the softer type, for such things as sheet tailplanes, rudders, and wings. In the medium and hard grades keep it for such items as wing spars, trailing edges, ribs, etc. It is easily recognised by its speckled or dappled colour on the surface, the odd man out in the bundle. Never put it back when making your purchases, rather keep it and put an ordinary tangent sheet back.

Spruce

This is a strong, springy, close-grained wood, about 3 times heavier than balsa, and because of this, is used in a thinner section than its balsa equivalent for such things as spars and trailing edges in large models such as gliders and radio-controlled scale models. Full size aircraft, of wooden construction, have always used Sitka spruce for the main structure of the airframe.

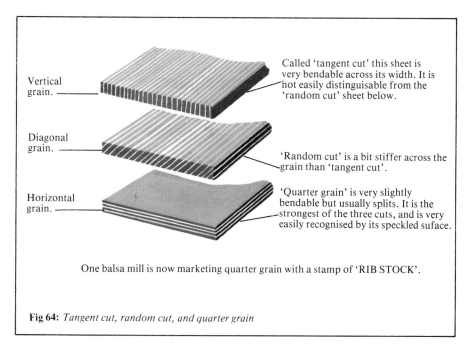

Vertical grain.

Called 'tangent cut' this sheet is very bendable across its width. It is not easily distinguisable from the 'random cut' sheet below.

Diagonal grain.

'Random cut' is a bit stiffer across the grain than 'tangent cut'.

Horizontal grain.

'Quarter grain' is very slightly bendable but usually splits. It is the strongest of the three cuts, and is very easily recognised by its speckled suface.

One balsa mill is now marketing quarter grain with a stamp of 'RIB STOCK'.

Fig 64: *Tangent cut, random cut, and quarter grain*

Obeche

This should not be treated as a substitute for balsa—it is a bit stronger and far heavier than balsa. It can be used for carving rubber model propellers and, when a bit of weight is needed, for noseblocks.

Jelutong

This wood is almost the same as obeche and has the same uses; it does, however, sand down better than obeche, giving a smoother surface. Use obeche and jelutong for carving moulds for cellulose and glass fibre.

Bamboo

Here is a light, tough, springy wood that has a number of uses when split down to strips. It sands down fairly easily and the surface is then silky smooth. It makes excellent struts, landing gears, etc, for small scale models, where it is cheaper and better than plywood for the same purpose. When split and sanded to very thin strips, it makes very good stringers in place of balsa wood for scale models. Always bear bamboo and cane in mind when a tricky problem in construction appears as one of the two, usually, is the answer.

Mahogany veneer

This is extremely useful for making propellers of all sizes for rubber powered models. When the wood is used in conjunction with locally produced Alcolin PVA glue for a propeller, the resulting unit is of a very high standard of strength and lightness, which has been found to surpass other known methods of propeller fabrication.

Cane or reed

Cane, or reed, of the basket-making type, is another excellent material for use in wingtips, tyres, cockpit coamings, tailskids, etc. It is very tough, light, and extremely easily worked by soaking in water, shaping, and allowing to dry.

Pine

This wood is fairly light and tough, not nearly as light as balsa of course, but it has its uses as spars and trailing edges for large models, and for 'stick' fuselages on small gliders it is excellent. I cut mine from old tomato boxes, being careful to check the grain direction and length on two sides.

Plywood

This material is an absolute necessity for all models, and comes in several thicknesses. All sorts of plywoods are available, and the ordinary material obtainable from the local timber merchant is usually not good enough. Birch plywood that is 'resin-bonded waterproof' is the type to use, and comes in sizes from the thinnest, $\frac{1}{32}$ in (0.7 mm), or $\frac{1}{16}$ in (1.5 mm), for facing ribs on models with detachable wings in two halves and dihedral braces in medium size models, and for undercarriage mounting plates in rubber powered models. Control line models have the nose section of profile models strengthened with this size of ply. 3 mm and 6 mm is used for wing tongues, undercarriage mounting plates, dihedral braces, and wheels, depending on what size of model these are for. 0.7 mm and 1.5 mm ply are also used for propeller blades on rubber powered models.

Birch dowel

Birch dowel, of small diameters, is used for wing-retaining elastic bands on numerous models, and for retaining the rubber motors on rubber powered models.

Plastics

Acetate sheet

This material is used for cabin windows, cockpit canopies, spats, cowlings, etc, and is best glued using acetone (without oil). When heated for moulding, it must be moulded rapidly, before it loses its heat. Because it is transparent, it should be doped, using coloured dope, but this has to be carefully done so as not to melt the material.

Expanded polystyrene

This material is used for a number of parts for models, the main one being cores for wings on control line combat models, and radio-controlled models. Cutting is best done with a hot wire cutter, using a car battery, or transformer, for power. The transformer is easier to use, and should be of not less than 2 amps and with tappings of 4, 8, and 12 volts. The wire, obtainable from dealers catering to the radio ham, is nichrome wire of about 0.013 in (0.3302 mm), and a second piece of about 0.022 in (0.5588 mm). This can be strung across a bow made of wood. The jig for cutting the foam should have rib templates of either plywood or aluminium, fixed at the root, and tip, of the proposed wing. The ability to cut the foam is governed by the length and diameter of the wire, and the voltage you put through it, so a little experimenting is in order to establish the correct set-up for the particular job you are doing. When you have it working properly, then start your wing at the leading edge, and pull the bow evenly back to the trailing edge, and off the edge of the plastic. If you pull the bow too fast the wire will drag in the centre, go cool, and drag all the more, and the edges will be overheated, causing the foam to 'draw away' from the wire. If you pull it too slowly, the whole surface will be overheated and become wavy. Only a bit of practice will get it right. Once you have that done well, then the leading edge and spar notches can be done. Do this in one rather quick movement of the wire, into and out of, the small jigs pinned to the foam wing core.

Below: Fig 65 *The basic foam styrene wing, when used for a radio-controlled model, still needs leading edge, trailing edge, spar and wingtips in balsa, and sometimes a hardwood insert for the undercarriage, before adding the balsa, or similar wood veneer on top and bottom surfaces to complete the structure.*

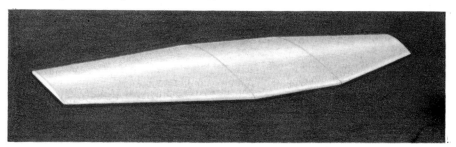

Be very careful to get these accurately lined up with each other on both ends of the wing. Glue the spars, and leading and trailing edge, with PVA glue only; *never* use balsa cement, it just dissolves the foam, as some other glues also do. If you do decide to use some other favourite glue, then test it on a spare piece of foam first, and also be sure it does not dry too rapidly before you can get the pieces into place. Cover the entire wing with soft, flexible, sheet balsa, again using PVA glue, and pinning, or weighting the sheet firmly to the foam and the leading edge and trailing edge. If you are good at using contact adhesives, and the subsequent fitting and laying of the balsa sheet, then do so, but again, test the adhesive on spare foam before trying it on your wing. Some modellers use brown wrapping paper to cover the wing, using contact cement as the adhesive. Finish the wing with any of the systems shown under covering and materials, making sure you have a fuelproof covering.

As the new CO_2 motors and small electric motors are also sweeping into favour, you will find that you can make at least the mainplane, tailplane, and rudder, for these models from foam. There is no earthly reason why the same parts, for rubber powered models, cannot also be made from foam, especially if you are in a hurry to try out a new idea, or if you plainly do not like the work involved in making these parts from wood. With a bit of ingenuity you could also make the fuselage for these small models, but you will have to add reinforcements for the undercarriage and motor. This reinforcement can be either hard balsa, or $\frac{1}{32}$ in (0.8 mm) plywood. For these models you can leave the foam in its natural state, or cover it with tissue paper, provided you first paint over the foam with a dilute coat of PVA glue, and allow this to dry before you apply the tissue. This will protect the foam from the effects of the dope applied to the tissue for finishing. Expanded foam is going to be more widely used as modellers find out the various ways to use this very versatile material.

Below: Fig 66 *A half fuselage glass fibre shell, with integral fin, for a 100-in (254 cm) span radio-controlled glider. Note the two sockets to hold the wing joining steel rods (See Figs 107 and 108) and the built-in tray to hold the receiver, batteries and servos. Partitions for the latter will be added to the tray when their correct positions relative to the Centre of Gravity have been established.*

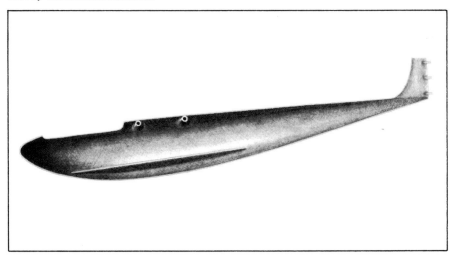

Glass fibre

This is a very handy material for all sorts of construction purposes. It is a bit heavy, and one has to remember this, and be careful to use it where weight is not too much of a problem. Glass fibre rods are used for fuselages on medium to large gliders, and some rubber models. It is also used for moulding complete fuselages in very thin shells, and then braced internally; also for spats, and whole cowlings, in scale radio models, in speed control line models, etc. There is a very good book on the market which gives the complete story on the methods of working this material.

Adhesives

Balsa cement

This is a cellulose-based material with thinners, plasticisers, and other additives added, to make it adhere far better than straight cellulose would. It is a strong rigid glue that even sticks to your fingers (remove it with thinners), and can be used as a gap filler on bad joints. It is supplied in tubes of two sizes and types which makes it very handy: one type is for ordinary construction at home, and this dries in about 20 minutes, depending on the temperature, and the other is for quick 'field repairs', and this dries in about 5 minutes.

PVA or white glue

This is very sticky and makes a tough flexible joint, and although it takes longer to dry than balsa cement, a good many modellers prefer it to cement. It is superior to cement in some cases. For instance, as a coat smeared over sheet balsa it gives a tough film that is flexible, and prevents the wood splitting. Cement, used in the same way, always cracks under severe impact. I always use the cement to make the joint, and then cover it over with a thick coat of PVA. These joints have yet to fail after many hard knocks on a test model. T-shaped butt joints with PVA only, as on a fuselage, I find allow a certain amount of distortion to creep into the finished frame, with a slight alteration in the tail-plane incidence, but the credit side shows that these joints never crack—PVA remains tough and springy. It is this springiness that causes the frame to 'move' out of true line, and this also allows the frame to 'move' and so avoid being broken at a joint. Glue dries slowly between two pieces of balsa. To cut the drying time, use the 'double gluing' method. With longerons pinned and uprights ready to be glued, place glue on the two ends of an upright, then wipe it around the sides too with a finger. Do all the uprights in this way, placing them on a plastic sheet to dry. Wipe glue in the same way on each position on the longerons and allow to dry. Place fresh glue at the ends of an upright, and fit it between the longerons then wipe the glue flat with a finger. Do each upright in the same way. It has several advantages over other glues too. Firstly it is lighter; the joint is always neat, as the glue smears disappear; you can wash it off hands and clothes; it does not warp; and it can be used to repair household items. Its only disadvantage is that it is not waterproof, but who is going to soak his model in water?

Contact adhesives and cold water glues

Many modellers use these on very specific jobs only, such as when laminating two balsa sheets. Here the glues like PVA, and cold water types, will induce a warp before the two sheets can be glued. In this case, use the contact adhesive.

Cold water glue is useful for gluing blocks of balsa, or other wood, to form a larger block that is to be carved and sanded to shape, as may be the case when a fuselage is being made to be used as a form for fibreglass.

Epoxy glues

These are handy for the person who dislikes soldering, or even welding. You can use epoxy to glue any two items you would have to solder, or join a metal part to balsa or to plywood, as when fixing an undercarriage to the fuselage. The 5 minute type can be used for quick field repairs.

Dope

This, like cement, is an odd word, and, like cement, is also a cellulose-based material. The big difference is that dope is useless for gluing wood (but some modellers use it for gluing the paper covering to the frame on light models), mainly due to the softeners, plasticisers, extenders, and retarders added. These latter are not found in cement. There are two kinds, cellulose nitrate and cellulose acetatebutyrate, commonly known as butyrate dope. The butyrate is the superior material in strength and water resistance, and needs no fuelproofer, but is more expensive than the nitrate. If you ask for dope when making your purchases at the hobby shop, you are generally given the 'nitrate' dope, and this is fine for all models. If you want to purchase the same thing in a hardware store you must ask for cellulose lacquer, it is exactly the same thing but is generally a lot cheaper at the hardware store, as are the thinners. The purpose of dope is to seal, tighten, and strengthen the tissue, silk, and nylon, used for covering models (on very small and/or light models it can be left off the covering, but the tissue must be handled very, very, carefully). It is always applied *after* the covering has been tightened up by spraying with water and allowing it to dry thoroughly. Silk and nylon are treated separately (see chapter 12). Dope can be applied with a brush or spray (the latter is best for small models and for decoration of an elaborate nature on all models). The brush can be used for the same purpose, but needs a bit of care, and practice, before using it on a model.

Fuelproofer

This is a polyurethane material that is painted on by brush, or it can be sprayed, over the entire model after the dope has dried. This only applies to models powered by glowplug, and some diesel motors. The motor bay must also be treated. Do not buy this material at any store other than your hobby shop, because there are different types of polyurethane, and some are not suitable for model aircraft, while some turn out with a distinct yellow cast which can spoil a model finished in white, or light colours.

Chapter 5

Construction methods: some simple models

To start with, we will take the simplest model possible, and take it right through to the flight stage. Its purpose is to satisfy a bit of basic construction, adjusting, balancing, and flying. A lot of what you have learned so far can be verified if you care to take the trouble to observe. Its big attractions are its simple structure—it is about the cheapest model you can build and is very resistant to crash damage. If you make it well, and balance it properly, and it has no warps, it flies extremely well in calm, or windy, weather.

Before you start building any model, you *must* get into the habit of reading every single note on the plan, to avoid getting into difficulties as the structure progresses. You have been warned!

Spitfire

Materials 1 1.5 mm by 76 mm balsa sheet, hard or medium. **2** One length 20 g (0.035) steel wire. **3** One length brass tube to fit wire. **4** 4 cm square plywood, 1.5 mm thick. **5** One tube balsa cement. **6** One bottle clear dope and thinners. **7** One bottle 'Alcolin' PVA glue. **8** Two size 64 rubber bands. **9** 10 mm diam by 20 cm dowel. **10** Planed pine plank 30 cm by 15 cm for cutting on. **11** Beaverboard (strawboard, ceilingboard), 60 cm by 130 cm for building on. **12** 3 mm cane or dowel 10 cm long. **13** Carbon paper. **14** Drawing pins. **15** Pins. **16** Metal edged ruler. **17** One packet 'NT' blades, snapper, and design knife, from art store. **18** Plasticine. **19** Sandpaper, one sheet No P80 and one sheet No P220. **20** Red, yellow, black and blue poster paints. **21** 20 mm bamboo strip. **22** One small triangular fine file.

Study the plan before you start. Work with care at all stages, especially 'balance' and 'alignment'.

Tracing 1 Only fuselage, mainplane, tailplane, and rudder have to be traced. **2** Use drawing pins to pin bottom of plan to beaverboard. **3** Slide balsa sheet under part to be traced. **4** *Watch grain direction.* **5** Pin balsa. **6** Insert carbon paper between plan and balsa. **7** Trace off all solid lines, using ballpoint and ruler, on all straight lines. Remainder freehand. **8** Raise loose end of plan, and carbon, to check tracing. Wing position on fuselage and tailplane slot, and centrelines on wing and tailplane, *must* be accurate. **9** Go over all lines on balsa with ballpen.

Cutting out 1 Use ruler to cut all straight lines. **2** Keep knife vertical when cutting. **3** Use light pressure on knife. **4** Take several cuts to get through wood, especially across the grain. **5** Glue split wood with balsa cement, after part is cut

Above: Fig 67 *The finished model Spitfire requires patience and care right from the start if you want a model that looks good and flies extremely well. Information in Fig 69c is vital to this end, as is the balancing as in 69a and 69b.*

out; keep part flat while glue dries. **6** Rough sand all parts to outline. **7** Fine sand to round off all edges. **8** Cut out shaded area piece 'A' on fuselage; keep it. **9** Trace off lines on blank side of balsa pieces. **10** Use compass to draw wheels on plywood. **11** Cut out carefully, and sand smooth. **12** Drill wheel centres. **13** Cut brass tube with fine file. **14** Bend wire to shape for undercarriage, catapult hook and tailwheel; cut off as shaped, and file rough edges. **15** Extend wing, and tailplane centrelines, to undersurfaces.

Assembly 1 Carefully cut along centreline, on undersurface of mainplane, to about halfway through thickness. **2** Turn wing right way up. **3** Carefully crack along centreline, so that wingtips are raised slightly. (Try not to break completely.) **4** Smear balsa cement into crack on undersurface. **5** Pin down one half of wing, placing waxed paper under glue. **6** Prop up other half of wing by 52 mm under wingtip. **7** Smear balsa cement over centre of wing top surface, between dotted lines (see wing plan). **8** Leave overnight to harden. **9** Balsa cement tailplane in fuselage slot. **10** Check squareness to fuselage as glue dries (front view). **11** Balsa cement rudder to fuselage; check true and square. **12** Balsa cement wing to fuselage; check true to fuselage (front view) and centreline on undersurface. **13** Leave 2 hrs to dry. **14** Insert brass tubes in wheels, and glue with PVA; leave to dry. **15** Using PVA, glue card discs to undercarriage wire, each side of wheel (see front view). Wheel most rotate freely. **16** Attach undercarriage, wire hook, tailwheel wire with very little PVA glue. **17** When dry recoat with **3** heavy layers PVA glue, drying between each. **18** Cut and sand piece 'A' to fit, and attach to fuselage using PVA glue. **19** Slightly dilute some PVA with water; complete step laid out top right of wing plan. **20** Paint (one coat only) this dilute PVA over rudder and tailplane both sides. **21** Smear fuselage, both sides, with one thick coat undiluted PVA; allow to dry. **22** Smear undiluted PVA over wing to fuselage joint in one thick coat. **23** Assemble

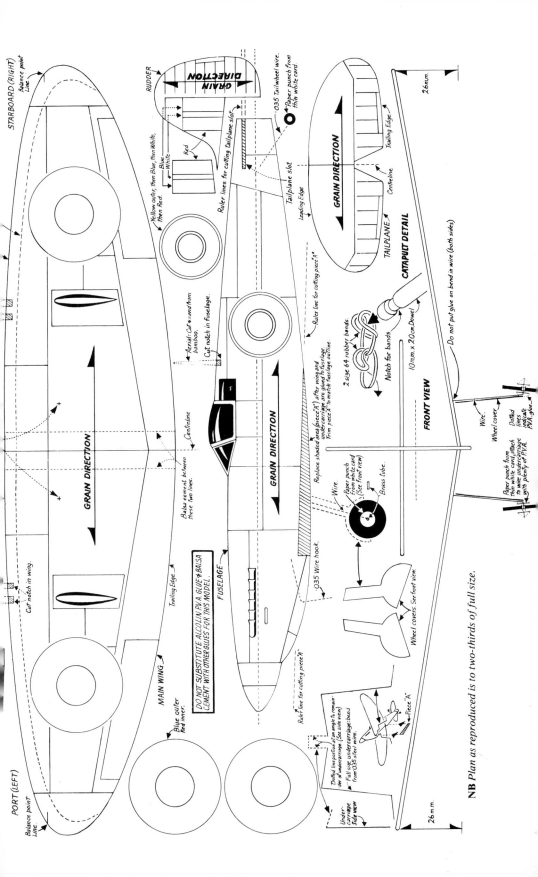

NB Plan as reproduced is to two-thirds of full size.

catapult (see detail). **24** Fine sand rudder and tailplane lightly to smoothness.

Decoration For best flights save weight by not doping or painting model. **1** Smear PVA over back of plan at all decals, and wheel covers. Dry. Repeat on front of plan. **2** Colour all decals. **3** Apply 50-50 thinned clear dope over decals. **4** Cut out, and attach to model with thin coat PVA. **5** Attach aerial, and wheel covers, with PVA. **6** Paint wheels with black poster paint. **7** When dry, apply thinned clear dope.

Balance *Lateral:* **1** Insert pin in nose and rudder. **2** Model should balance with wings dead level. **3** If required, add PVA to high wingtip until level. Allow to dry. **4** *Recheck. Pitching* **1** Balance model on pin points under balance points on wing. **2** Add small amounts of Plasticine to nose until model balances dead level.

Below: Fig 69a *Balancing the model. Sight directly over the top of the model to make sure the nails are directly under the marks at the wingtips. Add Plasticine to the nose until the model hangs dead level when seen from its side. Make the props as in the photo from pine and dowel. The dimensions are height 6-in (15.24 cm), base 4½-in (11.43 cm). The small square piece and the triangular piece are joined by a short piece of thick dowel. The nail is 3/8-in (.95 cm) from the apex. The nails are used for small models and the apex for large models. (See Figs 154 and 155.)*

Alignment *Note: this is vital.* **1** Place model at window, and face it into room. **2** Stand about 1 metre away. **3** Keep head steady, and sight with one eye only. **4** Check model against front view on plan, for twists or warps in surfaces. **5** If warp is noticeable, recheck from rear of model. **6** Keep checking until *exact* spot of beginning of warp is established. **7** Dampen (not wet) surface, top and bottom, from front to back, only at this spot. **8** Lay as much as possible of the surface (eg, wing) flat on the beaverboard. **9** Pin, or weight, surface close to damp area *across* surface. **10** Pin, or weight, surface that stands up, or is off the board. **11** Put 1 cm long card strip under surface edge that is pressing down, near tip of surface. **12** Leave 2–3 hrs to dry. **13** Recheck alignment against front view and repeat steps 7–12 if necessary. **14** Alignment must check against front view before flying.

Flying 1 Learn to find wind direction, by turning your head until you can feel the wind on your face and ears, giving an equal pressure on both sides. **2** Find large open grass park, or rugby field. **3** *Catapult elastic must be untwisted.* **4** Use very little catapult pressure. **5** Keep wings and fuselage level and fire into the wind. **6** Watch with care. **7** A wide level turn is fine. **8** Correct tight diving turn by moistening both sides of rear rudder, and bending 1 mm against turn direction—this correction must be permanent. **9** Hard dive straight ahead,

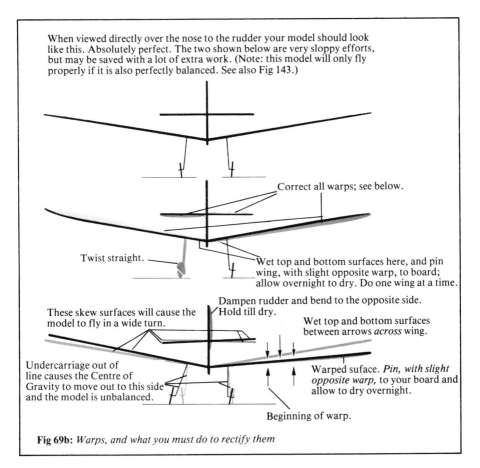

When viewed directly over the nose to the rudder your model should look like this. Absolutely perfect. The two shown below are very sloppy efforts, but may be saved with a lot of extra work. (Note: this model will only fly properly if it is also perfectly balanced. See also Fig 143.)

Correct all warps; see below.

Twist straight.

Wet top and bottom surfaces here, and pin wing, with slight opposite warp, to board; allow overnight to dry. Do one wing at a time.

Dampen rudder and bend to the opposite side. Hold till dry.

These skew surfaces will cause the model to fly in a wide turn.

Wet top and bottom surfaces between arrows *across* wing.

Undercarriage out of line causes the Centre of Gravity to move out to this side and the model is unbalanced.

Warped suface. *Pin, with slight opposite warp,* to your board and allow to dry overnight.

Beginning of warp.

Fig 69b: *Warps, and what you must do to rectify them*

remove $\frac{1}{2}$ pea size Plasticine. **10** Hard climb, stall and dive, *add* $\frac{1}{2}$ pea size Plasticine. **11** Persist with steps 3 to 10 until model flies level with only a wide turn; note turn direction. Now for full catapult power.

Assuming model turns naturally to the left: **1** Face into the wind. **2** Turn 90 degrees to your right. **3** Bank model with left (port) wingtip pointing vertically to the sky and catapult banked to match. **4** Fire level to ground. **5** A good flight is a climbing turn to about 25 metres height, with a roll out to level flight, and a long glide. **6** You should never aim the catapult more than 20 degrees up when using full power. **7** If your model turns naturally to the right, then reverse steps 2 and 3. **8** If the undercarriage becomes even slightly bent, it should be realigned properly (side and front view) to maintain correct balance.

Aerobatics or stunts, such as stalls, spins, rolls and loops are all possible with a well trimmed model. Use $\frac{1}{2}$ to $\frac{3}{4}$ pull on catapult to induce these manoeuvres; model should be fired with *wings and fuselage level with ground*.

Hints and tips 1 Before flying, always check for warps. **2** Work through testing schedule, steps 2 to 10 under Flying, above. This takes a few minutes and saves unnecessary repairs. **3** A drop of castor oil, rubbed into the catapult elastic, preserves it. **4** Never rest one model on top of another. **5** Save all left-over materials, including scrap, for repairs, and future models. 6 Use PVA glue for all repairs. **7** *Stay away from overhead power lines.* **8** *Never aim the model at, or towards, other people.*

When all is correct, the Spitfire performs very well indeed. If your model will not fly at all properly, no matter how you catapult it or adjust it, and it seems a complete failure, I suggest you start again, at the very beginning of this book, and find out where you have missed a point. By following each step carefully, your model will end up flying very well. It is up to you to *make* it fly!

A simple rubber model

Having learnt something that is extremely easy, the next step is probably even easier. We will deal with a ready-made model to speed things up a bit. 'Star Flyer' is a ready-made, quickly assembled model, which, with a bit of extra work, will give hours of fun. It is a good model to fall back on too, when a really difficult, or tricky, model may drive you up the wall, and it will restore your love of flying, and your confidence to carry on. It is sold by all model shops, and a lot of toy shops, and its smaller brother is 'Sleek Streak'. Both benefit from the same treatment, so whichever one you have, just read on.

On opening the plastic packet examine the wings, tailplane, and rudder, for cracks. Repair these by holding the crack twisted open (gently does it) so that, by using a match dipped in PVA, the crack can be covered on one edge with glue. Allow the wood to close, and help it shut, then spread the glue on each side with your finger. Put a smear of PVA glue on all edges of each wing, top and

Opposite top: Fig 70 *'Star Flyer'. Very inexpensive, and a superb model with which you can learn the basis of rubber-powered flight. Buy several while you're at it, the propellers alone are worth the outlay. Save the propeller and wheels, when the model eventually becomes very tatty, and use them on future small scale models.*
Opposite: Fig 71 *'Star Flyer', spread out with the PVA on top and bottom* edges *drying out while resting on matchboxes. The wings have had the top surface dampened and the cement smeared in a thin line across the centre of the underside of each wing, which is the surface seen in the photo.*

bottom surface, and lay each wing on a matchbox until the glue is dry. Now damp the top surface only, of the mainplanes, and smear a thin line of balsa cement, on the undersurface, in the centre, *across the grain*, and allow to dry on a match box. Smear PVA glue on all edges of the rudder and tailplane, top and bottom, and support on a match box, until dry. The idea behind this dampening of one surface, and balsa cement on the other, is to make the wings take up a slight permanent curve (for lift, remember). Put very little PVA glue on the base of the rudder, and insert it in its slot, and do the same for the tailplane. Before the glue dries, check the front view, constantly, for warps in the rudder, and tailplane. Constantly twist out any warps that may appear, until the glue is dry. Now mount the wings, without glue, in the plastic wing holder on the fuselage. Check front view for warps. Should there be a warp, simply try twisting it out, but be very sure the warp does not reappear 5 minutes later. If the warp persists, take that wing half off the mount, pin it to the board, with a slight opposite twist, and maintaining the curve. Redampen the top surface, and leave for about an hour or two to dry. Remount on the fuselage, and check that the warp is gone. Having rid the wing of all warps, only now can it be glued in the plastic wing mount. Do *not* glue the mount to the fuselage. When the wings are dry, assemble the entire model and rub a drop of castor oil well into the rubber. Never use Vaseline, car oil, or anything else like that. Glycerine is the only other substance you can use. As much oil, 3 in 1 or similar, as can be held on the sharpened end of a match, should be used on the propeller shaft. Balance the model by shifting the wing mount until it balances at about the middle of the wingtips. Mark the fuselage on the front, and back, of the plastic mount with a ballpen. Wind up the propeller, until there is about a half row of knots, face the wind (as you did with the glider), point the model up about 30 degrees, release the propeller first, and immediately give the model a slight push, or throw. It should climb rapidly straight ahead, or in a wide curve, until the rubber has run down. If it flies straight ahead, without climbing, shift the wing mount forward about $\frac{1}{16}$ in, and try again. If it had climbed too steeply, stalled and dived, then move the mount back by $\frac{1}{16}$ in. Continue either adjustment, until the model flies properly, and note where the mount is in relation to the ballpen mark. Now PVA glue the mount permanently. For even better flights, take the rubber off the back hook, stretch the rubber out until it is fairly tight, and then proceed to wind it up, using a hand drill with a hook mounted in the chuck.

At this point you have to be careful. Check the drill to see how many times the hook rotates to one turn of the drill handle. $3\frac{1}{4}$ turns of the hook to one of the handle, means that if you turn the handle 100 times, the hook will put 325 turns in the rubber. Work out the number of turns accurately, so that you know exactly how many turns you are putting into the rubber. For the first six flights, stick to about 150 turns in the rubber. Then you can increase the number, by about 25 turns, for the next 6 flights, and so on, to a maximum of about 300 turns. Naturally you will be counting the turns you put into the winding handle, on the drill. You must know what that means in turns on the rubber! Think about it, if you are in any doubt, until you know what is meant!

Incidentally, you will notice that the propeller shaft points down, when viewed from the side. This angle is called downthrust, and this is used on nearly every rubber, or powered, model, in varying degrees. Its purpose is to stop the nose of the model from rearing up, under the influence of the extra speed (extra lift, remember?) when the propeller is working at high speed, through high power, at the beginning of the flight. Check this by flying the model, under low power, by putting in very few winds. It does not fly nearly so fast, nor does the propeller 'pull' so hard, and the model does not climb as fast, because the lift from the wings is far less! Increase the winds, and you increase the power, propeller revs, speed, and lift! Simple isn't it? But very important! Notice that little spiral on the front of the propeller, and the way it locks the shaft to the propeller, when the rubber is wound up, and how it releases the shaft, when the rubber is fully unwound, so that the propeller can freewheel. That is exactly what it does when the model is flying; so that drag from the propeller is minimised when the model is gliding. If the rubber breaks, it must be replaced by one of equal, or slightly less weight. A fair substitute can be made from 3 size 64 rubber bands, linked as shown on the catapult glider plan.

Below: Fig 72 *Winding the rubber. Stretch the rubber out as far as possible (about 2½ to 3 times its normal length) and commence winding and counting the number of turns. Move slowly in towards the model as the winding proceeds until the last turns are put in near the tail. Grip the rubber with thumb and forefinger and at the same time unwind the drill slightly so as to free the rubber from the hook on the drill. Attach the rubber to the hook on the model. When fully wound like this, always grip the propeller by its hub, never by one propeller blade as this may bend and ruin the propeller.*

Chapter 6

Kits vs plans

The kit model is the cheapest way to start with. All the little bits, printed on, or die-stamped out of the sheet, are already there, together with all the strip wood in different sizes, bent wire for the undercarriage and other uses, wheels, covering materials, plan, etc. Usually you still have to buy cement, dope, and one or two other things, but it does save you from running around, because these things are pointed out to you in the shop. What this means is that you can start building the moment you reach home. This also means you do not have to stock up with expensive single items, like plywood for instance. This comes in large sheets, and is not cheap.

Building from plans, on the other hand, means you have first to make out a list of all the items: wood, wire, covering material, glue, dope, propeller, wheels, celluloid, plywood, etc, and then check your stock to see what may still have to be bought. Now that bit of plywood in the kit, for example, will save you having to purchase a large sheet, costing as much as a medium size kit, just to make one small part of the model. If you do take up aeromodelling as a hobby though, you will soon discover that building from plans is, even though you may have quite a bit of cash tied up in stock materials, costing you per model, about half of the price of the equivalent kit. Also, working from plans, you have almost a limitless range of models to choose from. Not so with kits. For instance, if you wanted to make a model of a 1910 Blackburn monoplane (an excellent subject for modelling and flying), you can get a plan, or draw one up, but you will not find a kit of the size and type of model you want.

Building from kits

The first thing to do is to get the creases out of the plan by folding the crease carefully the opposite way. Using thumb tacks, pin the plan fairly tight, and flat, to the beaverboard, or strawboard. Cover it with a sheet of greaseproof, or waxed paper, tacking this down flat also. Alternatively, you can also rub the end of a candle over the entire plan, but be sure you do the job very thoroughly. The reason for using these materials over the plan, is to prevent the glue from adhering to the plan, while construction is under way. Thin oil can also be painted over the plan to serve the same purpose (excess oil should be wiped off, with a tissue or rag), but this makes the plan transparent. This transparency can be useful, when you wish to make, for example, a right wing from the drawing of a left wing, simply turn the plan over, and you can see the drawing in the transparent oiled area.

Building from a plan

Should you be starting out with just a plan, then the first thing to do is carefully make up a list of all the materials you will need, including a ballpen, and carbon paper. Having bought all you need, begin by sanding off any fuzz on the sheets, and strips, using very fine sandpaper on a sanding block. Strip wood can best be done by laying all the same size pieces side by side, and sanding the lot together, then rotate them all 90 degrees, to sand them all again. Repeat until all sides are done. This not only ensures uniformity, but also speeds the job. Sanding is essential, because the glue cannot get a good grip on fuzz.

Trace off, directly from the plan, all the ribs, formers, wingtip pieces, etc (see under Spitfire catapult glider for tracing method). Only when you have checked that you have all pieces traced off can you tack the plan down as above.

Whichever method you are using, kit or plan, *you must study every little bit of the plan before you start.* That way, you know exactly how each part is to be made. It is sometimes impossible to proceed, without real problems, if you start off just anywhere. For instance, you could easily use the best wood, that should be used for the spars in the mainplane, in the tailplane and rudder. This could lead to disaster. The wood should, therefore, be graded before you start.

Wood selection (kit or plan)

All the strip wood should first be put into bundles of the same dimensions, eg, all the $\frac{1}{8}$ in by $\frac{1}{8}$ in together, $\frac{1}{4}$ in by $\frac{1}{2}$ in together, etc. Each bundle should now be divided into hard, medium, and soft. The easiest way is to simply dig your thumbnail into the end of each strip in turn. The more the resistance the harder the piece. While you are doing the test, you will come across some pieces you are

Below: Fig 73a *Hard, medium and soft strips should be kept in separate bundles with permanent labels. When new wood is bought it should be carefully graded and then added to the existing bundles. Do the same thing with sheet balsa. Later, with more experience you will be able to grade them as: hard, medium hard, medium, medium soft and soft.*

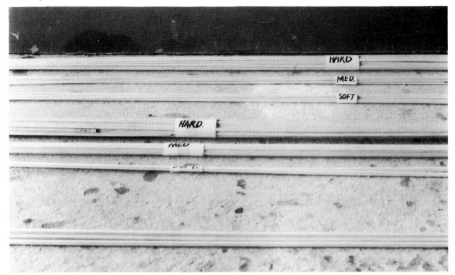

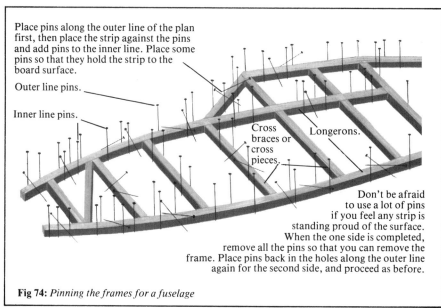

Place pins along the outer line of the plan first, then place the strip against the pins and add pins to the inner line. Place some pins so that they hold the strip to the board surface.

Outer line pins.

Inner line pins.

Cross braces or cross pieces.

Longerons.

Don't be afraid to use a lot of pins if you feel any strip is standing proud of the surface. When the one side is completed, remove all the pins so that you can remove the frame. Place pins back in the holes along the outer line again for the second side, and proceed as before.

Fig 74: *Pinning the frames for a fuselage*

unsure of, put them aside. Make three distinct stacks of the rest, and put a thin elastic band around the one end, and a piece of paper, marked *hard, medium* and *soft*, for each stack. Now go back to the pieces you were unsure of, and try to match them to the general 'feel' of a bundle. Put the medium and soft ones away, and open up the hard bundle. Select the hardest strips from this, for the mainplane spar, but you must check the grain direction. The grain should run, as near as possible, parallel to the edges of the wood. If it runs across the width of the strip, anywhere, reject it for this purpose, as it will only split under stress later. The last test is to hold the wood at one end, between thumb and forefinger, and press the other end against the table. A certain springback is felt on the end. Select the spars, in pairs, that have the most springback pressure. Now do the same with the leading edge, and the trailing edge. The tailplane spar, leading edge, and trailing edge, should be selected from the medium grade bundle, using the same care as you did for the mainplane. Rudder pieces are also selected from the medium grade bundle.

The longerons for the fuselage should be selected in the same manner as the spar, and if one pair of longerons has to curve more than the other pair (check this on the side view of the plan), then keep the stiffer pair of strips for the straighter side. The uprights, and crosspieces, should be cut from hard strips, for the section from the nose to behind the mainplane. Medium grade can be used from behind the mainplane to the tail, to save weight at the tail.

The sheets of wood are also selected as hard, medium, and soft. The hard sheets are used for ribs, outline wingtips, nose formers, and fuselage nose covering, etc, anywhere on the model where stress is expected. Medium sheets for sheet wings, sheet wingtips, fuselage formers behind the mainplane, and tailplane and rudder ribs, and tips. Soft sheets are used for sheet rudders, tailplanes, covering foam wings, and fuselage covering, etc, anywhere where practically no stress is expected.

Pinning, cutting and gluing

This is where most beginners spoil their first few models, and a spoilt construction will definitely end in a non-flying model, especially as they do not know what to do about it.

90 per cent of all wood strip in the framework needs pins, placed alongside each piece, to hold it, as close as possible, to the outlines on the plan, and to keep the strip flat to the board surface. Flat broad strips can have one, or several, pins pushed through the wood, but care must be exercised to avoid splitting some small pieces, cut from sheet balsa, as the grain, being straight, sometimes cuts across the curve, and this will split. This usually happens on the wingtips, and tailplane, and rudder pieces, on small models.

$\frac{1}{16}$ in sq and $\frac{1}{8}$ in sq (1.5 mm sq and 3 mm sq) should have the pins placed on either side of the strip, and some of the pins, on each side, should lean over the wood slightly, to hold the wood as flat as possible to the board surface. No matter how accurately the wood has been cut at the factory, it usually suffers from curves when viewed from one end. These curves are carried into the frame while building, and so it is very important to flatten the strips, as far as possible, so that the glue tends to keep the frame flat and true. Now if we remove the pins, when all the glue is dry, we will find that the frame is sometimes sprung, and has a twist or bend in it. This would be useless as it is, because on covering, the twist or bend is still there, and the covering, on tightening, tends to hold this, and we have a warped surface which must be straightened before the model can be expected to fly at all. This means taking the covering off, straightening the frame, and recovering. Oh dear! Oh dear! So, to avoid this frustrating situation, we must get rid of the twist while the frame is still pinned flat to the board. When the glue is dry, spray the entire frame with water. (You can also 'paint' the frame, using a large brush, and water.) Then leave it to dry overnight. *Never put it in front of a heater*, just let it dry out slowly, and naturally. You'll find that your patience will be well rewarded. In any case, the part can be drying all the time you are making other parts of the model, so you are not really sitting doing nothing during that time. The wings, tailplane, and rudder, on every model with a built-up frame, require this treatment of the frame. The fuselage, too, needs it when the basic frames are being built. After that it may only require it if, when joining the side frames, one frame will not bend as much as the other. Simply wet the longerons of the 'stiffer' frame, wait a minute or two, for the water to soak in, and then proceed.

Cutting sheet balsa

The sheet should be given a very light sanding, with fine sandpaper, on both the front and back, to get rid of any fuzz, but do not sand away the printing if the sheet is from a kit. Working from a plan, if you have traced off the parts such as wingtips, formers, ribs, tailplane, and rudder outline pieces, or if these are printed on the sheet balsa in a kit, you will have to cut out each individual piece. This is tedious but must be done, and properly, if your model is to fly well. Start by cutting the inside curve on the wing, rudder, and tailplane, outline pieces, making very sure not to cut on the line, but about $\frac{1}{32}$ in (0.7 mm) outside the line. Take several cuts to get through the wood, if it is at all hard, and do only these cuts, no others, until all the pieces are done. The straight lines are cut next, using the steel straight edge, and here it should cover the part being cut, leaving only the line exposed, just enough to see where it begins and ends. Cut exactly on the line, and a bit beyond each end. Lastly, cut freehand again, around the outer curve, also cutting just outside the line. When all the pieces are cut out, sand them on the inner and outer curves, to just leave a faint bit of the line. If you break a piece, balsa cement it, and pin it flat to the board, with a piece of waxed paper between it and the board, and leave it to dry for a couple of hours.

The cutting and sanding of ribs is treated separately, as these must all be identical. Having cut out all the ribs slightly over size, pin them together making a neat stack, and sand them down to size, with a clean surface top and bottom. If the wing is parallel, keep the front and back of the stack parallel. If the wing is tapered, be sure the ribs are stacked in the right order, and keep the front, and back, of the stack to the correct taper, as indicated by the first and last ribs in the stack. For tapered wings, separate the ribs into two stacks, for the left and right hand wings, and check that both stacks are the same by placing them back to back, before cutting the notches for the spars. Do the same for the tailplane ribs, and if the rudder has ribs, do these the same way too.

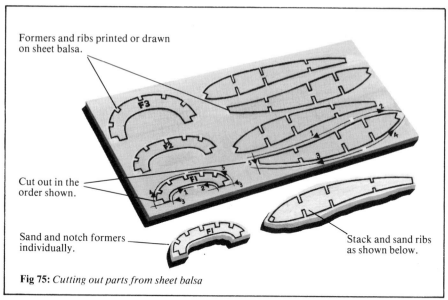

Formers and ribs printed or drawn on sheet balsa.

Cut out in the order shown.

Sand and notch formers individually.

Stack and sand ribs as shown below.

Fig 75: *Cutting out parts from sheet balsa*

Stack the ribs carefully. First press them individually from the top so that they are flush with the board. Then, using two straight edges, press the leading and trailing edges so that they are as flush as you can get them. Hold the stack firmly and pin as shown. Sand the leading edge straight and flush. Do the trailing edge the same way. Then sand the top and bottom surfaces smoothly to the outline. Use a sanding block for all this work.

Push the pins right into the stack.

Fig 76: *Stacking and pinning the ribs*

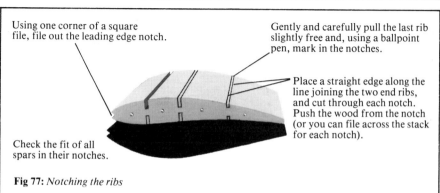

Using one corner of a square file, file out the leading edge notch.

Gently and carefully pull the last rib slightly free and, using a ballpoint pen, mark in the notches.

Place a straight edge along the line joining the two end ribs, and cut through each notch. Push the wood from the notch (or you can file across the stack for each notch).

Check the fit of all spars in their notches.

Fig 77: *Notching the ribs*

Geodetic ribs

The profile for these will be given on the plan, and here, as with any other rib shape, simply stack the ribs, and pin them, and sand them to profile shape, following the particular method, for the type of wing, except that the ribs will be angled to the line of the spars, and this angle will be, generally, about 45 degrees, also indicated on the plan. The reason for this is that this form of construction resists twisting of the frame, much more than the conventional construction, and so the ribs may be of $\frac{1}{32}$ in (0.79 mm) instead of $\frac{1}{16}$ in (1.5 mm) sheet, so saving a bit of weight, but the strength is the main thing. There is no more work involved than in conventional construction.

Sliced ribs

Sometimes you come across a plan that indicates the ribs must be 'sliced' from the sheet. Make the template from plywood or tinplate (an old jam tin cut open and flattened out), or sheet aluminium. Cut a strip off the end of a balsa sheet, about $\frac{1}{4}$ in (6 mm) wider than the length of the ribs for this, and start at the top of the strip, being careful not to split the wood when cutting the first rib.

Strip cutting

Another thing you can do with sheet balsa is to cut it into strips. There is a small 'stripper' on the market at the moment, but this is not very satisfactory, and a far better way is to use your straight edge, with a small sheet of sandpaper stuck to the underside, at the two ends and the centre, to stop it slipping. Hold it firmly down to the sheet and, using your knife, cut down the entire length of the

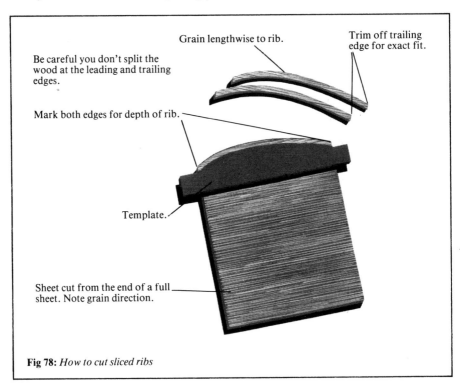

Grain lengthwise to rib.

Trim off trailing edge for exact fit.

Be careful you don't split the wood at the leading and trailing edges.

Mark both edges for depth of rib.

Template.

Sheet cut from the end of a full sheet. Note grain direction.

Fig 78: *How to cut sliced ribs*

sheet, taking several cuts to get through the wood. Things to watch out for are: that the grain of the wood runs true to the edge before starting, that you have lightly sanded it, and that the marks for the cutting are accurate. Keep the knife vertical while cutting.

Sheet balsa tailplanes and rudders

Sheet tailplanes and rudders can be very prone to warps, if you just stick them on, and hope for the best. Here are three ways you can prevent this. There is the usual method of inlaying a strip of the same sheet across the grain of the piece, and this strip is cut to fit near the centre of the piece. In the second method, the elevator can be a separate piece from the tailplane, and the fin separate from the rudder. The tailplane and the fin have the grain running along their length; the elevators and the rudder having the grain running at right angles to the grain on the tailplane and fin. In both these methods, pin the pieces to the board, with waxed paper between them and the board, and glue them with either PVA or balsa cement. The last method is to cut the tailplane and elevator in one piece from the sheet, and if it is not warped, then coat it, top and bottom, with slightly diluted PVA, but be very careful to put both the top, and bottom coats, on *at the same time*; do not let one dry before you coat the other, and you must not pin it to the board, even though it may now look warped. Simply hang it up to dry, and it will be perfect. Then sand it lightly, with fine sandpaper, and give it either another coat of PVA, or a coat of thin clear dope. Treat the fin and rudder the same way.

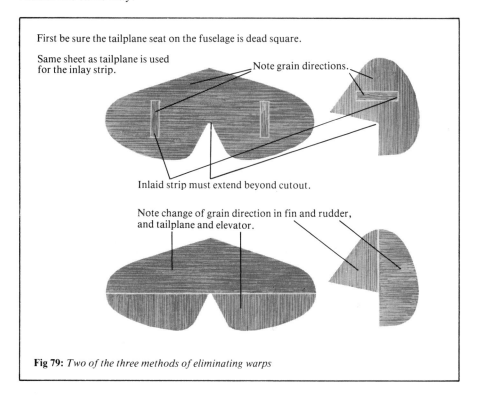

First be sure the tailplane seat on the fuselage is dead square.

Same sheet as tailplane is used for the inlay strip.

Note grain directions.

Inlaid strip must extend beyond cutout.

Note change of grain direction in fin and rudder, and tailplane and elevator.

Fig 79: *Two of the three methods of eliminating warps*

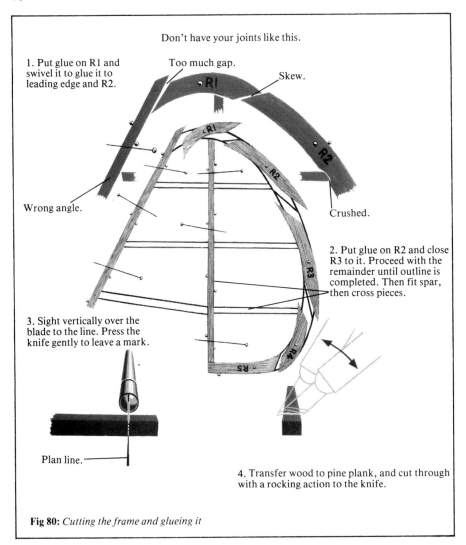

Don't have your joints like this.

1. Put glue on R1 and swivel it to glue it to leading edge and R2.

Too much gap.

Skew.

Wrong angle.

Crushed.

2. Put glue on R2 and close R3 to it. Proceed with the remainder until outline is completed. Then fit spar, then cross pieces.

3. Sight vertically over the blade to the line. Press the knife gently to leave a mark.

Plan line.

4. Transfer wood to pine plank, and cut through with a rocking action to the knife.

Fig 80: *Cutting the frame and glueing it*

Cutting strip framework

The cutting of strip balsa wood needs a mention here, because bad cutting affects the framework, causing trouble, such as an unaccountable warp, especially in wings, which can be a source of unbelievable frustration, and can so easily be avoided if the cutting is reasonably well done.

This being your first model, I suggest you start at the rudder because if you make a mess of it, it will not be a frightful loss, as you can always replace the wood cheaply and make a fresh start.

First pin the outline pieces in place, with one pin in the centre of each piece. Now swivel the piece slightly, to leave a gap between each, and put some glue on the edge of the first piece, then swivel it and its neighbour together, to close the gap, and glue these two. Continue right around the outline, until all the pieces are glued together.

With a new blade in the knife, trim one end of the strip that forms the spar (the vertical centre strip). Hold the strip against the inside edge of the outline on one side, and let it rest on top of the outline on the other side. Put the blade very gently in position, sight vertically over the outline inner edge, put the blade into this sight line, and press the blade gently to make a light slit in the wood, sufficient for you to see the mark. Remove the strip to the cutting block of pine, and cut through the wood at the slit mark. Try the fit of the cut piece. It must not be too tight, nor must it be too loose, and the ends should match the outline, as nearly as possible, and the cut should be vertical. Try to keep the blade of the knife vertical, and do not force the cut, rather rock the blade slightly, as you press it gently through the wood. Trim off a very thin shaving, if its fit is too tight, and try its fit again. When the fit is perfect, glue it in, and put pins on each side, to hold it firmly. Do each crosspiece the same way. When the glue is set, spray the frame with water, making sure the wood is really wet. Leave to dry right out overnight. Incidentally there is no need to discard a piece that is a bad fit, try to get it into the framework somewhere else, where a smaller piece is needed, and if it is still too small, put it in your scrap box. Also, if you get a piece that is about $\frac{1}{32}$ in (0.8 mm) too short, you can plug the gap with balsa cement, but do not have all your joints like this, because your model will turn out excessively heavy. You can cheat on a few joints, say about two, or three, per entire model, anything more means you are making a mess of it, and should try harder, taking greater care to do the job properly.

Every part of the entire frame has to be done with this sort of care, and try to make each joint better than the last—the way your model flies, and the way it looks, depend on it. Next time you visit your local hobby shop take a good look at the models there, they will inspire you to equal them.

Gluing the frame

There are two ways to use any glue. One is the right way, and the other is the wrong way. Too many beginners, old and young, use the wrong way, and their models look exceedingly ugly, because of the builder's ignorance in construction techniques, especially when using glues. The same model could look very good, if only the modeller had taken a bit of extra time to smooth the cement at the joints properly, and his model would also be much stronger.

The first thing to remember is that the balsa cement must be 'wet', or 'thin', it is absolutely no use at all, if it is 'thick', or like 'jelly'. If it is thick, then you can open the back of the tube by unrolling it, put in some thinners using an eye-dropper, and stir it gently, until the glue is wet. Carefully close the back again, and pinch it closed using pliers. This glue will take quite a bit longer to dry now, because the thinners are not the same as the original thinners used, when the glue was made at the factory. Sometimes this treatment of the glue makes it worse, and you have to throw it away. (It was useless as it was anyway.)

Because balsa cement dries fairly quickly, you have to make the joints without wasting any time. When making the fuselage for instance, put the glue on one crosspiece at both ends, then put one end to the longeron, to wipe a bit of the glue onto it, and the same with the other end, then put the crosspiece in place immediately. If you must chat, and wave the piece around while talking, you will find that the glue has dried slightly. This is a waste of glue, because the joint may hold, and seem all right, but in fact, it will not hold nearly as well as when the glue is wet, when the joint is made. 'Wet' glue will penetrate the pores of the wood, and therefore hold far better than slightly dried glue, which will not penetrate the pores as well. It is better to scrape that slightly dried glue off, and put fresh glue on the piece.

When gluing spars in a wing, start at one end. Put cement into a few notches, place the spar in position, and pin it if necessary, then put glue in the next few notches, push the spar into these, and so on to the end. Pin any spot where the spar does not stay in the notch. Before the glue has a chance to set, wipe off any excess, where it has squeezed up above the frame, with your finger. Where the glue is squeezed out sideways, smear this flat to the wood using a matchstick. If the glue is left to dry in blobs, you will find that these are very difficult to remove later, even when using very rough sandpaper. Covering over these blobs doesn't hide them at all, in fact they appear even more pronounced, and an otherwise well made model looks frightful. PVA glue usually dries without leaving any marks, but it is still a wise precaution to wipe it smooth, on the top surface of a frame, where the covering will go on.

Chapter 7

Built-up construction

Tailplanes and rudders

On small models of about 12 in to 20 in (30.5 cm to 50.8 cm) span, these are usually built flat, that is, they have no top curve or camber. This is a simple matter of building the outline to plan, and laying in the various spars, and crosspieces, and is usually finished by sanding the edges round and smooth. Sometimes however, further strips are glued on top of the frame, and these are then sanded to give a curved (lifting) top surface. Here again, all pieces should be pinned down, by placing pins on either side of each strip, making sure the whole frame is flat to the building board. Where the plan calls for a tailplane or rudder with ribs and spars, single or multiple, as these are identical to wings, they are all treated under the section on wings which follows.

Build in exactly the same way as the rudder in Fig 80, then add these strips.

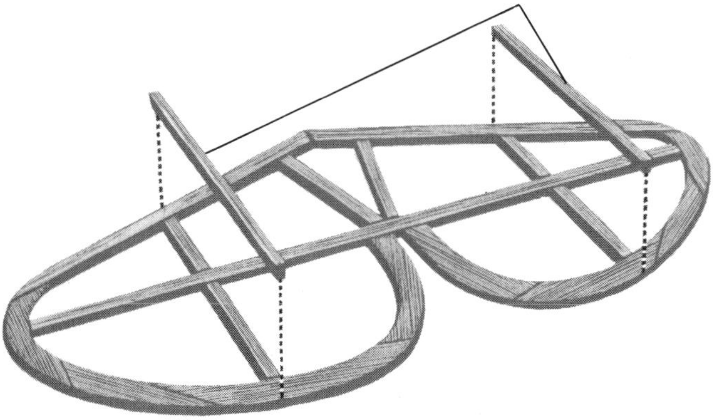

When dry sand the curve to the top surface as in the section below, while holding the frame firmly at the edge of the board.

Fig 81: *Small tailplanes*

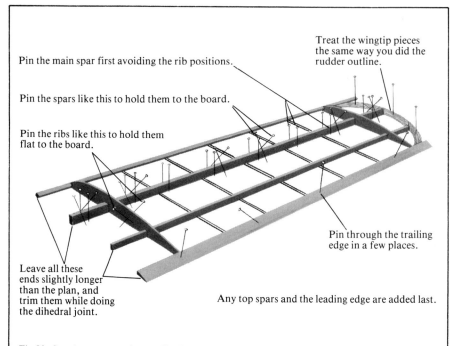

Pin the main spar first avoiding the rib positions.

Treat the wingtip pieces the same way you did the rudder outline.

Pin the spars like this to hold them to the board.

Pin the ribs like this to hold them flat to the board.

Pin through the trailing edge in a few places.

Leave all these ends slightly longer than the plan, and trim them while doing the dihedral joint.

Any top spars and the leading edge are added last.

Fig 82: *Starting construction on flat-bottomed wings, tailplanes, and rudders*

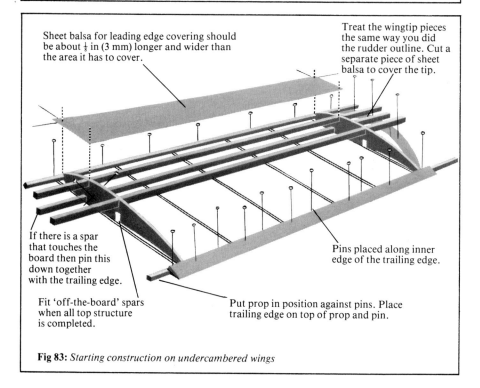

Sheet balsa for leading edge covering should be about ⅛ in (3 mm) longer and wider than the area it has to cover.

Treat the wingtip pieces the same way you did the rudder outline. Cut a separate piece of sheet balsa to cover the tip.

If there is a spar that touches the board then pin this down together with the trailing edge.

Pins placed along inner edge of the trailing edge.

Fit 'off-the-board' spars when all top structure is completed.

Put prop in position against pins. Place trailing edge on top of prop and pin.

Fig 83: *Starting construction on undercambered wings*

Wings, tailplanes, and some rudders with ribs of flat undersurface

Start by pinning either side of the thickest spar, the entire length of the plan of the wing, avoiding the rib positions. Trim the end at the tip very carefully, and leave the other end. Place any other spars on the undersurface, but do not pin them to the board yet. Pin them *after* the ribs are in position, mainly to keep them flat to the board. The ribs having been cut and sanded in stack form (as above), are placed in position and pinned if they do not lie flat to the surface. Check that each rib, as you place it, fits the spars properly; trim it if necessary. Put the trailing edge in position against the ribs, and pin it (the pins can be pushed through the wood), checking its fit. Using PVA, or balsa cement, glue in one rib at a time, spreading any excess glue, before gluing the next rib. *Make sure the rib is vertical, in line with the plan, and down to the board surface*; pin it to be sure it is right. If any rib is a loose fit, make sure you put a bit of extra glue on it, to hold it in place, or to fill any slight gap. Add the top spars (see under 'Gluing the frame' page 80) and the leading edge. The tip pieces are trimmed along their joint lines, until they fit, then pinned in their centres, swivelled open, edges glued, swivelled shut, and the excess glue wiped across the top surface. Allow to dry. They can then be easily fitted between leading edge and trailing edge, and glued.

When it is all done, and the glue has had a chance to set (about 2 hours for balsa cement and you can see when PVA is dry), spray the entire frame with water, using a detergent sprayer (with all the detergent thoroughly rinsed out), until the frame is well wetted. Allow it to dry out thoroughly overnight. Remove it from the board, sand the leading and trailing edge, if necessary, to shape them as the plan, and add the dihedral. (See under 'Dihedral joints', page 82).

Undercambered wings

Here we start by placing pins right along the inner edge of the trailing edge. Place the trailing edge prop against the pins, lay the trailing edge over the prop, and push pins through the trailing edge to secure it in place. Glue all the ribs to the trailing edge, pinning them to keep them upright and flush to the board surface, and glue on the leading edge. Find something else to do for the next hour or two, then continue by adding all the top spars, and allowing them to dry. If sheet balsa is to be used to cover the leading edge portion, cut this sheet slightly too wide, by about $\frac{1}{8}$ in (3 mm), test the fit, and when satisfied, working rapidly, put glue right along the leading edge and spar, and place the sheet in position. Pin the sheet at its centre and at each end, then work towards each end, pinning the sheet to the spar, and leading edge, as you progress. The tip pieces are trimmed along their join lines until they fit, are then pinned in the centre, swivelled open, edges glued, swivelled shut, and the excess glue wiped across the top surface. Allow to dry. They can then be easily fitted, between leading and trailing edges, and glued. Allow to dry completely. Cut and fit the sheet balsa to cover the tip, then glue and pin it in position, and allow to dry. Remove the wing from the board, and add glue to the ribs where they touch the top sheeting of balsa, then add the bottom spars, and allow to dry. Hold the frame, spray it thoroughly with water, shake off the excess, replace the wing on the board, again packing up the trailing edge and pinning it down. Lay weights on top, to keep the wing to the board, and allow to dry overnight. If a wing has a spar that touches the board surface, then that spar should be used, pinned down as well as the trailing edge, before proceeding as above.

Wings with two sides cambered

Here we may have a solid trailing edge, or one built of two sheets. The spar
may, or may not, touch the building board surface. Whether the trailing edge is
solid, or of two sheets (use the lower sheet), prop it up as per the plan, as well as
the leading edge. Put pins through the trailing edge, and at the front and back of
the leading edge. Test fit the ribs, and, when satisfied, glue them in place, and
allow to dry. Then glue in all the top spars, and where appropriate, the trailing
edge top sheet, and when dry, add the leading edge top sheet. Allow to dry.
Remove the wing from the board, and add the bottom spars. Allow to dry. Add
the leading edge sheet to the bottom surface. Allow to dry. Spray with water,
reprop the trailing edge, pin it to the board, and put weights on the top surface,
to keep the wing flat to the board surface. Allow to dry. To avoid all this hard
work, the ribs sometimes have balsa lugs left attached, so that the wing starts
off as though it had a flat undersurface. These lugs are removed last, when the
entire frame is completed.

Internal structure and two sheet covering

First make the entire wing structure, plus the dihedral, using the appropriate
method above for your particular wing. Cut the top and bottom sheets of balsa
slightly larger all around than the wing. This should be done by pinning the
sheets temporarily to the frame, using very few pins. Unpin the sheets, and lay
them out tidily on the board, in the same order that you remove them. Be
careful about this; do it again if you are slightly unsure. Glue together all the
sheets that form the top surface, using either balsa cement, or PVA. Do not
forget to use the waxed paper under the joints, and keep the sheets flat to the
board. Do the same for the lower sheet covering. Allow to dry. Use a brush to
paint the frame on the undersurface, covering all the ribs, spars, leading and
trailing edges, with a thick coat of PVA, and immediately lay the frame on the
lower sheet covering, centre the frame on the sheet, and pin it down to the sheet,
being very careful to ensure that the frame is well and truly flat down, and all
the ribs contact the sheet. The leading edge does not always contact the sheet;
just leave it like that. Allow the glue to dry. Now take out all the pins that will be
covered up by the top sheet, but leave those around the outside of the frame.
Unpin the top sheet from the board. Paint the top surface of the frame, as you
did the undersurface, and lay the top sheet in place. Centre it on the frame, and
pin it to the trailing edge with a few pins. Check that the leading edge is still
covered, and then proceed to pin that with a few pins. Check the covering is not
buckled and is down to the ribs. Do this by feeling if the surface is true to the
frame. Proceed to pin the sheet well down to the frame, and leave overnight to
dry.

Unpin the wing from the board, and glue and pin the lower sheet to the
leading edge. Trim the sheet, at the last rib, at the tip. Cover the tip with a
separate sheet of balsa. Do the other half of the wing the same way. Lastly,
cover the centre section, also in the same manner, being careful to keep the wing
true and untwisted at this stage.

Dihedral joints

The dihedral joints should be very carefully done. I cannot overemphasise the
importance of care here, even though the job is very simple. The main point to
watch is that the leading edge, trailing edge, and main spar, just outside the

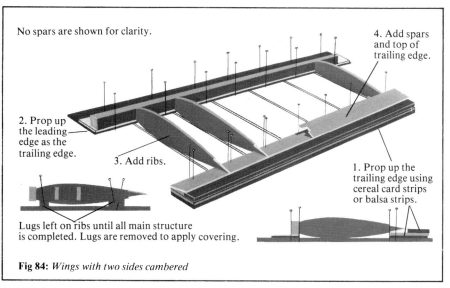

No spars are shown for clarity.

4. Add spars and top of trailing edge.

2. Prop up the leading edge as the trailing edge.

3. Add ribs.

1. Prop up the trailing edge using cereal card strips or balsa strips.

Lugs left on ribs until all main structure is completed. Lugs are removed to apply covering.

Fig 84: *Wings with two sides cambered*

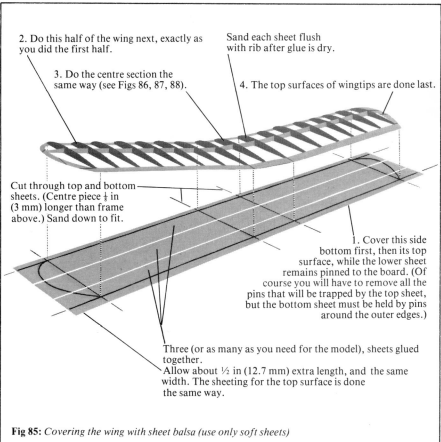

2. Do this half of the wing next, exactly as you did the first half.

Sand each sheet flush with rib after glue is dry.

3. Do the centre section the same way (see Figs 86, 87, 88).

4. The top surfaces of wingtips are done last.

Cut through top and bottom sheets. (Centre piece $\frac{1}{8}$ in (3 mm) longer than frame above.) Sand down to fit.

1. Cover this side bottom first, then its top surface, while the lower sheet remains pinned to the board. (Of course you will have to remove all the pins that will be trapped by the top sheet, but the bottom sheet must be held by pins around the outer edges.)

Three (or as many as you need for the model), sheets glued together. Allow about ½ in (12.7 mm) extra length, and the same width. The sheeting for the top surface is done the same way.

Fig 85: *Covering the wing with sheet balsa (use only soft sheets)*

When propped at one point only, either the trailing edge or the leading edge can sag slightly causing built-in warp.

Illustration is exaggerated to show the effect.

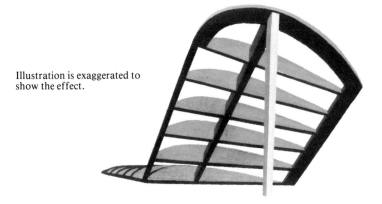

Fig 86: *How* NOT *to prop the wing for dihedral*

You can use one sheet of card as a prop, but make sure you place it under a rib near the wingtip, and check that the leading edge is not curved as shown. If the leading edge or trailing edge is curved then pin the wing flat to the board with a prop to give the opposite curve, wet the curved strip, and allow to dry overnight. Then proceed with the dihedral joint.

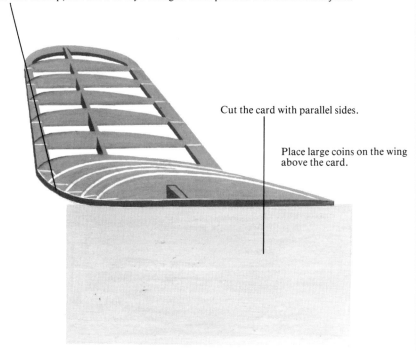

Cut the card with parallel sides.

Place large coins on the wing above the card.

Fig 87: *Dihedral joints*

joint, are all at the correct height above the board, at the same position. This will ensure that the angle at the leading edge, and the trailing edge, is the same throughout the joint. Although you have the correct height of leading edge, and trailing edge, at the tip, you sometimes find the angle at the joint varies, and this causes a warp, about half-way along the wing panel. It is a terrific hassle to fix it, when it is like this, once the glue has set. Also make sure you have a weight directly above the supports, because the cement at the joint sometimes shrinks so strongly that it lifts the leading edge, or trailing edge, beyond the angle you want. The extra work entailed is not much, and the benefits are obvious. If plywood dihedral braces are specified on the plan, do not rely on them to set the dihedral, but measure, and prop, the wing accurately as well.

Wingtips

On models of 12 in (30.5 cm) up to about 36 in (91.4 cm) span, where balsa is specified for outline wingtips, this can be substituted by $\frac{1}{8}$ in (3 mm) cane. Balsa tips cannot take much hard work, before they show signs of cracking up, and they do crack up rather easily if the model snags a wingtip, especially on the larger models. Cane, on the other hand, never breaks, rather it flexes and springs, so saving a lot of repair work. On 12 in (30.5 cm) span models it does

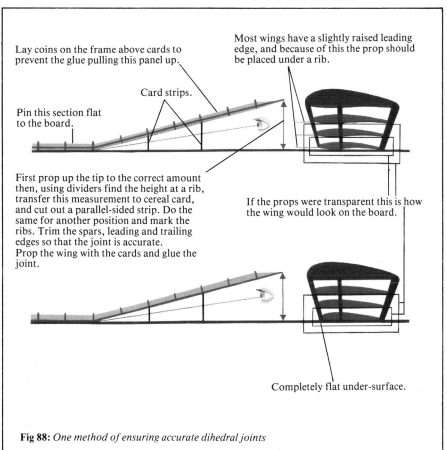

Lay coins on the frame above cards to prevent the glue pulling this panel up.

Most wings have a slightly raised leading edge, and because of this the prop should be placed under a rib.

Card strips.

Pin this section flat to the board.

First prop up the tip to the correct amount then, using dividers find the height at a rib, transfer this measurement to cereal card, and cut out a parallel-sided strip. Do the same for another position and mark the ribs. Trim the spars, leading and trailing edges so that the joint is accurate.
Prop the wing with the cards and glue the joint.

If the props were transparent this is how the wing would look on the board.

Completely flat under-surface.

Fig 88: *One method of ensuring accurate dihedral joints*

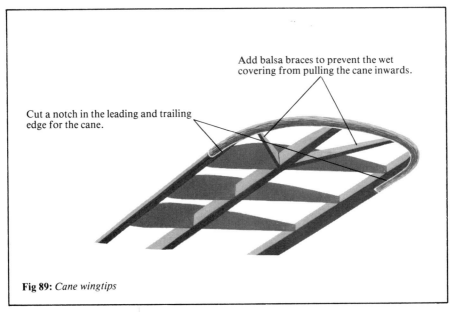

Add balsa braces to prevent the wet
covering from pulling the cane inwards.

Cut a notch in the leading and trailing
edge for the cane.

Fig 89: *Cane wingtips*

not give the 'heavy' wingtip which one might expect; in fact you do not even
have to sand it down. I find it works extremely well, even on the tailplanes. It
should be braced with balsa strips, to prevent it being pulled in by the paper,
when it shrinks after water spraying, the cane, of course, being damp for a while
after. Once dry though, the cane is back to its former toughness. When using
the existing plan of your model, all you have to do is to insert a row of pins
around the outside edge of the wingtip plan, wet the cane thoroughly, press it
against the row of pins, and keep it there, with a few pins on the inner edge,
until it dries. This will take about 3 or 4 hours, then remove the pins, notch, or
recess, the leading, and trailing edge, trim the cane to fit, and PVA it. If you try
to butt join the cane, you will find it does not hold very well, so always recess it
in a notch. It can also be sanded, so tapering it to fit the trailing edge is very
easy. Naturally, when it has to be used on larger models, the next size up, $\frac{3}{16}$ in,
or even $\frac{1}{4}$ in (4.7 mm or 6.3 mm), can be used. If curving it around pins becomes
a problem, then cut a form from soft wood like jelutong, to the inner edge of
the tip, and bind the cane in position, with string or rubber bands, until it is dry.

Fuselages
Box fuselage
Here, in fuselages, we find the most variations in construction methods.
Starting with the simplest, we have what is usually called the box fuselage.
Nowadays the basic structure is indicated on the plan by shading, and if there is
no shading, then the structure is very simple and straightforward. Start by
selecting four hard springy pieces for the longerons, and of these, select two that
are more easily bent, or curved, than the other two. The less curvable pair are
used for the straighter longerons of the frame. Use the offcuts, from these four
pieces, for the crosspieces, starting at the nose of the fuselage. The remainder of
the crosspieces are cut from medium or hard strips, depending on what you
have. The medium are preferable, as they save quite a bit of weight from behind

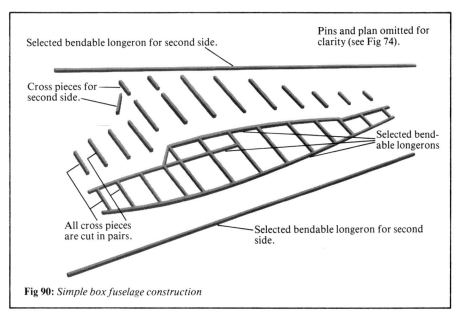

Selected bendable longeron for second side.

Pins and plan omitted for clarity (see Fig 74).

Cross pieces for second side.

Selected bendable longerons

All cross pieces are cut in pairs.

Selected bendable longeron for second side.

Fig 90: *Simple box fuselage construction*

the wing to the tail, which must be kept as light as possible. Soft strips can be used in this area, provided they are not very soft and/or brittle, but be careful when using very soft wood—it is not too clever to use this on fuselages. Pin the longerons, being careful that you follow the *outer* edge of the outline, especially where wing, and tailplane, fit. (The wing and tailplane angles have been carefully calculated, and the more accurately you follow the plan, the better the performance of your model, provided you keep the rest of the construction also as accurate as possible.) Cut the crossbraces, as you did for the rudder, but in pairs, so that both sides of the fuselage will be exact, and lay one from each pair above its position on the plan, and glue the other piece in place. When the glue is dry, spray or paint with water, and allow to dry thoroughly. Carefully remove the pins, and remove the side frame from the plan. Put the next pair of longerons in place, *using the same pin holes* that were used for the first frame; these are easily seen on the white paper of the plan. Glue in the crossbraces, as for the first frame, water spray, etc. Now while all this is drying, turn to the top view of the fuselage, and cut all the crossbraces in pairs too, and place them next to their appropriate positions. The next bit is slightly tricky, as there is not much to hold on to, and you must be very patient. The best procedure is to draw up, and cut out very accurately, a piece of card (use a cereal box), to fit two of the widest parts of the frame.

The idea is to cut two separate squares of card, large enough to have a square hole cut in each piece. The two cards act as a jig to hold the side frames square, while you add the top and bottom crosspieces. This hole should be as deep, as the side frame (at a crosspiece), and as wide as the frame will be (at the same crosspiece). The two pieces of card will fit the frame, fairly tightly, at two crosspiece positions. Slide each side frame into the two holes, tight to the side of each hole, and lined up with the crosspiece, from which you took the measurements. Glue in the appropriate top, and bottom, crosspiece. Allow the glue to dry for a couple of hours.

The measurements are taken from the side, and top view, of the fuselage, using the outer lines of the plan. Do all measuring with sharp dividers, and use set square and ruler to be sure all drawing is square and accurate. Cut out the card carefully. Check that the whole unit is square and accurate at this stage, check from above and from the side, prop if necessary, to maintain accuracy while the glue dries. The top can easily be checked, by placing the structure carefully over the top view on the plan, and sighted for alignment. The side view must be checked, by eye, that the frames are not skew to each other. Adjust at the tail to set them straight, by propping the rear of the longerons. When all is dry, carefully draw the tail ends together, and put a weak clothes-peg on, to hold it accurately closed. Here again, check side, and top, for proper alignment. Now glue in a few more top and bottom crossbraces, but do not hurry this, let the fresh pieces dry thoroughly first. Continue like this, adding a few pieces, and checking, until the tail is finished. While the tail is drying, work can proceed on the nose. Add two pieces at a time, and hold closed with a thin rubber band or two. Be careful you do not break something here, especially if you are using strong rubber bands. The card frames can now be removed. Now usually the undercarriage is built, and this will be covered under 'Wire bending' on page 107. Attaching the undercarriage is best done with PVA glue, rather than balsa cement, as the PVA is much more resilient than the cement, and very much tougher. Go over the nose joints with a smear of PVA glue, being careful to use a light smear on small models 12 in (30.5 cm) span. Larger models can take quite a thick smear.

Adding formers and stringers

Some plans show more pieces to be added to the above basic structure, and these usually consist of formers and stringers. The formers, cut and sanded, (some kits have them die-stamped, and we cannot work differently with them) should have the notches cut only in the first, and last, formers. Glue all the formers to the basic structure, in their respective positions, making sure they are square across the top and vertical from the side. Leave to dry. Now, placing a stringer in the first, and last notch, carefully mark the remaining formers, using a ballpen. Notch them at the marks. Select hard stringers for the undersurface, and the nose, softer ones for the top rear of the fuselage. Lay in one stringer at a time, after putting glue in the notches, and start in the centre of the fuselage. When this is all complete, roll up a piece of sandpaper and sand the wood between the stringers to a concave shape, if the model is to be covered with paper, silk, nylon, or any of the plastic films, like solarfilm, monokote, etc. This will prevent ugly bulges in the covering.

Sheet balsa covering

Sheet balsa covering of the entire fuselage is only done with soft bendable sheets; medium, or hard sheets, will add far too much weight. The further you can make a sheet go, in one area, obviously the less work you will have also, because there are less joints, you have less glue, and less weight. So wherever you can get a sheet to go further, by all means do that, but be careful you do not get a bulge that will not go down to the frame. Small free flight models up to about 30 in (76.2 cm) span, are covered (when this is called for on the plan), with $\frac{1}{32}$ in (0.79 mm) sheet, and above that size, use $\frac{1}{16}$ in (1.5 mm) sheet. Most control line models, covered this way, use $\frac{1}{16}$ in (1.5 mm) for the wings, and may

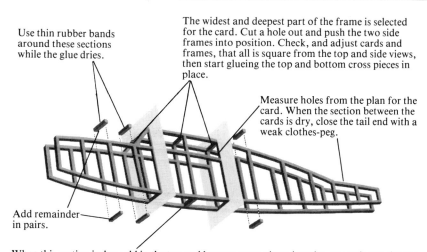

Use thin rubber bands around these sections while the glue dries.

The widest and deepest part of the frame is selected for the card. Cut a hole out and push the two side frames into position. Check, and adjust cards and frames, that all is square from the top and side views, then start glueing the top and bottom cross pieces in place.

Measure holes from the plan for the card. When the section between the cards is dry, close the tail end with a weak clothes-peg.

Add remainder in pairs.

When this section is dry, add in the top and bottom cross pieces in pairs, one pair at a time to nose and tail.

Fig 91: *Joining the two sides*

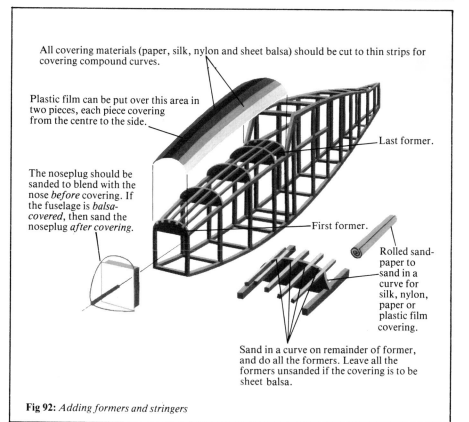

All covering materials (paper, silk, nylon and sheet balsa) should be cut to thin strips for covering compound curves.

Plastic film can be put over this area in two pieces, each piece covering from the centre to the side.

The noseplug should be sanded to blend with the nose *before* covering. If the fuselage is *balsa-covered*, then sand the noseplug *after covering*.

Last former.

First former.

Rolled sand-paper to sand in a curve for silk, nylon, paper or plastic film covering.

Sand in a curve on remainder of former, and do all the formers. Leave all the formers unsanded if the covering is to be sheet balsa.

Fig 92: *Adding formers and stringers*

use $\frac{1}{8}$ in (3 mm) sheet, or thicker, for the fuselage. Radio models use about the same sizes.

If the fuselage is to be covered in sheet balsa, then leave the formers unsanded (no concave sanding of the formers). If the stringer area is to be covered with balsa, this is sometimes, as in older designs, laid in between each stringer and involves quite a log of tedious marking and cutting. It is best to cut a strip of sheet, slightly wider than the gap between any two stringers, and then to lay this strip flat on the bench. Turn the fuselage, so that the two selected stringers cover, and lay on, the strip. Holding the fuselage steady, mark the strip using a ballpen. Cut the strip just outside the lines, and test fit it, noting where it does not fit, and sand this area, and test fit again. Continue sanding and fitting, until it fits, protruding very slightly above the stringers. Glue with balsa cement. Repeat on each pair of stringers, until the area is covered in. Sandpaper with medium, then fine sandpaper, until smooth, but being careful not to get the wood too thin. Test against a strong light, preferably outdoors. Another method is to damp the wood sheet, and gently ease it around a main curve, and continue round the fuselage as far as possible. Pin it with a few pins at the top of the curve, and down below, as far as the sheet reaches comfortably. Now take a ballpen (fine point) and holding the model to the light, sketch where it should be cut. Remove the pins, cut, and check the fit, cutting and sanding, until the piece fits with a bit of overlap, wherever possible. Now put PVA glue on each stringer, and former, redamp the wood, and try to get the pins into the old holes, and repin the sheet back in place. Only add more pins where they are needed, and leave to dry. Trim with the knife, and a small piece of folded

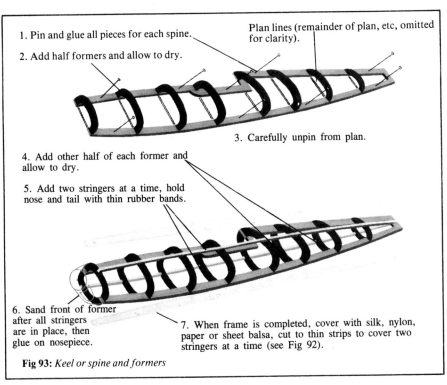

1. Pin and glue all pieces for each spine.

2. Add half formers and allow to dry.

Plan lines (remainder of plan, etc, omitted for clarity).

3. Carefully unpin from plan.

4. Add other half of each former and allow to dry.

5. Add two stringers at a time, hold nose and tail with thin rubber bands.

6. Sand front of former after all stringers are in place, then glue on nosepiece.

7. When frame is completed, cover with silk, nylon, paper or sheet balsa, cut to thin strips to cover two stringers at a time (see Fig 92).

Fig 93: *Keel or spine and formers*

sandpaper. Lay any other sheets needed in the same way, making sure they either overlap the first sheet, in which case you taper the edges, or make a good butt joint with it. Sand smooth all over.

Where a fuselage has compound curves all over, the only method is to use sheet, cut into strips, wide enough to cover the gap at the widest point, between the stringers. These strips should extend from nose to tail, with a slight overhang at one end. A start is made in the middle of each side. One complete strip is pinned and glued, starting from the nose, and working towards the tail, care being taken not to distort the underlying frame. Further strips are laid, working both sides simultaneously, above the first strip, towards the top. Then working the same way, towards the bottom. Each strip is also glued to the one next to it. Along the top, and bottom, centreline involves the cutting and fitting of innumerable small, narrow, wedge shapes, to seal the planking. It is then sanded smooth all over, ready for finishing.

Keel or spine and formers

This fuselage consists of a top and bottom spine, cut from sheet balsa, and assembled, and glued, on the plan, using pins pushed through each separate piece. Formers are cut, sanded, and notched. Each former is in two halves, and one half of each is glued to the spine, on the plan. When dry, remove from the plan and add the other half of each former. When dry, add two stringers, together, at the front, at the centre of each side, and work them into the notches, gluing as you go, until you reach the other end. *Make very sure you keep the two spines dead straight.* Put a thin rubber band, or two, over the nose

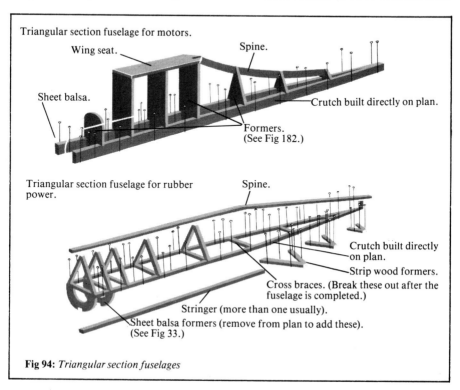

Fig 94: *Triangular section fuselages*

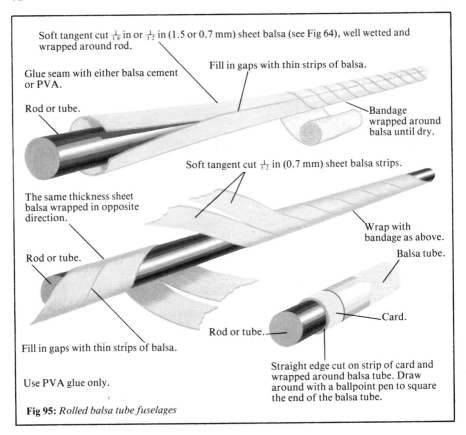

Soft tangent cut $\frac{1}{16}$ in or $\frac{1}{32}$ in (1.5 or 0.7 mm) sheet balsa (see Fig 64), well wetted and wrapped around rod.

Glue seam with either balsa cement or PVA.

Fill in gaps with thin strips of balsa.

Rod or tube.

Bandage wrapped around balsa until dry.

Soft tangent cut $\frac{1}{32}$ in (0.7 mm) sheet balsa strips.

The same thickness sheet balsa wrapped in opposite direction.

Wrap with bandage as above.

Balsa tube.

Rod or tube.

Fill in gaps with thin strips of balsa.

Rod or tube.

Card.

Use PVA glue only.

Straight edge cut on strip of card and wrapped around balsa tube. Draw around with a ballpoint pen to square the end of the balsa tube.

Fig 95: *Rolled balsa tube fuselages*

and tail, to hold the stringers in place. Proceed to add two stringers, one to each side at a time, until completed, continuously checking that the spines remain dead straight. This structure is covered with paper, if it is small to medium size. Larger models are covered with silk, nylon, solarfilm, etc, or can be covered completely with sheet balsa.

Triangular section fuselage

The triangular section fuselage is quick, and easy, when designed for motor power. This usually starts with a simple frame, or 'crutch', built directly on the plan view. Above this, formers are added, usually square in the nose, and triangular behind the wing to the tail. Then a spine is added on the section behind the wing to the tail. Front formers are covered with sheet balsa, after the insertion and gluing of the motor bearers and undercarriage (if used). Covering can then be tissue, silk, nylon, or solarfilm, etc. The triangular section fuselage, for rubber power, is started as above, but the formers are more generally built up, consisting of Vs of strip wood, built separately on the plan, and when dry, mounted in position on the frame. When dry, a strip wood balsa spine is added to the apex of the Vs. If formers are added to the other side of the frame, and stringers added over these, then the rubber motor may coincide with the position of the crossbraces in the frame. The crossbraces must be broken out, carefully, after the structure is completed.

Rolled tube fuselages

These are wrapped around some sort of tube or rod. This may be a wooden dowel, or aluminium tube, of the correct diameter. (Just be sure that whatever you use is straight, and will not bend too easily while you are working.)

A wide strip of balsa is simply wetted, and wrapped around the rod or tube, and held in position until it is dry, by wrapping with bandage. When dry, the overlap is cut through, and the two edges glued, with wax paper strip under the seam. Tape is put on, in strips, to hold the edges together while the glue dries.

Alternatively, the balsa strip can be quite narrow, and this is wrapped diagonally around the rod, or tube, after wetting thoroughly, and bandaged until dry. The bandage is removed, but the ends of the balsa strip are taped to the rod or tube to hold them firmly. A second strip of balsa is wetted, as before, and wrapped until it is dry. Taped at one end, it is then glued, and wrapped around the first strip, and taped at its far end, until the glue is dry. To get the ends square, simply cut a straight edge on a strip of thin card, or paper, wrap this around the end and, while holding it there, draw around the balsa tube with a ballpen. Cut just outside the line, and sand down to the line. A tapered rod is best wrapped with the wide strip method. Two thin sheets can be wrapped over each other, to form the tube of the same thickness as the main tube, if this was done with the diagonal winding method.

We have covered most of the common methods used in fuselage construction, so that your model can be tackled, and should now be a straightforward job. There are, of course, any number of combinations and variations to those I have given you here, but simply refer to one of these notes, for any particular construction you may have in your model, and I feel sure you will be able to cope with it.

Chapter 8

Fuselage additions and fittings

These can apply to any type of model, and are used in any combinations. They also have innumerable variations, but I will give you one or two examples, so that if your plan calls for a freewheeling propeller, but gives no details, you can make one and fit it with confidence that it will work.

Cellulose acetate cabin and windows

These are used on cabin semi-scale, and scale models, of all sizes and types. The smaller the model, the thinner the acetate should be, but *never* use cellophane, as it adds no strength to the cabin, it does not stick properly, and the creases are nearly impossible to remove. Cellulose acetate sheet can be obtained from your hobby shop, Kodak, or you may find it as the 'window' on some cardboard boxes, and as the transparent covering on some cosmetics. To identify it, put a drop of acetone (without castor oil) on one corner, and if it begins to dissolve, that is the stuff you are looking for. If it does not dissolve, do not use it. The cabin windows should be glued on before you begin to cover the model. Start at the front of the cabin. First take a sheet of ordinary writing paper and cut a very wide strip off the end. This strip should have a number of cuts in it, along its two long sides. Wrap it around the cabin front, and hold it in place with the fingers; of course it will not fit, but the idea is to see, roughly, how much to trim off, and where. Now hold it like that, and, with a ballpen, mark it as best you can, all around the outer edges of the cabin. Remove the paper, lay it flat, and carefully finish your lines, and round, or straighten them, to neaten them. Now cut out this pattern, leaving about $\frac{1}{8}$ in (3 mm) all around. Wrap the paper around again, to see how it fits. Try to adjust it, so that your sketch lines nearly fit. Readjust your lines where necessary. Now trim the paper down, close to the new line, and try the fit again. When it fits well (it does not have to be perfect), stick the paper to the acetate sheet, using tissue glue, or tape your pattern, face up. Use scissors to cut the acetate, peel off the paper pattern, and check the fit of the acetate. It should be slightly larger all around the edge of the cabin. Hold it in position and, carefully and gently, press pins through the acetate and into the wood, yes, even if the wood is $\frac{1}{16}$ in (1.5 mm) sq. The pins should go in near the joints but do not force the pins right through the wood, just the tip of the pin should penetrate, enough to hold the acetate in place. Use as few pins as you can. Take a thin piece of wire and dip it into a bottle of acetone (do not use your mother's, or wife's nail polish remover or acetone—it has oil in it which prevents it sticking) to collect a drop. Put this drop between the wood and the acetate, and it will run, by itself, neatly under the acetate. Repeat at each longeron and crossbrace in the cabin. Do not use too much, as it will over-melt the acetate, and cause it to sag in around the wood. Leave for at least an hour to dry. Remove the pins and the acetate should be firmly stuck. Trim any overlap, very carefully, with a knife. The side windows need an oversize strip of acetate, cut and stuck, as above, without a pattern. When dry, trim close to the wood.

Cockpit canopies

Some canopies can be made by simply bending a strip of acetate to shape, and pinning and gluing as above. Of course, you can use a paper pattern to make it, if you feel you may not get it right first time. The acetate can be laid on the side view of the cockpit, taped down, and then scratched with the point of a compass, used with a ruler, to trace it onto the acetate. This will leave a definite mark. Trace off the top view next to this, and then the side view again, next to that. Cut out along the outer lines, and fold it along the scratch lines. Pin and glue it to the frame, as above. Do the front piece, by the 'cut and try' method, as above.

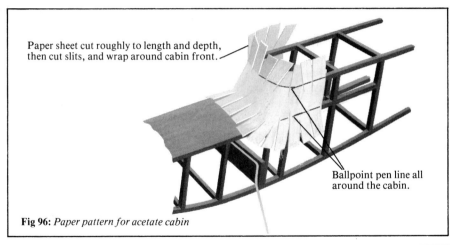

Paper sheet cut roughly to length and depth, then cut slits, and wrap around cabin front.

Ballpoint pen line all around the cabin.

Fig 96: *Paper pattern for acetate cabin*

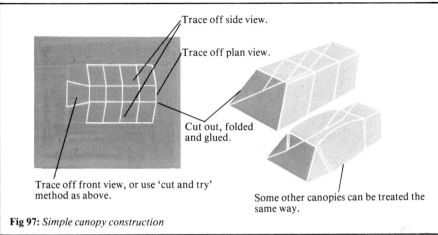

Trace off side view.

Trace off plan view.

Cut out, folded and glued.

Trace off front view, or use 'cut and try' method as above.

Some other canopies can be treated the same way.

Fig 97: *Simple canopy construction*

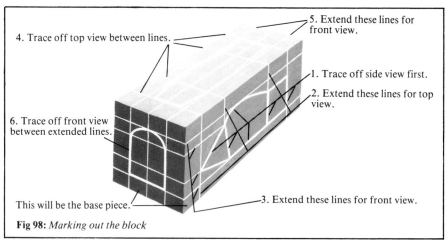

4. Trace off top view between lines.

5. Extend these lines for front view.

1. Trace off side view first.

2. Extend these lines for top view.

6. Trace off front view between extended lines.

This will be the base piece.

3. Extend these lines for front view.

Fig 98: *Marking out the block*

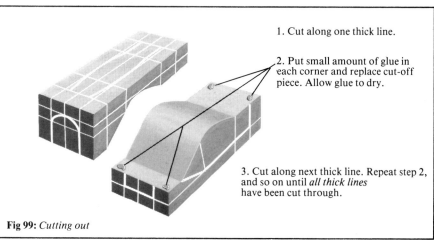

1. Cut along one thick line.

2. Put small amount of glue in each corner and replace cut-off piece. Allow glue to dry.

3. Cut along next thick line. Repeat step 2, and so on until *all thick lines* have been cut through.

Fig 99: *Cutting out*

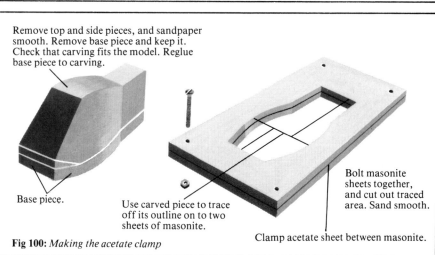

Remove top and side pieces, and sandpaper smooth. Remove base piece and keep it. Check that carving fits the model. Reglue base piece to carving.

Base piece.

Use carved piece to trace off its outline on to two sheets of masonite.

Bolt masonite sheets together, and cut out traced area. Sand smooth.

Clamp acetate sheet between masonite.

Fig 100: *Making the acetate clamp*

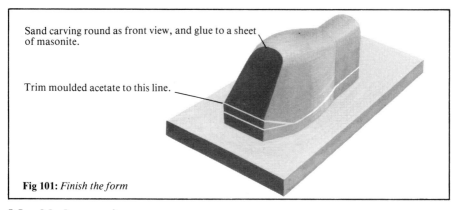

Sand carving round as front view, and glue to a sheet of masonite.

Trim moulded acetate to this line.

Fig 101: *Finish the form*

Moulded canopies

Kits supply these, but if you cannot get a suitable canopy from your model shop, when you are working from a plan, then you have to make one. This is interesting, and not too difficult. First get a block of soft wood like jelutong, or obeche. Do not use pine, as its grain will show up on the moulded piece. Cut and plane the wood to oversize, about ¼ in (6.3 mm) all around, it does not have to be perfectly square, but do your best. Now trace off the plan, the side view, top view, and front view. Transfer these, using carbon paper, on to the block, making sure they all line up to a line drawn around the block. Extend parallel lines, touching the edge of the top view, to the end of the block. Trace the front view between these lines, and fitting between parallel lines, extended from the side view. Using a jigsaw, hand held or power type, cut out the side view just outside the lines. Do not worry about it, if you cut it a bit wobbly. *Do not* try to recut it. Simply cut it right through. Put a tiny spot of balsa cement on one or two spots, and put the pieces accurately together again, and allow time for the glue to set hard. Now cut out the top view, and reglue it as before. Then cut out the front view, cutting at an angle, roughly the same as the angle of the curve (if it is curved). Remove only the top, and side pieces, not the base piece. Sand the sides first, then the top, and lastly the front. When it is cleaned up to this point, only then can you sand the front view curve in. Remove the base piece, but keep it. Check that the carving fits the model. Glue the base back on. Take two pieces of $\frac{1}{8}$ in (3 mm) sheet masonite, about 2 in (5.8 cm) larger all around, than the base of the carved piece. Place the carved piece centrally on one piece of masonite, and trace off its edge, using a ballpen. Bolt both pieces of masonite together, and cut out and sand the hole until it is smooth. Clamp a piece of cellulose acetate between the sheets of masonite, and hold, or support this, over an electric heater, about 18 in to 24 in (45.7 cm to 60.9 cm) away, above its surface. Watch the acetate carefully. When it is warm enough, it will sag, and 'steam', and now is the time to press the carved form, gently, into the hole in the masonite. Press firmly, until it is right in, and hold it in, while removing the entire unit from the heater. Continue to hold it, for about half a minute, while it cools. Remove the bolts, and gently ease out the moulding. Trim it, using scissors, and glue it to the model, using trimmed off acetate dissolved in a small pill bottle, about half full of acetone. Hold the canopy to the model, and apply the glue using a straightened paper clip. Hold it for a minute or two and then leave it to dry for about an hour.

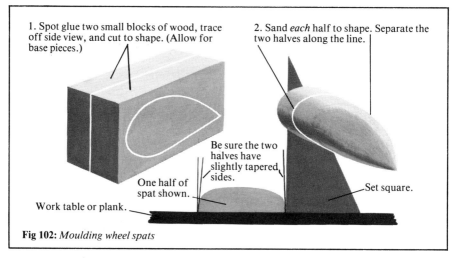

1. Spot glue two small blocks of wood, trace off side view, and cut to shape. (Allow for base pieces.)

2. Sand *each* half to shape. Separate the two halves along the line.

Be sure the two halves have slightly tapered sides.

One half of spat shown.

Set square.

Work table or plank.

Fig 102: *Moulding wheel spats*

Other mouldings

You do not have to stop at canopies, there are wheel spats, radial engine cowls, and complete nose mouldings, as well as any other part you wish to mould, that have a very thin wall, with a good finish to the surface, like air scoops, and cowling 'bulges' of all kinds, depending on the aircraft you are modelling. Once you get the hang of this moulding technique, you can do quite a few 'impossible' things with it. Some parts like wheel spats, and small wheels, should be made in two halves, trimmed, sanded 'wet', with the sandpaper laid on a flat surface (very important for a good finish to the joint), and then glued together. For wheels you only need to make half a wheel, out of wood or metal, to do your moulding.

Wing attaching methods

There are four ways the wings can be attached to the model. Small models of about 12 in (30.5 cm) span, have the wings glued directly to the fuselage, as are the tailplane and rudder. Models a little larger have only the tailplane and rudder glued on, the wings being held to the fuselage with rubber bands hooked around dowels glued in the fuselage. Larger models have the tailplane and the wings held on with rubber bands. Radio-controlled models generally have only the mainplane fixed with rubber bands. Some models, whether radio-controlled or not, have their wings attached by means of wing tongues of plywood, or they have wire dowels to attach the two halves of the wing to the fuselage.

When gluing the wings to the fuselage on small models, you should spend a bit of time on the job, to ensure that the wing is true to the fuselage in the side view (to ensure the correct angle of incidence), and in the front view, so that it is true to the tailplane, and in the top view, so that it is true to the centre line of the fuselage. The top of the fuselage that forms the wing seat is also a very important area. If you have spent a lot of time getting the wing completely accurate and then, say, the fuselage is a bit roughly done, the wing seat area will probably be a bit skew. This is noticed when the wing rocks on top of the fuselage. This must be rectified before you can attach the wing. The same goes for the tailplane and its seat. You can now see why it is so important to do every part of the construction properly, and not try to rectify it at this stage.

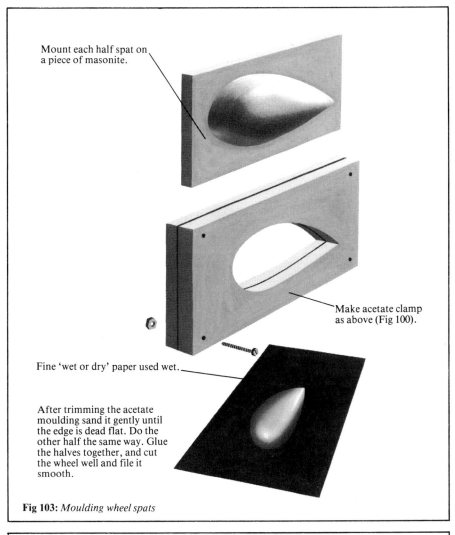

Mount each half spat on a piece of masonite.

Make acetate clamp as above (Fig 100).

Fine 'wet or dry' paper used wet.

After trimming the acetate moulding sand it gently until the edge is dead flat. Do the other half the same way. Glue the halves together, and cut the wheel well and file it smooth.

Fig 103: *Moulding wheel spats*

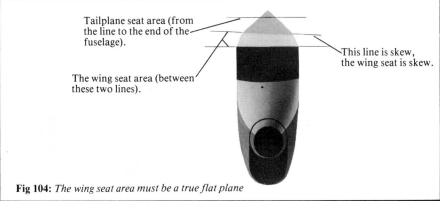

Tailplane seat area (from the line to the end of the fuselage).

This line is skew, the wing seat is skew.

The wing seat area (between these two lines).

Fig 104: *The wing seat area must be a true flat plane*

The same remarks can be made for the case where the wings are attached with rubber bands. *Do not* try to force the wings down with extra bands, this will only warp the wing and make things worse.

If, on a model with a glow plug, or diesel motor, you find that oil is getting on to the contact area between the fuselage and wing, you can rectify this slipping by gluing very fine emery cloth to the wing and the fuselage at the contact points. This will hold the wing firmly, and yet give way in a rough landing.

The plywood tongue, fixed either to the wing or the fuselage, plugs into a plywood, or balsa and plywood, box. This box is either in the fuselage, or the wing. However this is arranged, it must be very carefully made, to ensure that the wing (both halves of it), line up absolutely true. Let us suppose the box is in the fuselage, and the two tongues are in the wing roots. First make the box, using the cut tongues to ensure a good fit. Remove the tongues after the box is completed and the glue has dried. Place the box in the fuselage. Prop the fuselage square to the building board. Put the tongues into the box. Fit the wings to the tongues, *but do not glue them*. Prop up the wing panels for dihedral. Attach balsa strips, of deep section, to the wing panels with rubber bands. Carefully check the strips, in side view and top view, for true alignment. When both checks agree, then glue the tongues to the wing panels, and the box to the fuselage, without disturbing this true set-up, and allow at least all night for the glue to set properly.

The wire dowel method of attaching the wings is preferred by some modellers because the method allows a certain amount of flexibility to the joint. (The plywood box and tongue is strong and rigid.) The wire dowels should be cut, using either a hacksaw (with a very fine-toothed blade), or filed from two sides and broken. Grind the ends smooth, and very slightly tapered. Paper tubes are formed for the dowels by coating the dowel very thinly with wax, and wrapping the paper tightly, and gluing it, while it is being wrapped. The tube must have a thick wall. Allow a lot of time for the glue to dry—a day or two at least. Remove the tubes, and clean off the wax from the wire.

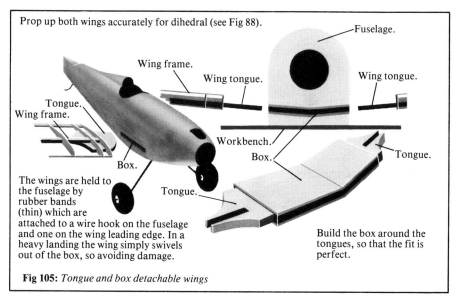

Prop up both wings accurately for dihedral (see Fig 88).

Fuselage.

Wing frame.

Wing tongue.

Wing tongue.

Tongue.
Wing frame.

Workbench.

Box.

Tongue.

Box.

Tongue.

The wings are held to the fuselage by rubber bands (thin) which are attached to a wire hook on the fuselage and one on the wing leading edge. In a heavy landing the wing simply swivels out of the box, so avoiding damage.

Build the box around the tongues, so that the fit is perfect.

Fig 105: *Tongue and box detachable wings*

A different model wing and fuselage shown solid for clarity. Dihedral props also omitted.

Two straight thick strips held to the wings, in line with the ribs, are used to check that the wings have exactly the same angle of incidence.

Rubber bands looped around the frame to hold the strips.

Check front view of wings and side view using the strips.

Fig 106: *Tongue and box. Check for the angle of incidence of the wings*

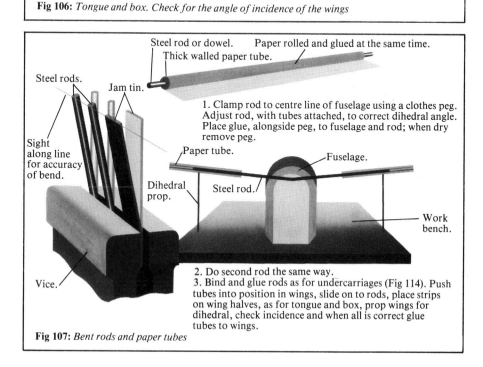

Steel rod or dowel.   Paper rolled and glued at the same time.
Thick walled paper tube.

Steel rods.   Jam tin.

1. Clamp rod to centre line of fuselage using a clothes peg. Adjust rod, with tubes attached, to correct dihedral angle. Place glue, alongside peg, to fuselage and rod; when dry remove peg.

Sight along line for accuracy of bend.

Paper tube.

Fuselage.

Dihedral prop.   Steel rod.

Work bench.

Vice.

2. Do second rod the same way.
3. Bind and glue rods as for undercarriages (Fig 114). Push tubes into position in wings, slide on to rods, place strips on wing halves, as for tongue and box, prop wings for dihedral, check incidence and when all is correct glue tubes to wings.

Fig 107: *Bent rods and paper tubes*

Assemble everything as in the diagram, with a clothes peg holding each rod at its centre. Use the two strips rubber-banded to the wings. Prop for dihedral. Check wing incidence from the front view as well as with the two strips. When this set-up is correct, glue the rods to the fuselage. Bind and glue the rods as for undercarriages (see Fig 114).

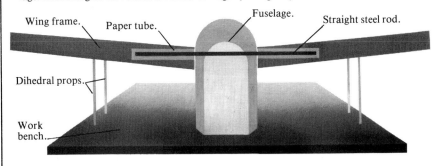

Fig 108: *Straight rods and paper tubes*

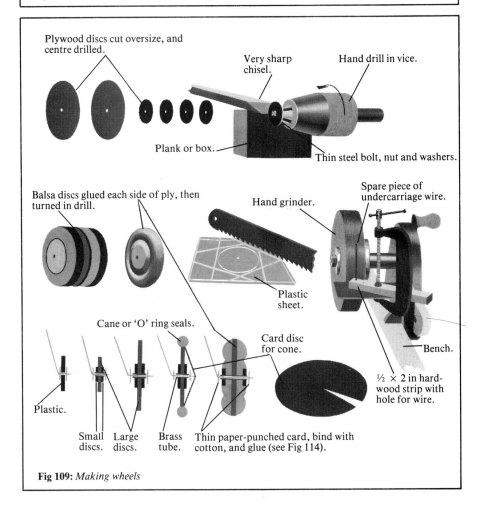

Fig 109: *Making wheels*

Put both pieces of wire in the vice, and line up their ends. Using a thick iron bar (about $\frac{1}{4}$ in by $\frac{1}{2}$ in) (6.3 mm by 12.7 mm) placed about $\frac{1}{2}$ in (12.7 mm) above the vice jaws, and in contact with the wires, tap this bar with a hammer to bend both wires at the same time, to the same angle. A strip of jam tin, flattened and then bent to the correct angle for the wires, should be placed in the gap of the vice jaws, to check the angle of the wires.

The same care is needed when gluing the parts to the wing and fuselage, as for the plywood tongue and box above.

Wheels

When working from plans these have to be made, and their construction is sometimes detailed on the plan. If not, then they can be purchased, or if your shop does not have them, you may be able to scrounge a pair, especially the very small ones from a toy car, even buying a cheap one at the bazaars is sometimes worth it. (They have ready moulded tyres and hubs in some cases. The cheap tinplate type are nearly always a good source.) If you own a lathe, then your problem is just the time to make them, but I must assume you have none of the advantages above, but you may have a hand grinder, or a disc sander, or just a hand drill.

The hand drill is not the best method, but it will serve. Draw the wheels and discs on plywood, using a compass. Cut out the pair of discs for your wheels, and two pairs of small discs; this need only be roughly done, but all should be cut oversize. Drill the centres for a thin steel bolt, and attach the nut and bolt to the disc, with a washer on each side. Mount the drill in the vice, being careful not to overtighten the vice. Chuck the bolt in the drill, and use the drill as a hand-turned lathe. A sharp chisel, or knife, should rest on a box, or plank, that serves as a tool rest. Turn the drill at high speed, to cut properly, and take very light cuts, do not try to force the cutting speed. Each disc is done in turn and, when the cutting is completed, use very fine sandpaper to smooth the wood while turning it. Balsa wood tyres and hubs can be added before the turning is done, so that the plywood and balsa are cut down together, and the centres can be cut, to accept the small discs. Brass tube is cut to the depth of the wheel, glued with PVA, and the small discs glued to the wheel to complete it. Paint the entire wheel with the PVA glue to strengthen it.

Here's how you can make a very true running pair of wheels. Small wheels can be formed from a flat sheet of plastic about $\frac{1}{16}$ in (1.5 mm) thick, taken from a pencil box top, or any other broken household plastic container. These containers are made of polystyrene, a plastic that gives a metallic ring when flicked with a finger. It is the same plastic that is used in plastic kits. (Do not use plastic squeeze bottles.) This polystyrene sheet is quite easy to work, being shaped on a hand grinder. First drill the holes, using a drill that gives a clearance to the wire. The drill should preferably be mounted on a stand to ensure truly vertical holes. An electric drill should not be used, as its speed is too high, and this will melt the plastic. In this case, turn the chuck by hand, and feed the drill in slowly. Now use a pair of dividers, to scribe the circles, for the wheels. Using a hacksaw blade, held in the hand, and worked flat across the surface, make several cuts around each piece, to release it from the sheet. It is only necessary to cut into the surface to about half-way down. Bend the sheet sharply along the cut line, to separate all pieces. Using the hand grinder, grind off a section until it is just flush with the scribed circle. Take a small piece of hardwood, aluminium, or plastic, about $\frac{1}{2}$ in sq by 2 in (12.7 mm sq by 5 cm), and drill a hole right through, to accept a spare piece of undercarriage wire, about $\frac{1}{2}$ in (12.7 mm) from one end. Take a piece of spare undercarriage wire, about $1\frac{1}{4}$ in (3.1 cm) long, and bend a small bit of the end to a right angle. Insert this wire in the hole, with the bent end underneath, and clamp the wood strip to the rest on the grinder, so that the wire is in line with the grinding wheel. Drop a disc onto the wire, and loosen the clamp, just enough to be able to adjust the position of the wood strip, until the flat ground on the wheel disc just touches the grinding wheel lightly. Clamp the wood strip tight. With the left hand, hold the wheel disc firmly, and rotate the grinder with the right hand. Now, *slowly* force the wheel disc to rotate on the wire, while rotating the grinding wheel at high speed. Continue until the wheel disc is perfect. Do the same with all the discs. If necessary, place each disc on a pin, held in a clothes-peg, dope the discs black, and leave to dry. This method can also be used with a disc sander, and any size, perfectly true disc, can be formed in sheet plastic, plywood, or metal, for wheels and thrust buttons, and propeller hubs for rubber powered models. Always use a piece of brass tube, to act as a bearing for the wire shaft, and glue the tube to the wood, using plenty of PVA glue.

To test a wheel, before the glue dries, for any wobble, insert a piece of wire in a matchbox, put the wheel on the wire, and spin the wheel by blowing hard on its edge. correct any wobbly running, by bending the wheel over, and leave to dry.

Tyres can be made, by taking a piece of cane of the right diameter, and long enough to go around the circumference, plus 1 in (2.5 cm) of both wheels, and soaking it in warm water for about an hour. In the meantime, place pins around the inner line of the 'tyre', making sure you have the waxed paper over the plan, remove the cane from the water and wind it around the pins, being sure to put in at least $1\frac{1}{2}$ turns per wheel. Pin the ends tight to the inner row of pins, and leave to dry overnight.

The cane can also be wound around a pill bottle, or metal canister, of slightly less diameter than the inner line of the tyre. Here, if you need a few tyres, you put on as many turns of cane as you can. Wind elastic bands tightly around the ends and leave to dry. Trim the end of the cane, wind it around the wheel, and nick a mark in the cane where it meets the trimmed end. Remove the wheel and cut the cane. Test the resulting tyre for its fit. Both ends should meet perfectly. Black dope the tyre, silver dope the wheel. Silver dope one side of stiff paper, or thin card and, when dry, cut a disc very slightly larger than the inner edge of the tyre on the plan. Cut a straight wedge shape out of the disc, being sure the cut starts exactly at the centre, and that the wedge shape is narrow. Put balsa cement on the back of the cut edges of the disc, and over the cut out V shape. Pull the edges of the V cut together, and place the V, to cover the joint, on the back of the disc. Clamp with a clothes-peg, and allow to dry. Put PVA glue around the edge of the wheel, and put the tyre on, and pin it to hold it, using about four pins. When dry, slip the wheel on to the axle, and PVA glue a paper washer on the axle end and, while the glue is still fresh, bind cotton thread tightly on the axle end, spreading the glue on the cotton as you go. Leave to dry. Add the cone to the wheel, gluing it with PVA. Should you want fat-tyred, modern wheels, then use thicker cane for the tyres, and possibly add a balsa disc to one, or both sides, of the wheel, adding a thin card disc to each side, with the spokes drawn in, or the discs left plain doped silver, as on a P40 Kittyhawk.

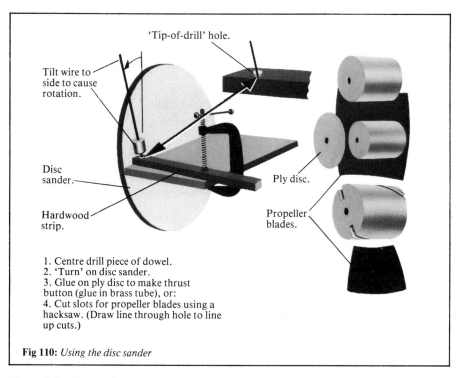

'Tip-of-drill' hole.

Tilt wire to side to cause rotation.

Disc sander.

Hardwood strip.

Ply disc.

Propeller blades.

1. Centre drill piece of dowel.
2. 'Turn' on disc sander.
3. Glue on ply disc to make thrust button (glue in brass tube), or:
4. Cut slots for propeller blades using a hacksaw. (Draw line through hole to line up cuts.)

Fig 110: *Using the disc sander*

Nose blocks and thrust buttons

All rubber powered models have one or the other. Small models up to about 12 in (30.5 cm) span need only the plastic thrust button, because the hole that it fits in the nose is usually large enough to allow the wound rubber motor back through the hole. Let me explain. The rubber motor is usually pulled to stretch it, to about three times its normal length, before winding begins. As winding progresses, so the person winding walks slowly back towards the model, until the model is reached at the end of the winding. This allows many more turns to be put into the rubber than is possible by simply winding the propeller around while still in the model. On reaching the model, and on releasing the winder, it will be found that the rubber has knots that take up about three times the original width of the motor. If the hole in the nose is too small, the rubber will not fit back into the fuselage. If this is found to be the case in a small model, then the nose opening must be opened up by cutting a square hole that will be large enough to allow the rubber back in. A separate square of balsa is made to fit the hole, and this piece is capped by a slightly larger piece of ply. The thrust button may be glued into this new thrust block, or the button put into your scrap box. Do not just dig a hole out, it should be quite carefully worked out, not too small for the wound rubber motor and not too large to spoil the nose lines, and weaken the nose. (The model may hit on the nose, under full power, and this force can sometimes push the whole nose in if the hole is too big.) The plastic thrust button makes a good bearing for the propeller shaft, and should therefore be used if possible. If, on a small model, it is found to disturb the balance, then exchange it for a brass tube that does not give a sloppy fit to the propeller shaft. The shaft should fit quite snugly, but it must rotate very freely.

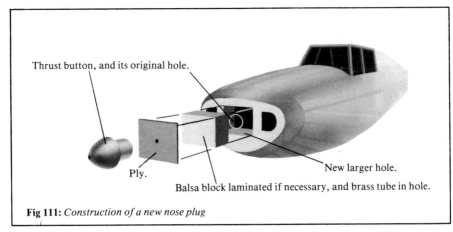

Thrust button, and its original hole.

Ply.

New larger hole.

Balsa block laminated if necessary, and brass tube in hole.

Fig 111: *Construction of a new nose plug*

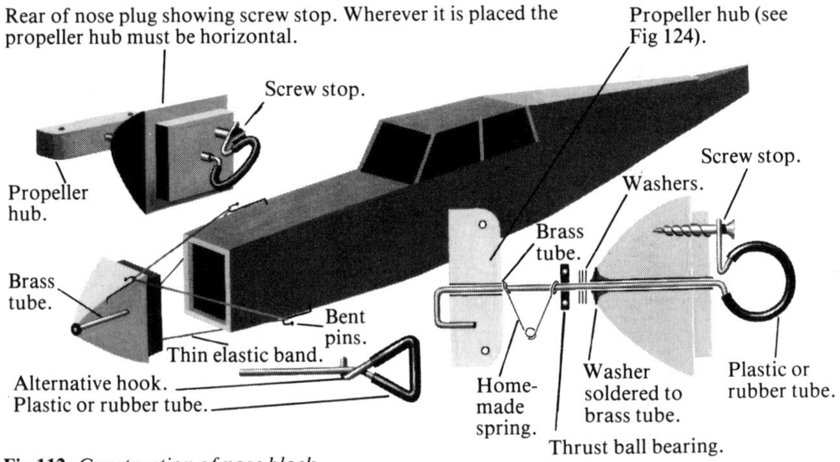

Rear of nose plug showing screw stop. Wherever it is placed the propeller hub must be horizontal.

Propeller hub (see Fig 124).

Screw stop.

Propeller hub.

Screw stop.

Washers.

Brass tube.

Brass tube.

Bent pins.

Thin elastic band.

Alternative hook.

Plastic or rubber tube.

Home-made spring.

Washer soldered to brass tube.

Plastic or rubber tube.

Thrust ball bearing.

Fig 112: *Construction of nose block*

The hole in the new block, for the brass tube, should be drilled vertically, which means you should use a pedestal drill, or drill press. On models of about 25 in (63.5 cm) span and bigger, the tube should have a small metal disc soldered on the front end, before gluing the tube into the block, to prevent the tube being pulled back by the rubber. If this is not possible, then allow the tube to protrude, front and back, by at least $\frac{1}{16}$ in (1.5 mm) and put plenty of PVA on the projecting ends to hold it strongly.

Larger models have only the noseblock and this must always be fitted with a brass tube, as above, together with a ball thrust bearing, which adds to the free running of the propeller. The noseblock tends to fall out when the motor is unwound, so it is best to add a pin to diagonally opposite longerons; and diagonally opposite these, two pins to the noseblock. Connect all four pins with a thin rubber band. Use plenty of PVA glue around all four pins. These are not always specified on the plan but should be used because, if the noseblock falls drunkenly forward when the model is high in the sky, the propeller will not freewheel, or fold, and this will spoil the ensuing glide.

Chapter 9

Undercarriages

Wire bending

Undercarriage wire bending can be a lot easier than it appears to be. The same applies to bending propeller shafts for rubber models. If you find you cannot manage the job when using pliers, then use a vice to hold the wire while you force it to shape. The big secret is simply to keep all the bends in their own particular planes. If you try to bend wire at a shallow angle to the gap in the pliers, it will always slip.

This means, of course, that if you ensure that the bend is going to be made at right angles to this gap, the wire will not slip, and you will have a far neater job. A word of caution—make very sure you do not get a sharp bend in the wire, as this will weaken the wire. Keep all the bends well rounded, to preserve the wire strength. Cutting the wire, especially the thicker gauges, is best done by filing through from opposite sides. Grip the wire in the vice for this job, and use a triangular file. When half way through, bend the wire backwards and forwards a few times and it will snap at this point. File the rough ends smooth.

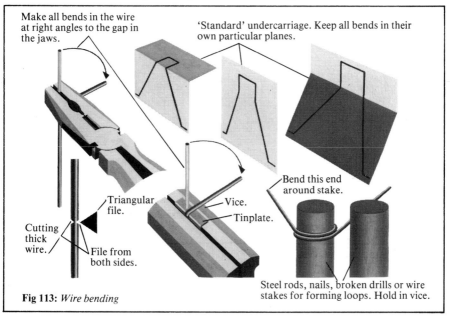

Make all bends in the wire at right angles to the gap in the jaws.

'Standard' undercarriage. Keep all bends in their own particular planes.

Triangular file.

Vice.

Tinplate.

Cutting thick wire.

File from both sides.

Bend this end around stake.

Steel rods, nails, broken drills or wire stakes for forming loops. Hold in vice.

Fig 113: *Wire bending*

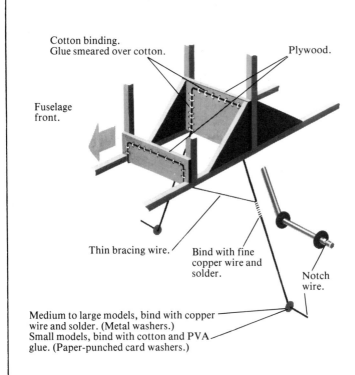

Cotton binding.
Glue smeared over cotton.

Plywood.

Fuselage
front.

Thin bracing wire.

Bind with fine
copper wire and
solder.

Notch
wire.

Medium to large models, bind with copper
wire and solder. (Metal washers.)
Small models, bind with cotton and PVA
glue. (Paper-punched card washers.)

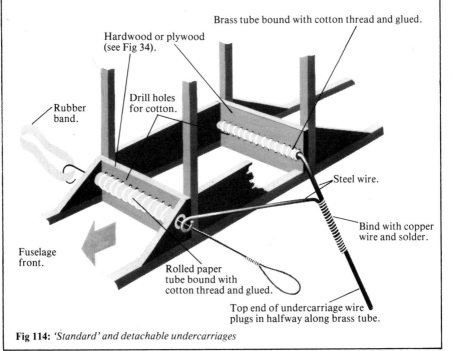

Brass tube bound with cotton thread and glued.

Hardwood or plywood
(see Fig 34).

Drill holes
for cotton.

Rubber
band.

Steel wire.

Bind with copper
wire and solder.

Fuselage
front.

Rolled paper
tube bound with
cotton thread and glued.

Top end of undercarriage wire
plugs in halfway along brass tube.

Fig 114: *'Standard' and detachable undercarriages*

'Standard' undercarriage

Most undercarriages for rubber, glow plug, diesel, electric, and CO_2 powered models, of all sizes and shapes, use the standard wire undercarriage, which is basically the shape in the sketch. Variations are made in the centre portion and its shape. This type is sewn and glued to a plywood sheet, or former, which is glued and securely braced in the fuselage.

Detachable undercarriage

An independently sprung, and detachable undercarriage can be used on medium to large models, free flight, radio-controlled, and control line. It is useful for storage, as well as being capable of taking a really hard knock. An appropriately sized brass tube, is PVA glued to a hardwood crossbrace in the fuselage, and a $\frac{1}{4}$ in (6.3 mm) inside diameter, or larger, paper tube is glued to a crossbrace further forward. Rubber bands pass through the paper tube, and are secured to the wire hooks. The bands are pulled through the tube with a piece of soft wire. These bands hold the undercarriage together, and allow independent springing. The model illustrated weighs 3 lbs (1.36 kg), and the undercarriage works extremely well, the wire showing none of the usual signs of bending permanently backwards.

Unusual undercarriages

When an undercarriage poses a problem of, say, excess weight, and complication, as in the case of the Fieseler Storch as illustrated, then see if you can improve on the plan. This particular model is only 18 in (45.7 cm) span, and has a very narrow chord, so its wing area is small for this size of model. Here bamboo, and wire, were resorted to as indicated. If wire had been used throughout, the model may have been too heavy to fly. Also, if balsa had been used for some of the struts, these would have collapsed on the first landing. As it is, this undercarriage has independent springing, and is very strong and light, so the model flies extremely well, despite the drag from so many struts.

The Bleriot undercarriage shown overleaf uses $\frac{1}{8}$ in (3 mm) round cane, together with bamboo and wire, for the same reasons as the model above, also it is more in keeping with the full size aircraft and therefore looks great on this small span 15 in (38 cm) model. Aluminium tube could have been used in place of the cane, but it may have become (very easily) bent, and would then have been a headache to maintain in good condition. A flat birch sucker stick, suitably cut down, and sanded, could have been used instead of the bamboo pieces. When joining the cane or bamboo struts to wire, as in the Storch undercarriage, first put a thin smear of PVA glue around the wire, and around the cane or bamboo and, when dry, put a thin smear of PVA on one piece and quickly bring the other piece in contact. Hold together for a minute or two until they are stuck, then add quite a lot of PVA right around both pieces. This binds them firmly in a very flexible, but tough, film of PVA, and on small models it is not necessary to bind the joint with cotton.

The wire part of the undercarriage looks too skinny on scale, or semi-scale models, and this can easily be rectified by slipping on a piece of plastic tubing, or embedding the wire in a strip of cane, or covering it with paper or cartridge paper. Cane should have a groove cut into it with a knife, and PVA glue used to hold the wire in the groove. Paper should be writing paper, for small models up to about 18 in (45.7 cm), and cartridge for larger models. Always coat the sheet of paper with a thin coat of dope first. When dry, coat again, using PVA. Allow to dry, then fold the paper, and cut out the strut shape. Coat again with thin PVA, and place it over the wire, and press it firmly together with the fingers until set. Put a coat of PVA over the entire strut and, when it is dry, dope the colour you want. This paper-covered strut is very resistant to wear and tear, and the paper and PVA, keep thin wire quite rigid and straight, although still flexible enough to take landing shocks.

Bamboo undercarriage

On very small, and not so very small models, where many struts are involved such as a float-plane, you may find wire to be too heavy, or thin enough but not rigid enough, for the job. Here, you will find bamboo an absolute godsend as a substitute for wire. On the model illustrated, an all balsa float-plane glider, the struts were all made from $\frac{1}{32}$ in by $\frac{1}{64}$ in (0.79 mm by 0.39 mm) bamboo strips, PVA glued. This proved to be extremely tough, as the model suffered many hard knocks during its test life (being catapulted straight into the ground on many occasions, by mistake), and the struts have never shown any signs of cracking, splitting, or joint separation. Wire would have been far too heavy and floppy for this model. Should you use bamboo for the undercarriage on small models, it is a good idea to put a wire spring at the top end, and a wire for the axle at the lower end. These can be held in place with PVA only. (The model discussed above had no wire at all for the struts, or anywhere else, except for the catapult hook.)

Below: Fig 115 *Fieseler Storch rubber-powered scale model showing the use of bamboo, paper and wire for undercarriage struts. Wing and tailplane struts are balsa. (Note mahogany veneer propeller. See p.126). 1 Thin bamboo strips. 2 ½ paper cone. 3 Rolled paper tube with bamboo struts. 4 Bamboo struts move freely in fuselage hole. 5 Steel wire. 6 Doped paper strut cover. 7 Thin bamboo struts.*

Above: Fig 116 *Bleriot rubber-powered scale model showing the use of round cane, bamboo, and wire in the undercarriage. Bamboo wing bracing pylons (bracing wires not attached at this stage) and bent cane for the tail-skid.* **1** *Fine bamboo strips.* **2** *One continuous, thick, bamboo strip.* **3** *Round cane.* **4** *Bamboo strips.* **5** *Round cane 'tyres'.* **6** *Steel wire.* **7** *Paper cones.* **8** *Steel wire.* **9** *Cane cut down and sanded.* **10** *Round cane.*

Below: Fig 117 *An 8-in span floatplane catapult glider was built for the sole purpose of gaining some idea of the difference in the amount of drag when flown with, and without, struts and floats.*

Dummy engines and exhausts

Dummy engines can be built up in a number of ways, depending on how much weight can be carried by any particular size model. Up to 18 in (45.7 cm), the cylinders, whether inline or radial, should be made of paper (writing paper), rolled to size around a pen, pencil, dowel or similar round object slightly thinner than needed. Keep the layers to about three or four, and glue the paper as you roll it. Mount and glue a piece of dowel, which is a fairly close fit in the paper cylinders, and should be the correct height of a cylinder, into a hole in a scrap of balsa. Put the paper cylinder on the dowel, and sand the top of the cylinder to the correct height. When all the cylinders are sanded, PVA glue them all to a sheet of the same paper. Cut the cylinder and top free by cutting, with scissors, around the top, tight up against the cylinder. On radial engines, the crankcase can be cut and sanded from laminated sheets of balsa wood. Mark the centre with your compass point, and draw in the outer circle of the crankcase, and its centre hub. Add a smaller, drilled and sanded piece, made as the crankcase. Drill through the hub, and crankcase, for the nose button, or noseblock. Silver dope, and sand, until it is really smooth and neat. Draw two circles, one for the outer edge of the crankcase, and one for the centre hole, on a piece of cereal box, making sure you leave a very visible mark with the compass, at the centre. Using a protractor, mark out seven (51.4 degrees) or nine (40 degrees) cylinder positions. Place the crankcase over this drawing, and pin the card to the back of the crankcase, using several pins. Check that it is accurately placed. Glue the cylinders to the crankcase using PVA glue. When it is dry, go over the whole motor with slightly thinned (use water) PVA glue, dry, then give it a second coat. Push new, clean, pins into the crankcase at a slight V angle, and close up to the cylinders, to represent the push rods. Larger models can have thin steel wire, bent, and pushed into the pin holes, in place of the pins. PVA glue the top and bottom ends of the push rods. On small models, the bolts on the crankcase can be simulated with pin pricks, along pencilled lines, put on the crankcase using a compass. Rub out the pencil lines after all the bolts are done. Bolts may also be represented with dents, put in with an old, dry, ballpoint pen. On larger models, bolts are represented by pushing a small diameter, sharpened, brass tube in place of the pin pricks. If the dummy engine is to be used on a glow plug, or diesel powered model, simply cut away one of the cylinders, and part of the crankcase, to allow the motor to fit snugly, but do allow space for air to pass around the cylinder for proper cooling and exhaust expulsion. A motor that runs well on the bench, and refuses to speed up in the model, is usually being suffocated in its own exhaust fumes. When given space, and therefore air in which to 'breathe', the engine runs properly. Whatever you do to make your dummy engine, do not use balsa for the cylinders, it is easily broken or damaged in a hard landing on the nose. Hardwood, like birch doweling, is a bit heavy when used for the cylinders. It does, however, make an excellent dummy motor for a static or exhibition model, especially if you have a lathe to turn up all the pieces. Inline engines, on most aircraft, are cowled in, and very few actually show the cylinders. First World War aircraft, such as the Halberstadt D I, Fokker D VII, and others, had part of their cylinders showing, and these can be made, as indicated above, and trimmed to suit the particular model you are building.

The cylinders are wrapped with cotton, or thin cord, to represent the fins. Do not use fuse wire, copper wire, or iron wire (unless, of course, your model needs

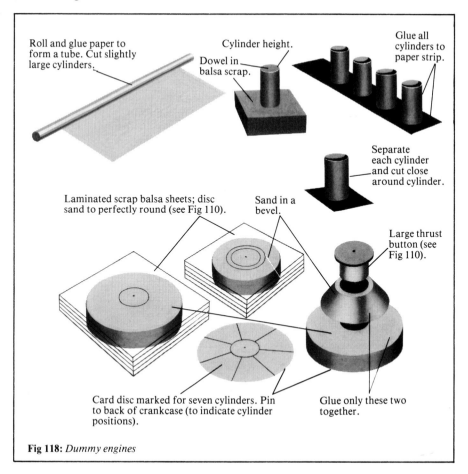

Roll and glue paper to form a tube. Cut slightly large cylinders.

Cylinder height.

Dowel in balsa scrap.

Glue all cylinders to paper strip.

Separate each cylinder and cut close around cylinder.

Laminated scrap balsa sheets; disc sand to perfectly round (see Fig 110).

Sand in a bevel.

Large thrust button (see Fig 110).

Card disc marked for seven cylinders. Pin to back of crankcase (to indicate cylinder positions).

Glue only these two together.

Fig 118: *Dummy engines*

a lot of weight in the nose), it is just too heavy for small 18 in span models. Larger models of 25 in (63.5 cm) span, and larger, may have thin aluminium wire bound around the cylinders. Fix the cotton, or aluminium wire, with PVA glue, smeared on the cylinders before wrapping. Try to leave a slight gap between each row, about the same thickness of gap as the thickness of the wrapping material. Paint with black dope.

Exhausts

Exhaust pipes are easily made in two ways. Long straight types, as on the First World War SE5, can be made by wrapping paper into a tube, around a dowel, wire or any other mandrel, even another paper tube, as above. Close the front end with a balsa plug. More elaborate exhausts, and inlet manifolds, as on the First World War Albatross DII to DVa, can be very easily made from cane. Sand down a thick piece of cane, if the thinner piece does not fit the plan. Keep it round, by wrapping coarse sandpaper around the piece, and sanding in one direction, preferably away from you, until it is nearly done to the right diameter, then repeat the sanding with fine sandpaper. When it is smooth, and round, then proceed as for the wing tips method.

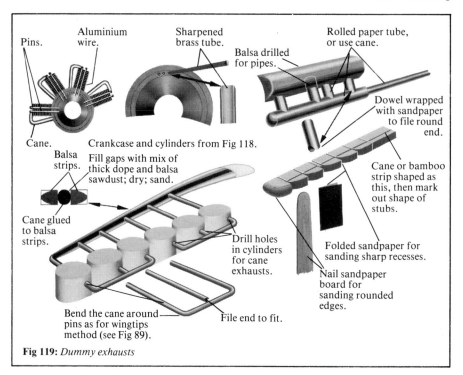

Pins.

Aluminium wire.

Sharpened brass tube.

Balsa drilled for pipes.

Rolled paper tube, or use cane.

Dowel wrapped with sandpaper to file round end.

Cane.   Crankcase and cylinders from Fig 118.

Balsa strips.

Fill gaps with mix of thick dope and balsa sawdust; dry; sand.

Cane or bamboo strip shaped as this, then mark out shape of stubs.

Cane glued to balsa strips.

Drill holes in cylinders for cane exhausts.

Folded sandpaper for sanding sharp recesses.

Nail sandpaper board for sanding rounded edges.

Bend the cane around pins as for wingtips method (see Fig 89).

File end to fit.

Fig 119: *Dummy exhausts*

Exhaust stubs, as on the Spitfire of the Second World War, have to be more carefully made. A strip of cane is marked out, for the position of each stub, on an appropriate diameter of cane, or preshaped strip of bamboo. Cut, and then sand, each stub to shape, using a nail manicuring sandpaper board. Separate the entire strip of stubs from the main strip and dope, with a mixture of a little silver dope stirred into a small amount of black dope, in a separate container. Glue to the model using PVA.

Auto rudders

These are used on towline gliders and contest power models. If we had the rudder offset permanently, this would be fine for the glide in both cases, but would be impossible for the towline in the case of the glider and just as impossible for the power model while the engine is running during the climb. They would both veer to one side, and continue to turn, until they hit the ground.

So we use a straight rudder for the towline and the power climb, the rudder being held straight by a line from the rudder to the towhook where the towline ring pulls against the line. When the towline slips off the towhook, at the top of the tow, this line is pulled back by a rubber band on the opposite side of the rudder and the rudder moves over against a stop, and the model can go into its circling glide. The same thing happens to the power model, except that the rudder line is worked by the timer that cuts the motor, allowing the rudder to move over a fraction of a second before the motor cuts so that the model enters the turn as the motor cuts. This prevents the stall that the power model will suffer, after its steep climb.

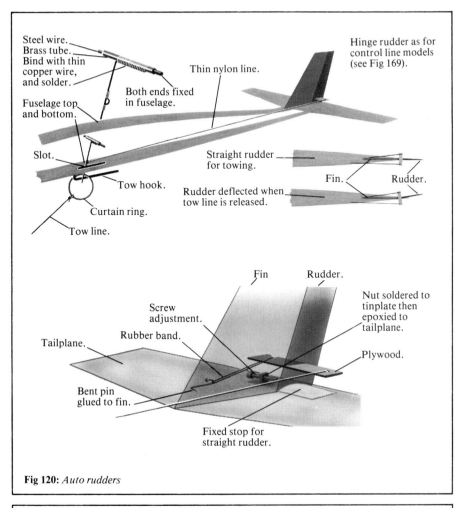

Steel wire.
Brass tube.
Bind with thin copper wire, and solder.

Fuselage top and bottom.

Slot.

Tow hook.

Curtain ring.

Tow line.

Thin nylon line.

Both ends fixed in fuselage.

Hinge rudder as for control line models (see Fig 169).

Straight rudder for towing.

Rudder deflected when tow line is released.

Fin.

Rudder.

Fin   Rudder.

Nut soldered to tinplate then epoxied to tailplane.

Screw adjustment.

Rubber band.

Tailplane.

Plywood.

Bent pin glued to fin.

Fixed stop for straight rudder.

Fig 120: *Auto rudders*

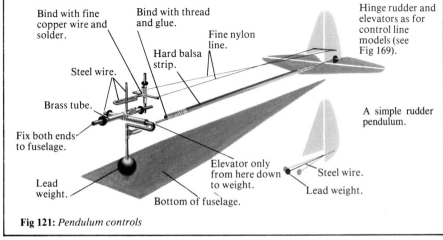

Bind with fine copper wire and solder.

Bind with thread and glue.

Fine nylon line.

Hard balsa strip.

Steel wire.

Brass tube.

Fix both ends to fuselage.

Lead weight.

Bottom of fuselage.

Elevator only from here down to weight.

Hinge rudder and elevators as for control line models (see Fig 169).

A simple rudder pendulum.

Steel wire.

Lead weight.

Fig 121: *Pendulum controls*

Pendulum control

This system is sometimes used on power scale models, to help maintain a good flight path. It is not possible to use it on rubber powered models, because of the rubber motor being in the way. The movement of the controls should be very free, but not sloppy, and the pendulum weight should not be excessive but should be sufficient to move the controlled surface against a slight pressure. The swing of the pendulum weight should not be too great, and is best limited by stops, as a large movement of the weight causes a change in the position of the centre of gravity, which causes instability.

Dethermalisers

Here you can use either a fuse, or a mechanical timer, to raise the tailplane after a set period of time, about one to three minutes after launching the model. The purpose is to put the model into a hefty stall, so that it descends vertically, tail down, and so save it from flying away for miles. It is used on free flight gliders, rubber, and powered models, the tailplane being activated by a rubber band in tension, pulling the tailplane to an angle of about 45 degrees against a stop. When a fuse is used, this is cut to the required length, inserted through a rubber band holding the tailplane against the tensioned band, and lit at the moment of launch. After the period of time, the fuse burns through the band, which releases the tailplane, allowing the tensioned band to pull the tailplane up, the model stalls and descends. The mechanical timer does exactly the same thing by releasing the tailplane after a set period of time.

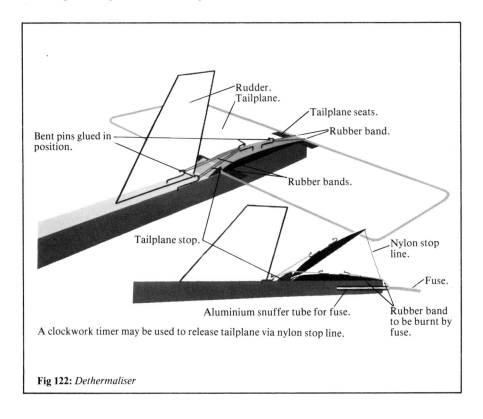

Fig 122: *Dethermaliser*

Chapter 10

Propellers

Freewheeling propellers

Freewheeling propellers are usually simpler to make than folding types, so use them if you are on your first few models. Although they do slow up the glide slightly, they do not spoil it nearly as much as a propeller that remains still when the motor has unwound. We will show some simple, but effective, types here. The first, and very efficient it is too, is the one we came across on the Star Flyer, remember? It is about the simplest one around at the moment, and would be very hard to beat; in this case you can wind the motor, using the hand drill, from the back. Another freewheeler is shown in the sketch. It can be used on a model from 18 in (45.7 cm) to about 25 in (63.5 cm) span. For larger models use wire one size up in gauge (16 gauge prop shaft, and 18 gauge spring). Start the propeller shaft front loop first. Put two 6 in (15.2 cm) nails close together in the vice, and close the vice tightly. Insert the wire shaft through the gap between the two nails, and wind the wire as far as you can around one nail. Open the vice, so that the two nails can be spread slightly, to get the wire between them. Close the nails together, close the vice tightly, and continue to wind the wire around. When you have completed a loop in it, remove it from the vice, and take the nails out. Put the loop in the vice, and wind the end of the wire around the shaft. Form the end of this section, using large pliers, to the shape in the sketch. Incidentally, note which way the wire is wound, when forming the loop. Now tackle the spring in the lighter gauge wire, also using nails and the vice. These nails are much thinner of course, 16 gauge will do. Assemble as in the sketch, and bend the hook for the rubber last. Everything should be very free moving, to ensure that it works properly. Also the motor should not be too tight between the front and back hooks when it is unwound. Another type is also shown, and is good if you have a sturdy hub for the propeller, where the tube fits into the blade. Bend the wire, as above, starting at the loop in front, and ending with the rubber hook. Do not convert this to a folding propeller. The previous one can be converted to a folding type.

Folding propellers

The first propeller, described above, can be converted to a folding type by cutting through the blades at a point that allows the blades to lie flat along the sides of the fuselage, when viewed from the top. If the hub is from balsa, it may be substituted by a mahogany, or birch block of wood, or even aluminium. When using wood for the hub, the holes must be bushed with brass tube. Each

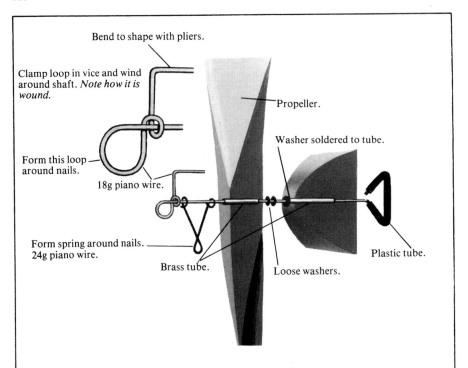

Bend to shape with pliers.

Clamp loop in vice and wind
around shaft. *Note how it is
wound.*

Propeller.

Washer soldered to tube.

Form this loop
around nails.

18g piano wire.

Form spring around nails.
24g piano wire.

Plastic tube.

Brass tube.

Loose washers.

Fig 123: *Free-wheeling propellers*

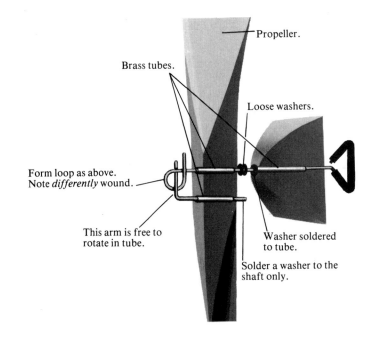

Propeller.

Brass tubes.

Loose washers.

Form loop as above.
Note *differently* wound.

This arm is free to
rotate in tube.

Washer soldered
to tube.

Solder a washer to the
shaft only.

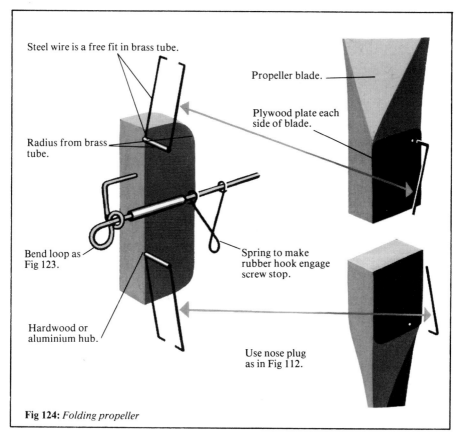

Steel wire is a free fit in brass tube.

Propeller blade. ——

Plywood plate each side of blade.

Radius from brass tube.

Bend loop as Fig 123.

Spring to make rubber hook engage screw stop.

Hardwood or aluminium hub.

Use nose plug as in Fig 112.

Fig 124: *Folding propeller*

blade should have plywood at both sides of its base, and this must extend, slightly, beyond the wire prongs. The blade is held in position against the hub, and the prongs are pushed into tiny holes made with a pin. Bind the prongs with cotton, and cover the entire blade base with a thick coat of PVA glue.

The folding propeller produces the least drag of all propellers on rubber powered models. Its main drawback is that as the blades fold, so a slight shift of weight occurs, which can upset the balance if the blades are heavy, so keep them as light as possible without sacrificing adequate strength.

Carved and built-up propellers

Some manufacturers are still, after 30 or more years of practice, turning out models, even so-called duration models, with notoriously small propellers. Some scale models are miserably heavy, and the ads tell us that this thing was 'engineered by our experts'. I doubt if any aeromodeller was anywhere within a thousand miles of some of these kits. However, if your particular kit model glides well, but goes no further than a few yards, the chances are that it has one of these shrunken propellers. The propeller should be *at least* $\frac{1}{3}$ of the wingspan to make any rubber powered model fly. Do not throw that plastic propeller away, put it in your scrap box for any tiny model you may make in the future. Ideally, each model should have its propeller specially designed for it, and this would also match the rubber motor. Naturally, this would be a case for a book

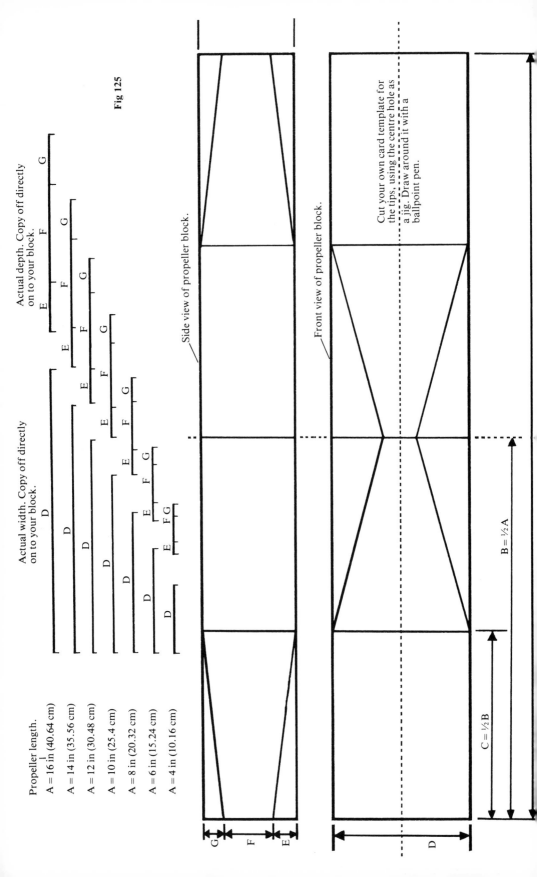

Fig 125

Actual depth. Copy off directly on to your block.

Actual width. Copy off directly on to your block.

Propeller length.

A = 16 in (40.64 cm)

A = 14 in (35.56 cm)

A = 12 in (30.48 cm)

A = 10 in (25.4 cm)

A = 8 in (20.32 cm)

A = 6 in (15.24 cm)

A = 4 in (10.16 cm)

Side view of propeller block.

Front view of propeller block.

Cut your own card template for the tips, using the centre hole as a jig. Draw around it with a ballpoint pen.

B = ½A

C = ½B

on the subject, so the best I can do to help you get a better performance is to give you an idea of what is needed. Try this method and I feel sure your model will be improved. This is an average good propeller, which can be scaled up or down, to suit most models. You will realise after a bit of use that it could be improved by, say, giving it less pitch or twist, or making the blades narrower, or slightly longer, or slightly shorter, or a combination of some of these factors. So, to begin with, measure your model's wingspan, and divide by 3. That will be the length of your propeller from tip to tip. Choose a blade size from the diagram which is slightly smaller than one half of your propeller size, this is to allow for the hub which is carved separately, if you decide to make the built-up type. This is certainly the easiest way, and the quickest; it is also very tough and light.

Carved propeller

If you, for some reason, prefer to carve a propeller, then we will start with this one. You can use balsa, jelutong, mahogany or any soft, close-grained wood. I do not recommend knotty pine, even if you do have a piece that is clear of blemishes, as the grain is too prominent. The main thing is to use a wood that is light, and fairly easy to cut and sand. If your model is very light, and the nose does not need much weight, then use balsa. If it needs a bit of weight, then use either jelutong, or mahogany which is slightly heavier than jelutong. The method of carving applies to any wood. First cut and plane the wood to the outer dimensions you have worked out from the diagram. Be sure the block is fairly accurate as far as being square. Mark the centre all around, and drill the centre hole to suit the shaft, using the drill press, or drill stand. Now mark out the rest of the propeller as in the diagram. Start cutting along the plan view lines

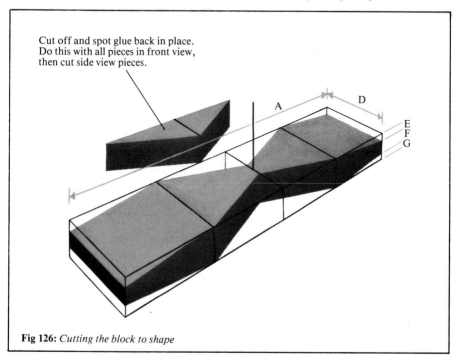

Cut off and spot glue back in place. Do this with all pieces in front view, then cut side view pieces.

A   D

E
F
G

Fig 126: *Cutting the block to shape*

first. These cuts should be just outside the lines, and as vertical as you can
manage. A bandsaw, or jigsaw, for this job, is very useful, but not altogether
necessary, as you can use a hand jigsaw. Save each piece as it is cut off. (See
Moulded canopies for cutting method, page 97). When all the plan pieces are cut
and replaced, then only cut the pieces from the side view (but do not replace the
pieces) and also remove the top pieces, leaving the basic propeller. Make the
card template for the tips with its centre hole. Mount this to the front of the
propeller, using the drill, centre the template over each half blade, and trace
around the edge, using a ballpoint pen. Carefully trim down with the knife,
watching the grain and cutting direction. Sand the outline down to the line. Now
start carving the blades down, on the top surface to a curve, but do not get the
surface flat and stop just short of the edges. Turn the propeller over and carve
the undersurface down until each blade surface is flat. Now, using coarse sandpaper, sand the undersurface of each blade to a slight hollow that matches the
top surface curve, and brings the trailing edge to nearly a sharp edge. Carefully
sand the top surface of each blade to the profile shown, and round off the
leading edge. A jelutong, or mahogany, propeller for large or medium size
models, should have blades with an average thickness of $\frac{1}{8}$ in (3 mm), and small
models $\frac{1}{16}$ in (1.5 mm), and the hub should remain thick, and blend smoothly
into the blade. Balsa blades can be roughly twice as thick, to avoid being broken
too easily. Finish by sanding with very fine sandpaper, clear dope, allow to dry,
sand again, and dope again. Balance the propeller, with its shaft in place, on
two match boxes. Rest the shaft on top of the boxes, note which blade is heavy,
and give the opposite blade tip an extra coat of dope. Allow to dry, and retest.
Never put on too much dope, as it soon makes things far too heavy.

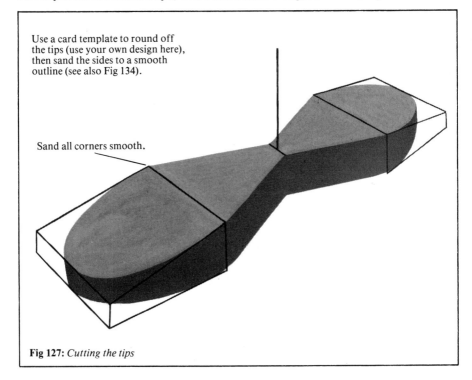

Use a card template to round off
the tips (use your own design here),
then sand the sides to a smooth
outline (see also Fig 134).

Sand all corners smooth.

Fig 127: *Cutting the tips*

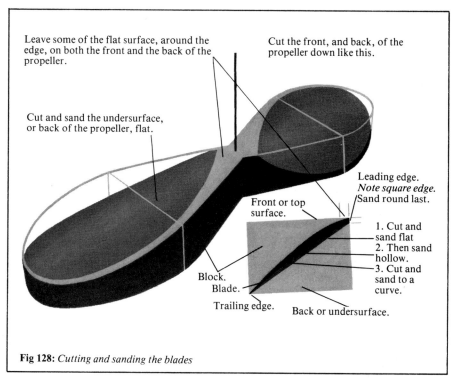

Leave some of the flat surface, around the edge, on both the front and the back of the propeller.

Cut the front, and back, of the propeller down like this.

Cut and sand the undersurface, or back of the propeller, flat.

Leading edge.
Note square edge.
Sand round last.

Front or top surface.

1. Cut and sand flat
2. Then sand hollow.
3. Cut and sand to a curve.

Block.
Blade.

Trailing edge.

Back or undersurface.

Fig 128: *Cutting and sanding the blades*

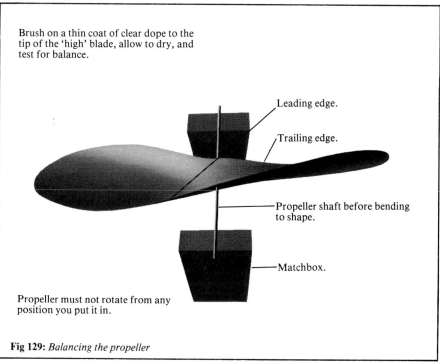

Brush on a thin coat of clear dope to the tip of the 'high' blade, allow to dry, and test for balance.

Leading edge.

Trailing edge.

Propeller shaft before bending to shape.

Matchbox.

Propeller must not rotate from any position you put it in.

Fig 129: *Balancing the propeller*

Built-up propeller

Another method uses mahogany veneer. This saves a lot of time, effort, and wasted wood, and gives very thin, tough, almost perfectly balanced blades. Mahogany veneer is obtainable from hardware shops, builders' merchants, and timber merchants, in 1 in (25.4 mm) wide strip, or in sheet form—both are suitable. Of course, any light veneer can be used, except the brittle types like kiaat. This is hopeless stuff for propellers. Sometimes mahogany veneer gives the impression it is very brittle, especially across the grain, but do not let this bother you, it will turn out just fine. Make your template on cereal box card, sanding the edge smooth—this is for the blades. Using this template, trace off around the edge with a ballpen, to give another template, which is cut down for the reinforcing pieces. Mark both with 'top' and centre lines, so that the curves will always coincide. Trace off the number of blades you need on the veneer, together with the reinforcing pieces. Carefully mark in the centre lines on all pieces. Be sure the grain runs along the length of all pieces. (If the template is wider than the veneer strip, then butt join two or more strips to make the required width, using PVA glue.) *Do not pin.* Cover with waxed paper, and lay weights over the surface to hold everything completely flat. Allow the glue to dry very thoroughly.

For 18 in (45.7 cm) span models, take a beer can which is roughly $2\frac{5}{8}$ in diameter by $4\frac{5}{8}$ in deep (6.6 cm by 11.7 cm), and has completely smooth sides, and dope it black. Cut a template from the cereal box card, making an angle of 10 degrees from the vertical. Stand the can and the card on the table and, using a sharp point, scratch lines down the can all around it, spacing them about 1 in (2.5 cm) apart. Cover the can with thin polythene sheet, and tape it down.

Cut out all the pieces on the veneer, being especially careful with the reinforcing pieces. Put elastic bands around the top and bottom of the tin, and place the blades, one at a time, tucking the top and bottom of the blades under the bands, and aligning the marks on the blade with the scratch marks. Now take each reinforcing piece, and put a thin smear of PVA glue on each piece, and on the blade where it fits, and assemble. Put at least two bands around the tin in the centre area. Leave to dry for about one hour, then immerse the tin in water to soak the wood for a short while. Remove the tin, and leave to dry overnight. Remove all the bands, except the top and bottom and, using fine sandpaper, sand the edge of the reinforcing pieces to blend with the blades, and give the blades one thinned coat of PVA. Leave to dry. Brush on one thin coat of clear dope, and leave to dry. Remove all the blades, and lightly sand the leading edge round, then brush on thinned PVA to the back of the blades.

The propeller hub can be made of mahogany, or birch (which is the wood used for making dowels). Cut and plane the wood to a square section, the diagonal of which is the same length as the bottom of the blades, and be sure to have the wood about 6 in (15.2 cm) long at least. Allow $\frac{3}{16}$ in (4.7 mm) for the blade, $\frac{1}{8}$ in (3 mm) for the centre, and another $\frac{3}{16}$ in (4.7 mm) for the other blade, on a propeller of about 6 in (15.2 cm). This means you cut a piece $\frac{1}{2}$ in (12.7 mm) long for the hub, and it is a good idea to cut one or two more hubs, in case you spoil one and keep the remainder of the strip in your spares box. Centre drill the hub, on the pedestal drill, to suit your propeller shaft. As it is very easy to get the diagonals mixed up in this next operation, I suggest you mark both ends of each piece with a ballpen, so there can be no mistake. As the propeller will rotate in a counter-clockwise direction, when finished, you should put the wire

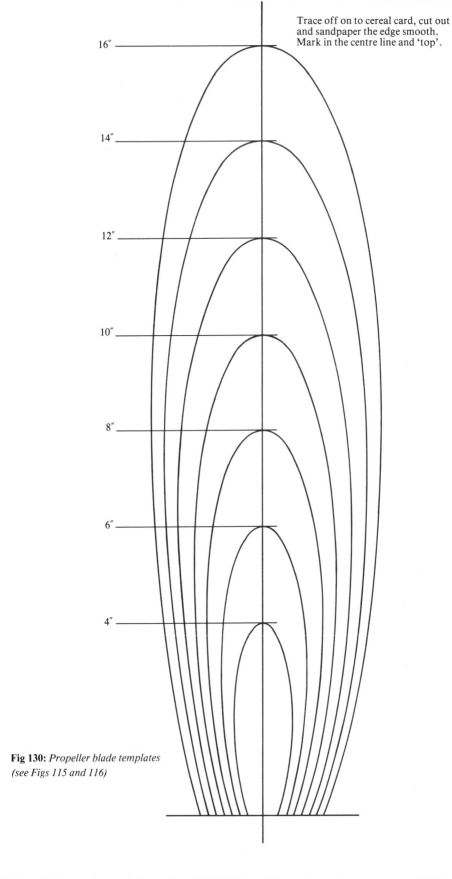

Trace off on to cereal card, cut out
and sandpaper the edge smooth.
Mark in the centre line and 'top'.

16″

14″

12″

10″

8″

6″

4″

Fig 130: *Propeller blade templates*
(see Figs 115 and 116)

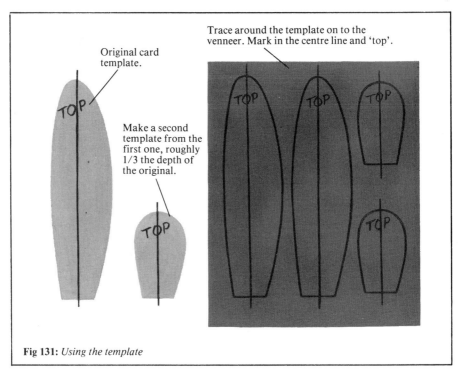

Original card template.

Trace around the template on to the venneer. Mark in the centre line and 'top'.

Make a second template from the first one, roughly 1/3 the depth of the original.

Fig 131: *Using the template*

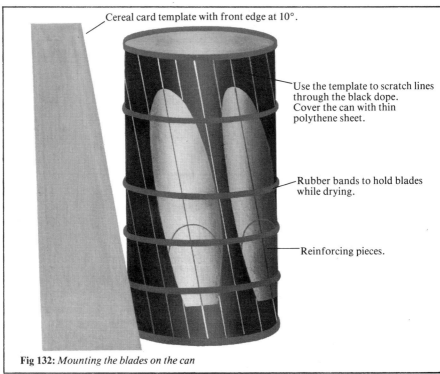

Cereal card template with front edge at 10°.

Use the template to scratch lines through the black dope. Cover the can with thin polythene sheet.

Rubber bands to hold blades while drying.

Reinforcing pieces.

Fig 132: *Mounting the blades on the can*

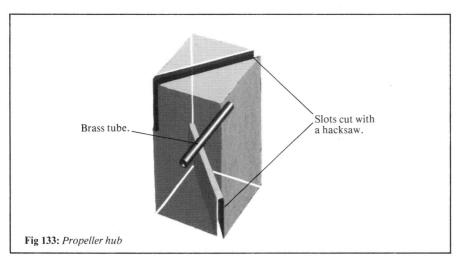

Brass tube.

Slots cut with
a hacksaw.

Fig 133: *Propeller hub*

into the shaft hole, and then mark both diagonals with reference to the sketch. Now it will make no difference which side you call the front. Mount it in the vice, and very carefully cut the diagonals down $\frac{3}{16}$ in (4.7 mm), using a hacksaw. If the cut is not wide enough, lean the saw over so that the teeth rub down one side to gently scrape the side down. If you spoil it, throw it out, and have another go on the other piece. It simply *must* be quite accurate. Using plenty of PVA in the slots, and also on the base of the blades, insert them in the hub, making sure they do not flop over. If they do, then push pins into the hub at the edge of the blades, to support them until dry. Check that the blades are true to each other from the front and the side. When dry, file away the four corners, to blend the hub into the blade; then give the joint a coat of PVA, allow to dry, and give the entire propeller a coat of thin clear dope. Balance the propeller on its shaft, adding a small amount of dope to the tip of a blade that is light. Allow to dry, and retest.

The tin can be used for $4\frac{1}{4}$ in (10.7 cm) blades, which should have a slot depth, in the hub, of at least $\frac{3}{16}$ in (4.7 mm), and the diameter of the finished propeller will be about $8\frac{5}{8}$ in (21.9 cm), which is about right for 25 in (63.5 cm) span models. Larger models will need a longer tube, with a slightly larger diameter. The idea is to have roughly the same proportions as the tin. Models of about 20 in (50.8 cm) span and up, can have two blades PVA glued together, to give one blade of adequate strength. As an alternative to this method for the blades, you can use $\frac{1}{32}$ in (0.7 mm) plywood for the blades, on models from 18 in (45.7 cm) to about 30 in (76.2 cm) span; 30 in (76.2 cm) and up, use $\frac{1}{16}$ in (1.5 mm) plywood for the blades. These plywood blades should be soaked in very hot water for about half an hour, then immediately wrapped, using thick string, around a 1 litre cold drink bottle, and set at about 5 degrees to the vertical. Heat to dry and soften the plywood glue in front of an electric heater, about $1\frac{1}{2}$ ft (45.7 cm) away, for about 2 hours. Remove from the heat, allow to cool, and then remove the string. Sand the leading edge of the blade round, and the trailing edge of the blade to a sharp edge. Assemble as above. Props for about 12 in (30.4 cm) wingspan, need only be about 4 in (10.2 cm) diameter and these, cut from mahogany veneer strip, need no reinforcing piece; just add a thick coat of PVA to the hub/blade joint.

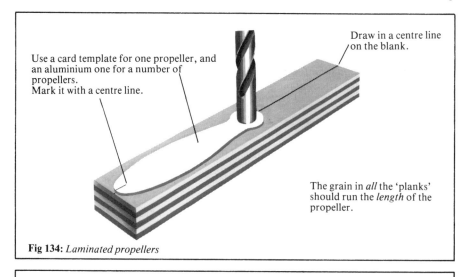

Use a card template for one propeller, and an aluminium one for a number of propellers.
Mark it with a centre line.

Draw in a centre line on the blank.

The grain in *all* the 'planks' should run the *length* of the propeller.

Fig 134: *Laminated propellers*

The finished propeller shows 6 'planks' used in its construction which is correct for scale models of WW1 aircraft. This shape of propeller is fine for flying the model, but true scale shape would be very much narrower and longer than this, and the thickness of the 'planks' would be half that shown. A change in the shape of the propeller would give a different shape to the outline of each 'plank', so aiding your carving.

Fig 135: *The finished propeller*

Laminated propellers

These are mainly used on scale models of the pre-Second World War era but, as they are quite decorative, there is no reason at all for you not to use them on any model that you feel could use this type of propeller. The glue that you use is of some importance, because it affects the strength of the finished job, and its subsequent use. For a small model using say, a CO_2 motor, PVA glue would be sufficient in strength, or you could also use cascamite, but for models with glow plug engines, a tougher glue will be necessary, and it should also be fuelproof. As each propeller is different, and the power used will vary so enormously, we will only deal with the general method of construction. To highlight the effect, two different coloured woods should be used, but their strengths should be nearly equal. If you have mahogany and birch this is fine, because these two woods give a pleasant contrast in colour. First cut and plane, or sand, the two woods to the side view depth of a layer, and the front view width, and length, allowing a slight bit extra in the width and length. Make sure you have enough 'planks' for the propeller, from both the woods to be used. If you cut, and plane, a long strip of each of the woods, then all you have to do is to cut it to the number of lengths of 'plank' you need. Arrange the planks to alternate the types of wood, and then glue and clamp them to dry, wiping the glue that is squeezed out before it dries. Drill the centre hole first, using a drill press or stand, to be sure the hole is dead vertical. Now lay out the front view, and carry this around to the side view. Proceed as for propellers carved from a solid block.

Chapter 11

Covering and materials

Preparing the frame (except microfilm)

Before applying any covering to a model, always sand the entire frame lightly, using very fine sandpaper, along the outer edges, to remove any fuzz or cement blobs. On small models, about 18 in (45.7 cm) span up to about 36 in (91.4 cm) span, apply a thin coat of clear dope to the same outer edges, dry, and sand lightly again with fine sandpaper. Larger models, covered with tissue, can have two or three coats of thin dope. When covering with silk or nylon, apply the thin coat of dope, dry, sand, and apply one or two thick coats of dope. This is to stick the material to the frame, and should be applied just before the actual covering takes place. Thick dope is about 60 per cent dope and 30 per cent thinners. Covering with solarfilm, or monokote, or any other plastic films, should only be done on the undoped, but sanded wood of the airframe.

Below: Fig 136 *An 8-in (20.3 cm) or 10-in (25.4 cm) span model is fun to fly in the lounge, if you make sure it can circle without hitting things.*

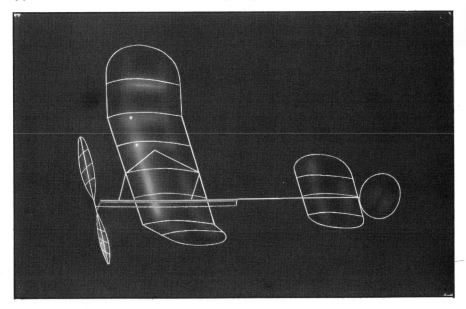

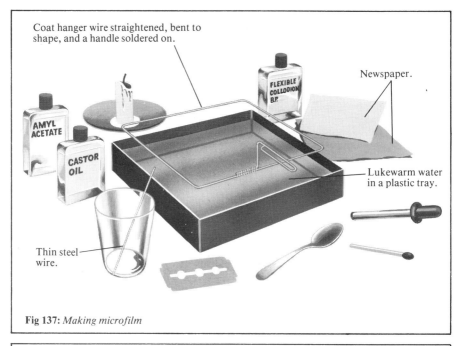

Coat hanger wire straightened, bent to shape, and a handle soldered on.

Newspaper.

Lukewarm water in a plastic tray.

Thin steel wire.

Fig 137: *Making microfilm*

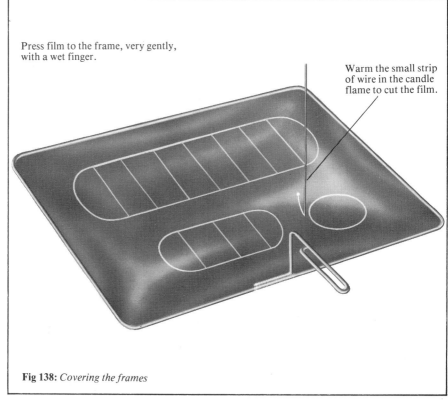

Press film to the frame, very gently, with a wet finger.

Warm the small strip of wire in the candle flame to cut the film.

Fig 138: *Covering the frames*

Microfilm

This is the lightest covering material there is, and it is used only on 'indoor' models. It can be purchased from dealers in 'indoor model' supplies (see modelling magazines for addresses), or you can make it at home. Should you decide on the latter course then the first thing to do is to collect the following: one wire coat hanger (cut the hook off and straighten the wire to get rid of the kinks, then bend it to a square to fit the container, and bind the end to the 'handle' with thin wire); a square plastic container about 2 in (50.8 mm) deep filled with cool water to near the top (use a clean sheet of newspaper to wipe the surface of the water, to remove anything on the surface); a teaspoon; a small glass; a match; an eye-dropper; a double-edge razor blade; 6 in (15.2 cm) of thin wire; and a candle.

You will have to try out a few mixtures first to get your particular ingredients to work properly, so use small quantities to begin with. From your chemist or wholesale supplier, get a bottle of amyl acetate, and one of castor oil and, if he can supply it, a bottle of 'flexible collodion BP' which contains ether and castor oil. Do not buy the acetone collodion; it does not work properly. Take the teaspoon and fill it with the collodion, and put it into the small glass. Dip the match into the castor oil and use it to put in ten drops, and with the eye-dropper put in 30 drops of amyl acetate. Mix with the teaspoon. Pour this solution as close to the surface of the water as possible, slowly, in one spot. It should spread out to the edges of the dish quite rapidly. If it does not spread properly, then make a mental note of how many more drops of amyl acetate you will add to the next batch. Before pouring this, remove the first trial film from the water, and clean the surface again with the newspaper. Allow the film about a quarter of an hour to dry, then wet the razor blade, and cut the film free from the edges of the container. Hold the frame just over the film, and use your finger to roll the film onto the edge of the wire. Holding the wire handle, tip the container so that the water just begins to pour over the edge, and slide the wire, with the film, off the surface of the water. Hang the film up to dry. Gently press a frame (tailplane or rudder) on the film, pressing the film very carefully to the frame with a wet finger. To trim the film, run a piece of thin wire, heated in a candle flame, around the edge of the frame, about ⅛ in (3 mm) away from the frame. If the film will not stick to the frame, add one or two drops of castor oil to the mix, and if it dries out too sticky, reduce the number of drops of castor oil. The film should, ideally, be smooth, very slightly tacky, and springy. Adjust the amount of amyl acetate to get the mixture to spread properly, and the amount of castor oil, to the stickiness and/or or the springiness you need. If you cannot get collodion, then use dope, and thin this with the amyl acetate, not thinners. Now the formula varies a bit from the first one, in that you use one teaspoonful of dope, one of amyl acetate, and half a teaspoon of castor oil. Here again, adjust the amount slightly, until you get the mix to work as above. Note that the film will stick to the wing frame by itself; you must *not* dope the frame, or try to stick the film with any glue whatsoever.

Tissues

These are one of the lightest, and cheapest, of the covering materials. First is what is known as 'Jap' tissue, and this is very soft and pliable tissue that is practically soundless when handled and has very good shrinkage when wetted. Its main drawbacks are that it is porous and comparatively expensive. It has a

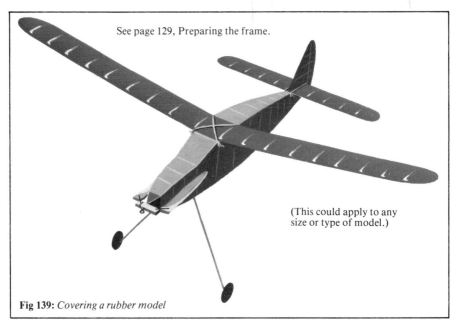

See page 129, Preparing the frame.

(This could apply to any size or type of model.)

Fig 139: *Covering a rubber model*

definite grain in one direction, but do not rely on this to tear it into strips: always cut it with scissors or a sharp blade. It is used on all rubber powered models of 12 in (30.4 cm) span, to the largest, about 40 in (101.6 cm) span, small to large gliders, and small to medium free flight models, and control line models, such as small stunters. It is best not to apply too much dope to this material as, being porous, it absorbs dope into the pores of the paper, and rapidly puts on weight, without getting any stronger. One or two thin coats of clear dope are sufficient to strengthen it, and that is all you need. Sometimes it is best not to dope it in order to save weight, but care is then needed in handling the model, as it is very easily damaged.

Kite tissue is slightly heavier than Jap tissue, but it is about one tenth of the price, and some grades have equal, if not better shrinking properties than Jap tissue, while other grades do not shrink nearly as well. It is not nearly as porous as Jap, is much stronger, and therefore does not need nearly as much dope to tighten it, so saving a lot of weight. Some of the latest material can even be reshrunk with water several times, which is very handy when eliminating warps. You can also buy it at nearly any stationers, and some hardware stores. Its wet strength is very good so that, when applied with a water medium glue, it does not tear easily. The last grade of tissue is 'bamboo' paper, and this is a very strong, heavy, porous material, which is used mainly on the larger models. Apply it after dampening it between damp towels, as the other tissues, but add an extra coat or two of clear dope to seal the pores.

Cutting out
Before you start, hold the tissue up to the light to see if it has a grain. Try tearing a narrow strip down the side if you cannot see any grain. If it has a grain, then lay the tissue so that the grain runs the *length* of the item to be covered. If it has no grain, then you can lay the tissue any way you like.

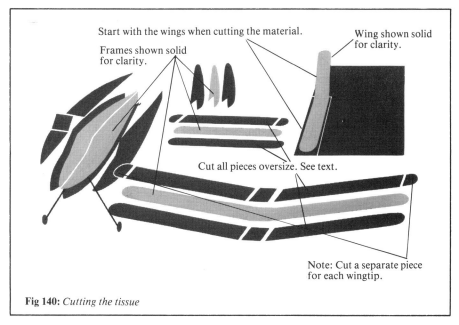

Start with the wings when cutting the material.

Wing shown solid for clarity.

Frames shown solid for clarity.

Cut all pieces oversize. See text.

Note: Cut a separate piece for each wingtip.

Fig 140: *Cutting the tissue*

Place the material on a large flat surface, such as a table. Put the wing over it, near one edge, and cut the tissue about $\frac{1}{2}$ in (12.7 mm) oversize all around, with an extra bit at the dihedral joint. This is for the undersurface. Cut the tissue again, leaving 1 in (25.4 mm) all around; this is for the top surface. Do the two fuselage sides with $\frac{1}{2}$ in (12.7 mm) all around, as also the top and bottom. The tailplane and rudder are done last, and here again you need only about ½ in (12.7 mm) all round. I suggest you start covering the rudder first, as it is the easiest to do, and any mistake is not a waste of a large piece of tissue, and time.

Covering with tissue

The way your model will fly will depend on how well you cover the wings, tailplane, and rudder. These must be true in front, side, and rear views. If they turn out twisted or warped, the model simply will not fly until all the warps are eliminated. If any warp is slight, it can usually be rectified with a little work, but if it is bad then the best remedy is to recover the part properly so that there is no warp. It has to be right the first time. If you were to put the covering on, without any preparation, it *may* turn out well. It usually does not. The method, and the order given here, if properly done, gives a very satisfactory result. Later, when you can do the covering well, you will probably have worked out your own method.

Paint tissue paste on the entire outline of the rudder on one side only, and carefully place the sheet over it. Pull the sheet tight across the middle and, working out to the top edge, keep pulling the material tight using only your thumbs with light pressure. *Do not strain to get it tight.* The main idea is that it should not be too slack, and all wrinkles must be worked out.

Before it dries too much, check it for flatness, by laying it on the building board. It should be completely flat and true. If not, then free the tissue very carefully where it is pulling the frame skew, and relay the tissue, until the frame does lie perfectly on the board. There should be no gaps around the outer edge anywhere. Weight the frame to the board, and allow to dry thoroughly, while trying a fuselage side.

Proceed as for the rudder, except that it is best to get the tissue drawn tight between the nose and tail first, press it down at these points, then proceed to thumb it down tight across the fuselage, starting from the middle and working out to the nose and tail. Allow to dry. When the rudder is dry, trim the paper all around the edge to about ⅛ in (3 mm) away from the frame, nick the paper radially at all the curves, paint the back of the tissue with paste (thinly of course), and fold the tissue over and down on the back of the frame. Do the same for the fuselage. Now do the other side of the rudder in exactly the same way as the first side, ending by trimming the tissue, nicking all around, and pasting the trimmed edge down on the back. Allow to dry. Put the remainder of the sheets on the fuselage, in the order 1–6 as shown. Pieces 5 and 6 should be put on as a single sheet only if the side view of the nose is straight. Should it be curved, then use separate strips of tissue to cover. Where two sheets of covering material meet at a corner, the first sheet should be trimmed flush with the edge of the wood, and the second sheet should overlap the first by about ⅛ in (3 mm). This overlap should be pasted down flat over the first sheet. The tailplane is next. Starting on the undersurface, apply paste to the outer edges and to the centre rib/s. Place the piece of tissue and first stretch it tight between the tips. Press the tissue to the centre rib/s, pull it tight across the tailplane, to the leading and trailing edge, at the centre. Now proceed to thumb it tight, working from the centre, to each tip in turn, removing all wrinkles as you go. Test for flatness as you did for the rudder and rectify all faults. Allow to dry. Do the under-surface of one half of the wing in exactly the same way, also testing for flatness. Back to the tailplane, and cover the top as you did the undersurface (except for the tips, if it has a curved top surface; these should be done separately). The wing should have the undersurface completed in stages, each stage being a section between dihedral breaks. Test each for flatness as before and, when complete, tackle the top surface in the same way. Never be afraid to check for warps at any stage of the covering, and *always* weight, or pin, the part to the board while the paste dries. *Never use a heater or hairdryer to speed the drying.*

Undercambered wings

On undercambered wings, each rib must be given a coat or two of thick clear dope (two-thirds dope, one-third thinners) on the undersurface only, immediately before covering. Place the tissue in position, press it down along the end rib, pull gently to the tip rib, press it to this rib, and then press it to each rib in turn and back to the end rib. *Make sure it is stuck to each and every rib all along the undersurface of each.* Allow to dry. Now paint the outer edges with tissue paste, and glue the edges down. If you mess it up (it is not easy on the first try), remove the outer edges first, then soak the dope along the ribs, one at a time, with thinners, and peel the tissue off, and discard it. Start again while the dope on the ribs is still soft. If necessary, go over the ribs a second time, or more, with thinners, to keep the dope wet, while you are applying the new sheet of tissue.

Water spraying and doping

When all the covering is done, and the paste is all dry, go over all the overlapped tissue joints, with a thin coat of clear dope. *This is important.* Allow to dry.

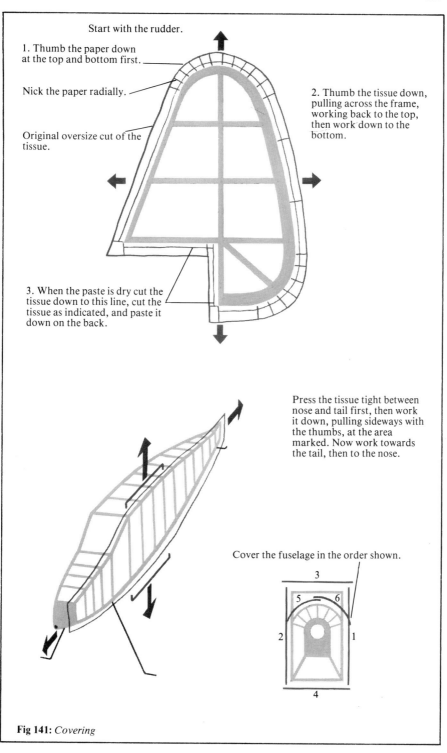

Start with the rudder.

1. Thumb the paper down at the top and bottom first.

Nick the paper radially.

Original oversize cut of the tissue.

2. Thumb the tissue down, pulling across the frame, working back to the top, then work down to the bottom.

3. When the paste is dry cut the tissue down to this line, cut the tissue as indicated, and paste it down on the back.

Press the tissue tight between nose and tail first, then work it down, pulling sideways with the thumbs, at the area marked. Now work towards the tail, then to the nose.

Cover the fuselage in the order shown.

Fig 141: *Covering*

Using a fine water sprayer, spray the entire model *except* one wing half. Pin, or weight, the rudder, tailplane, and the wing half, flat to the board. Leave overnight to dry. The fuselage needs no pinning. Note that, although the paper appears dry, the frame is still slightly damp, so leave everything to dry right out overnight. Leaving the wing, rudder, and tailplane still on the board, pinned or weighted, apply one thin coat of clear dope, and leave to dry. Use the same dope to do the fuselage. Water spray the other half of the wing and pin, or weight it. Turn the rudder over, pin, and dope. Remove the tailplane, and dope the undersurface and, when touch dry (about 5 minutes) replace on the board with pins or weights, and leave for several hours. Dope the top of the wing, and allow to dry. Now dope the undersurface of the wing, one half at a time and, when touch dry, replace on the board with pins or weights, and leave for several hours. The reason this is a bit tedious is that whenever you wet, or dope a wing, tailplane, or rudder, you must keep it flat until it is dry, otherwise a warp may set in. So be careful, and patient, until it is all done.

If you end up with a number of wrinkles on the model, do not worry about it. Read the section below on warps, and the section on flying further on, and try the model first. I doubt if there is a modeller alive who has not, no matter how experienced, had one or more wrinkles, or a warp, on a model at some stage of his life. So join the happy crowd! We all get it wrong sometime!

Alignment

Assemble the model and check that all the surfaces are true, flat, and not warped. This is done by comparing it to the front view on the plan. (You do not really need the front view, but it will help you while you are still learning.)

Place the model at the window, facing into the room. Seat yourself about a metre away and facing the model. Using one eye only, sight directly over the nose, to the tail and, keeping your head still, sight each wing panel. Lower your line of sight, still keeping that one eye looking directly over the nose, until you

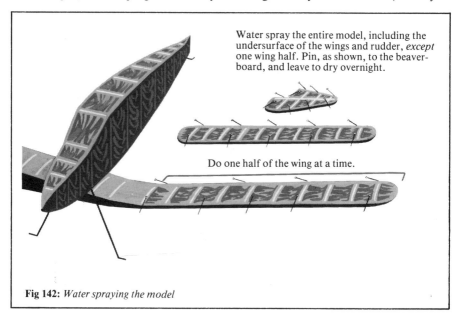

Water spray the entire model, including the undersurface of the wings and rudder, *except* one wing half. Pin, as shown, to the beaverboard, and leave to dry overnight.

Do one half of the wing at a time.

Fig 142: *Water spraying the model*

can just see the lower surface of the wing. Check each wing panel. If they are not identical, check again. Notice any warps, and make a mental note of where they are. Now do the same with the tailplane. Turn the model around, prop the tail up. Check this as you did for the front view, doing the wing first, then the tailplane, and do not forget the rudder. Having made this check, it will not harm to do it again, to be dead sure you know where, and to what extent, any warps occur. Now take each wingtip, and sight directly along each leading edge, and trailing edge, noting where either of these may be curved up, or down. This will help you to understand any warp you may have seen on the first check, and therefore how to deal with it.

Warps

A warp that is small or slight can be left until you have tried the model on the flying field. A warp that is, say $\frac{1}{8}$ in (3 mm) out on the wingtip of a large model may, or may not, be serious. Check the plan to see if the designer has specified 'washin' or 'washout' on that tip. If you have 'washout' when the plan calls for 'washin', then you have to correct that. Now you may or may not have to remove the covering to fix it. If the wing is covered with tissue, silk, or nylon, first try holding the wing in front of a radiator-type electric heater, about 2 ft (60.9 cm) away, and turn the top and bottom surfaces, slowly, to face the heater. Do this for about 5 minutes, then twist the wing to the correct twist, plus a bit, hold it like that, remove it from the heater, and hold the new twist for a minute or two until it is cooled completely. Check to be sure the warp has gone; if it is still there, then the only thing to do is recover the offending panel. Check the frame after stripping the covering. If the warp is still there, then the frame must be corrected. This can be done by pinning the frame to the board, with a slight opposite twist, wetting it thoroughly, and allowing it to dry out overnight. Unpin the frame, check that its warp has gone, and then recover it.

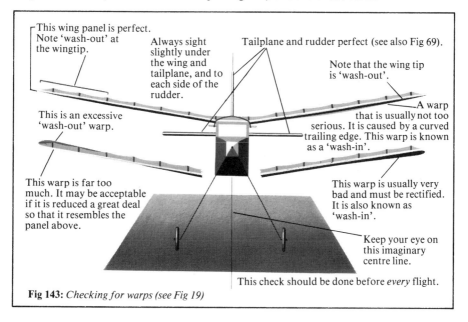

This wing panel is perfect. Note 'wash-out' at the wingtip.

Always sight slightly under the wing and tailplane, and to each side of the rudder.

Tailplane and rudder perfect (see also Fig 69).

Note that the wing tip is 'wash-out'.

This is an excessive 'wash-out' warp.

A warp that is usually not too serious. It is caused by a curved trailing edge. This warp is known as a 'wash-in'.

This warp is far too much. It may be acceptable if it is reduced a great deal so that it resembles the panel above.

This warp is usually very bad and must be rectified. It is also known as 'wash-in'.

Keep your eye on this imaginary centre line.

This check should be done before *every* flight.

Fig 143: *Checking for warps (see Fig 19)*

Silk covering

This is used mainly on medium to large models, and is extremely tough, porous, and needs a bit of practice to get a good result. Do not be put off by that last statement, anyone can learn to do it. First cut the material, as for tissue covering, for all the parts, leaving about an inch (2.5 cm) oversize all around for each part. Make up a mixture consisting of one part balsa cement to four parts dope (the dope being thinned 50–50 with thinners). Have a shallow basin of cold water nearby, a bottle of thinners, a water sprayer, and your box of *clean* pins. Now start with the rudder, it is the smallest part, and if you make a mistake it is not a waste of a lot of material. Take the two pieces of material and soak them in the water, and dope the outer edge of the frame, one side only, using the mixture above. While the dope is still wet, get the one piece of material on to the frame. When lifting the silk from the basin, try to get it as 'opened out' as possible, and hold it by two corners. From there, lower the bottom edge over one side, and let it fall into place as you bring the material down to the other edge of the frame. While doing this, try to get the threads of the material to come out parallel to the centre spar of the frame. With the material in place, press it on to the frame, in the centre of the lower edge, and pull it tight to the centre of the top edge. Using your thumbs, press it flat to the top and bottom edges, pulling the silk tight as you go. Two things to watch at this stage. Keep the strands of the material straight, and parallel to the centre spar and, at the same time, make sure the material is stuck to these two edges and is not creeping back; thumb it down until it does hold. Press down the centre of the other two sides, and again thumb it down, pulling sideways as you go, watching the straightness of the threads. At this stage, watch that the silk is not too dry, it should be kept damp with the sprayer. Work out any wrinkles, so that the silk is smooth over the entire surface. If the dope dries at any point, so that the silk will not stick, simply brush on thinners at this point—not too much, it works very well if you give it a second or two to work on the dope. Then thumb it down again. Once the silk is flat to the surface, and the threads are straight, it can be pinned (push the pins in only sufficiently to hold firmly, *not* right through the wood) to hold the silk from creeping while the dope dries. Place the rudder on the board, with weights on the corners, and allow to dry. Trim off the excess silk with a new blade in the knife, right against the edge of the wood. Cover the other side the same way, but trim the silk, leaving about $\frac{1}{4}$ in (6.3 mm) all around the edge, nick around any curve, and dope this edge down, smoothly, on to the first side. Using 50-50 thinned dope, dope one side at a time, and weight it down on the board until it is dry. (Smell the surface, and when you cannot smell the dope, then it is dry.) Give the silk about three coats of this thin dope. If you get any 'dry spots' on the covering, then add a teaspoon of talc powder, to a teaspoon of thin dope, mix well, and apply this to the dry spots. If while doping, the dope soaks through the silk and forms drops on the inside of the covering, then stop. Make the dope mix 'thicker' by adding undiluted dope to your mix, keep the dope thin enough to brush on, and not so thick that it will not spread properly.

Where wings have an undercambered rib, this should have the cement dope mix applied along the entire lower edge of the rib, as well as the entire outer edges, when covering. Make sure you have plenty of the mix applied for silk and nylon, as the strain set up when these two are doped is considerable. The rest of the model is covered in the same order as for tissue.

Nylon chiffon covering

This material is put on to the frame in exactly the same way as for silk, using the same dope cement mix. The only difference is that you do not wet the material, since it will not shrink tight as silk does. You have to get it as tight as you can, and then dope it. The dope will help by shrinking the material slightly, over and above what you have done when you put it on. Because this material is porous, one has a tendency to put on too much dope in an effort to seal the surface properly. When this happens, or you feel you are going to do that, rather put on two thin coats of dope, and then cover the whole model with tissue, spray the tissue with water, allow to dry, and then give it a coat of thin dope. This treatment gives a very good finish to the model, and saves a lot of weight.

Plastic films

These are obtainable at hobby shops only, and come in rolls of various colours. They are light, tough, smooth, pre-coloured, and have a special adhesive on the back which is only exposed after removing the backing sheet. They can be used on all types of model, and all sizes, except the smaller rubber powered models, and small gliders. Their big attraction is the speed with which they are applied, plus the fact that they need no doping or other treatment, and you do not have to dope the frame. Cut the film, with the backing film in place, slightly larger than the part to be covered, as you did for silk, etc, peel the backing off, lay the film in place on the frame. Warm an electric iron and test it on a spare piece of film: it should be just hot enough to curl the film, but should not melt it. At that temperature press the iron lightly, but firmly, to the film on the frame, to tack the film to the wood. You do not even have to pull the film tight, simply tack it down, all around the edges, and then go around again to get the film pressed, and stuck, to the entire outer wood surface. (Do not stick it to the tops of the ribs, just the outer edges.) Now hold the iron just above the surface (about $\frac{1}{2}$ in (12.7 mm) away) and *slowly* move it around; this will shrink the film tight. Trim, leaving about $\frac{1}{8}$ in (3 mm) overlap, and press this down to the back surface of the wood, with the iron. Presto! Finished—like magic! Beautiful!

If you have a warp in a wing, simply twist and prop the warp out on your board using weights and packing, and move the iron about over the surface as you did to shrink it, and the warp vanishes. Do the same on the undersurface to take the strain out. The only snag is that all these films are not as strong as silk or nylon, but they are nevertheless a boon to modelling, and if you are one of those unfortunate people who suffer from a complaint such as bronchitis, then all your models should be covered with this material. Dope and fuelproofer have those fumes that, if inhaled for the time it takes to dope and fuelproof the model, can, and do, bring on a case of bronchitis, in which case you should drop all the tissue, silk, and nylon covering materials, and only use the films.

Colour finishing

Never do any doping while you have a cold or 'flu. The fumes from the material will only aggravate the condition and make it worse. Rather wait until you are better, and even then, make sure you work in a well ventilated room.

Dope always adds weight and so must be treated with due caution. The smallest models suffer most, especially scale models. Control line models are the only ones that do not get affected nearly as much, because they have plenty of power to overcome the drag of the extra weight. We will, therefore, start with the small models, and work through to the larger ones. The classic finish is coloured dope but, fortunately, we are not confined to this method only, as you will see. So let's take the small ones, 12 in to 25 in (30.4 cm to 63.5 cm) span, free flight, 'duration', and scale, first, and see how much we can do to give them a bit of colour. Silver dope is the lightest of the colour dopes, and this colour is used on a great number of pre-Second World War scale aircraft, also it is used on just about all scale aircraft on such items as wheel discs, propellers, engine cowls, etc. Black dope is also used on these parts, and so I would suggest that if your models cover the above range, these two colours are basic necessities for scale models. Duration models are coloured to each individual's own taste, and so you must pick colours that suit you, and here you should stick mainly to coloured tissue, and to coloured dopes that will be used very sparingly. In both scale and duration types, besides the main use of coloured tissues, you can add to the range by using food colouring dyes, or photographic colouring dyes, or inks used in artwork. All of these last items require spray painting to do a satisfactory job. It is just about hopeless to try to do them in any other way. When it comes to colouring the model itself, start by using coloured tissue for the overall colour scheme, and add to this with colour dope, *only where absolutely necessary.* Remember that coloured tissue can be covered over with another coloured tissue, and give almost any desired scheme. White tissue can be sprayed over with, say, a very fine mist of silver dope to give a metallic effect, or it could be sprayed over with a coloured food dye in one colour for the wings and tailplane, and another colour for the fuselage and rudder. As cutting masks on the tissue paper is impossible, then the coloured tissue is cut to the desired coloured shape, and doped onto the existing coloured tissue, so giving an effect as would be obtained with mask and spraying. On scale models, the control surface outlines can be drawn on, using indian ink and a pen (ruling or nib type). A ruler must be used to get the lines straight, freehand use of the pen only spoils the job, and is best left off the model. Lettering can be cut from tissue and doped on or, if a suitable Letraset type can be found, use it, but be careful with Letraset, try it on a spare piece of paper first, and dope over it very thinly to see if you can get it right before putting it on your model. You can also use a very thin coat of PVA over Letraset if you find the dope method spoils the letters.

Spraying colour dope

This is a subject that would require a book to deal with all the ins and outs of spray painting. Your local book shop or public library may be able to help you with a book on the subject if you want to know more about it. However I have found that most modellers can do a reasonable job, after a bit of practice on spare pieces of card, and so I will only give a few pointers on some of the dos and don'ts. *Never mix any two brands of dope—stick to one brand for each model.*

Colour schemes

When the model is covered and given a coat or two of thin clear dope, keep the wings, tailplane, rudder, and fuselage all separate and remove the engine from the fuselage. Now you have to make up your mind about the colour scheme the model will have. As this is a very personal thing, I cannot tell you what you must do, and what colours you must use. The plan may have a scheme, as for instance on a scale model, or you may decide you want it your way, and ignore the scale colour scheme. You can find colour schemes galore in magazines on flying at the local library or book shop. I sometimes work out my own, or I may find a label in the grocery cupboard that has an excellent colour scheme and design that can be adapted to suit the model. The same thing can be said for any magazine, advertisement, newspaper, comic, books, etc. Just look around you, and you will find it. There is no fixed law for colour schemes, but there are good and bad schemes. The good ones you will generally find in the printed matter I have suggested above.

Masking and spraying

This simply means you do one colour at a time and isolate the rest while you spray that colour. Suppose you want the model overall white, with orange and red stripes, outlined with black. First you mask off the undercarriage and cabin with newspaper, roughly cut to shape, and held in place with Scotchtape or masking tape. Mix the white dope with thinners (50 dope and 50 thinners), and do the same with the orange, red, and black, the black obviously in a small quantity. Collect two used, large, Marmite jars, that have been well cleaned and dried, for each of the colours. Mix one colour and thinners in one jar, put a clean, old, stocking over the mouth of the spare jar, and hold it in place with an elastic band. 'Dent' the stocking into the mouth slightly, stir the thinned colour, and pour it into the stockinged jar, slowly. Remove the stocking, wipe the lip of the jar, and put the lid on properly. Do this with all the colours.

Put the white into the spraygun, and try spraying a spare piece of coloured card first. The thing to watch is that you press the trigger *before* you start at the

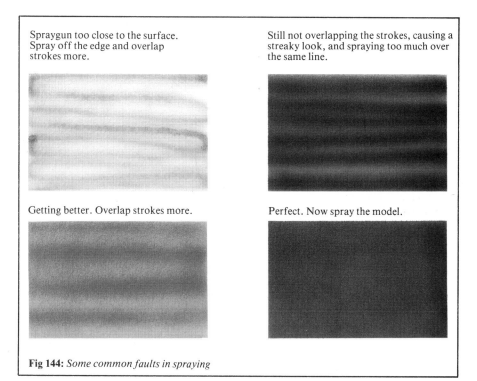

Spraygun too close to the surface. Spray off the edge and overlap strokes more.

Still not overlapping the strokes, causing a streaky look, and spraying too much over the same line.

Getting better. Overlap strokes more.

Perfect. Now spray the model.

Fig 144: *Some common faults in spraying*

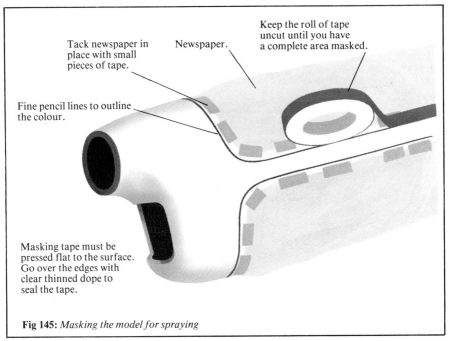

Keep the roll of tape uncut until you have a complete area masked.

Tack newspaper in place with small pieces of tape.

Newspaper.

Fine pencil lines to outline the colour.

Masking tape must be pressed flat to the surface. Go over the edges with clear thinned dope to seal the tape.

Fig 145: *Masking the model for spraying*

edge, keep it depressed until off the other edge. This is important. Keep the spray going along the length of the card, not in patches, nor suddenly across the width. Try, also, to keep you arm movement at an even speed, and at a constant distance above the card, and do not flex the wrist—it is an arm and body movement. The card will show up with blotchy patches if you do not get it right. Ask someone to watch and rectify your mistakes. When you can spray an even coat thinly, then you are on the right path, and can begin to spray the model. Spray the entire model white, in thin coats, and allow each coat to dry for about 5 minutes before doing the next coat. Do not go on too far, as white is deceptive, and you can put on far too much. Allow to dry for at least 4 hours in summertime (see directions on the tin).

With a soft pencil, 2B or 4B, mark out the stripes, using a ruler to draw the lines. Cut newspaper into about 3 in (7.6 cm) wide strips, and tack these in place with small pieces of tape. Keep the strips about ⅛ in (3 mm) away from the line. Tape is placed to touch the line, and cover the edge of the paper strips, and rub the tape firmly to the model's covering—there should be no tiny bumps in the tape. Mask all the areas to be sprayed, on the wings, tailplane, rudder, and fuselage, then cover the remainder with newspaper, so that the model is entirely hidden, and only the areas to be sprayed are exposed. Go over all the taped edges with clear dope, using a brush to seal the edges before spraying. Spray in the orange on all exposed areas, and allow to dry.

Lift the tape very carefully at one edge, and peel it back gently, keeping this free section flat to the surface, sticky side up. Remove all the tape and newspaper. Mask the red areas, and cover the model again with newspaper, then proceed as above. Do the same with the black.

Points to watch are: always use dope that is well thinned, make sure the spraygun nozzle is properly cleaned, before, during, and after spraying. *Always*

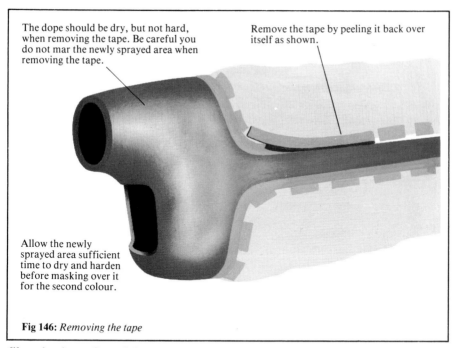

The dope should be dry, but not hard, when removing the tape. Be careful you do not mar the newly sprayed area when removing the tape.

Remove the tape by peeling it back over itself as shown.

Allow the newly sprayed area sufficient time to dry and harden before masking over it for the second colour.

Fig 146: *Removing the tape*

filter the dope. Spend time on getting the mask down flat to the surface, seal the edge of the mask with clear dope before spraying, and learn when to remove the tape so that it does not crack the edge of the colour; usually this can be done the moment the dope is *touch* dry. Be especially careful when using white and yellow; white can become far too heavy, before it is seen to be 'solid' white. Yellow too, needs to be quite heavily applied to 'cover' another colour.

Brushing on colour dope

If you do use a brush for applying the dope, the brush should be red sable (from a good art store), of about 1 in (2.5 cm) width, and flat. Always, *always*, rinse the brush out in thinners after use, and do not just put it down anywhere, so that the bristles get thoroughly crushed, and spread out. No! That brush is expensive, and it will last just about your lifetime, if you nurse it. Rough it up, and it will go very quickly. There is no better brush for applying dope. When brushing any dope, clear or coloured, thin it down about 40 dope and 60 thinners—it should be quite thin. Put on one coat rapidly; do not brush backwards and forwards too often in the one spot, remember that dope is drying very fast, and scrubbing like this will only mess the job up. Paint it out in long, quick strokes, only enough to smooth it, and then leave that patch. Dip the brush in the dope, gently wipe the excess off on the edge of the tin and, over-lapping the last patch slightly, quickly smooth out the brushful. The best bet is to try this out on a piece of card first, until you get the hang of it, and then try it out on your model. No matter what the experts with the brush might tell you, you simply cannot match a sprayed job, especially on very thin transparent colouring. Try it yourself to be sure, but the brush will give you a satisfactory job.

Control line models, except combat models and some stunters, and large free flight, and radio control models, about 5 ft (152.4 cm) and up, can take about 4 coats of dope, or as many as needed to get the colour 'solid'. Do not go on putting the dope on after this point is reached, it is a waste of time, and dope; and makes the model too heavy and therefore tricky to fly. Large control line models of the sport and scale types, can, and do, take quite a lot of dope to decorate them, and suffer no visible effects on their flying ability. This is because their motors are very large and powerful for the size and weight of the model, by comparison with, say, a free flight model. Combat control line models do not last all that long, and they do not need the extra weight of dope anyway, because that would affect their manoeuvrability.

Gloss enamel paint

One thing that a lot of modellers have missed, is that you can use ordinary household gloss enamel paints on rubber powered models of both duration and scale types and on all gliders, as well as diesel powered models that use straight 'undoped' fuels. The only thing to watch for, when using this enamel paint, is to first give the entire model at least one coat of thin clear dope. When applying the enamel, be sure to paint it on in slightly diluted form, keeping it well stirred all the time, and each coat should be 'stretched' as far as each brushload will go. Then put the model under a cardboard grocery box (well dusted out) overnight, to dry. Most of the time you will only need two coats, and the model will be really beautiful. This paint treatment is slightly lighter, and a lot cheaper than dope, and it remains pliable all its life if you buy good quality paint. Its only drawback, when compared with dope, is that it takes longer to dry, but this is a minor detail when one considers all the advantages. *Never* use this paint though, on any glow plug powered model, without first testing it thoroughly on a piece of wood, or some other material, to see if the paint will stand up to the fuel, and whether or not it will accept fuelproofer.

Fuelproofing

On all models that are powered by glow plug motors, and diesel motors run on 'doped' fuels, there is the last item to the covering schedule that cannot be avoided, and that is to fuelproof the entire model. The ingredients of these fuels always get sprayed back over the entire model, when it is in flight, or whenever the motor is running, and these minute drops of fuel, even though burnt in the cylinder, turn the usual dope, or paint finish, into a sticky goo, and ruin the entire covering, and framework around the engine within a short time. To prevent this happening, we always fuelproof the entire model before the motor is finally installed. This entails painting the model again, after all the doping is finished, with a polyurethane clear lacquer. Some dopes, such as butyrates, are fuelproof and need no further treatment (*always* check before using on your model). The engine, and fuel tank bays especially, which always have fuel in them, should be painted out completely (underside of exposed framework too), at least twice, to be sure no tiny part is left unprotected. A coat of PVA is fuelproof and this is always pliable, in contrast to the polyurethane, which sometimes turns out very brittle. The only drawback to the PVA is that it makes the covering matt. The usual fuelproofer is a polyurethane lacquer that comes in two parts, and must be mixed before applying with a brush. Here you must follow the instructions that come with the pack. I have found that some polyurethanes can be diluted, without harming the product, by first mixing as directed, and then diluting with grade 'A' thinners. Try yours in a small quantity first. Paint it onto a doped cardboard sheet, dry, and test by leaving the raw fuel on it for at least ten minutes, wipe the fuel off, and note if the fuelproofer is still protecting the dope. The point in thinning it is that you can then apply two, or three, thin coats of fuelproofer, which gives you two or three times better chance of covering the entire model properly, without having unprotected areas, especially the engine bay, and fuel tank bay. Do not forget to do the area under the wing, and tailplane, where they lie on the fuselage. Never get the fuelproofer on to rubber, or plastic tyred wheels, or on the windscreen and windows; mask these, using newspaper and tape. The plastic films, like solarfilm and monokote, etc, are all fuelproof, but it is a good idea to put fuelproofer along all the overlapped edges to seal them properly, and the engine and fuel tank bays, on models covered with these films, should be given a couple of coats of either PVA or polyurethane.

Epoxy paints

The epoxy colours are also very good, and they give a far superior finish to the model. They are capable of being sprayed or brushed, but you have to be a very neat and careful worker, as these materials call for the utmost care when being used. You must read the directions on the tins, and you *must do exactly* what they say, to avoid the many problems they can give you if you are at all careless. Like dope, they should not be used when you have a cold or 'flu, and never inhale the fumes—work outdoors to be very sure you remain healthy.

Decals and transfers and cut-out designs

These can be made on gummed brown paper if you prefer to have transfers. Office equipment, or art material shops, stock brown paper rolls in several widths, and these rolls have gum arabic spread thickly over the one side. This is the glue side of the paper, on which you can do any drawing. First coat the gummed side with at least two coats of thin dope, and let this dry. Now over this you can paint with poster paints, or black waterproof ink. When dry, give the drawing a coat or two of thin dope, and allow to dry for several hours. Transfer the design to the model, after soaking the paper in warm water for a minute or two to soften the glue. Another method is to use clear doped typing paper, on which you can draw your designs with poster paint which has been mixed with some PVA (Alcolin) glue. These colours are diluted with water to a workable consistency. You may find you have to go over the design a second time with paint, to get the desired depth of colour, or if the first coat was too thin. Do this only after the first coat has dried. Cut the design out, using scissors, and glue it to the covering with PVA. These decals can be painted over with clear dope, or polyurethane fuelproofer.

Do not use coloured dopes to make these decals, because the dope is difficult to use, and is far heavier than the poster paint. (Dope has the pigment bound with a lot of clear dope; poster paint has the pigment bound with a very small proportion of gum and all the water evaporates, leaving mainly pigment.) Dope also has a tendency to leave a lumpy surface, especially if you put on one or two coats to get rid of the streaky appearance. Poster paints, on the other hand, turn out completely smooth and flat.

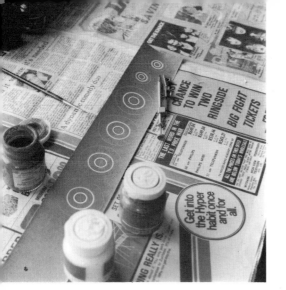

Fig 147a *Tape a length of gummed paper down to hold it while you work. Set the springbow compass to the size of circle you want. Use the small brush to load the compass pen with poster paint and draw in the outline of the circle. Set the compass to draw a slightly smaller circle than the first one. (The two lines should just touch to give a thick line.) This will give you the outer thick line shown. Do the same for the inner thick line.*

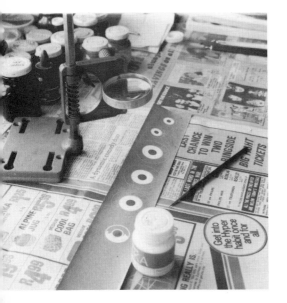

Fig 147b *Use the brush to fill in the colour between the two thick lines.*

Fig 147c *Outline the next colour the same way and fill it in as you did for the first colour. Do exactly the same for the third colour, and let the whole job dry for about half an hour.*

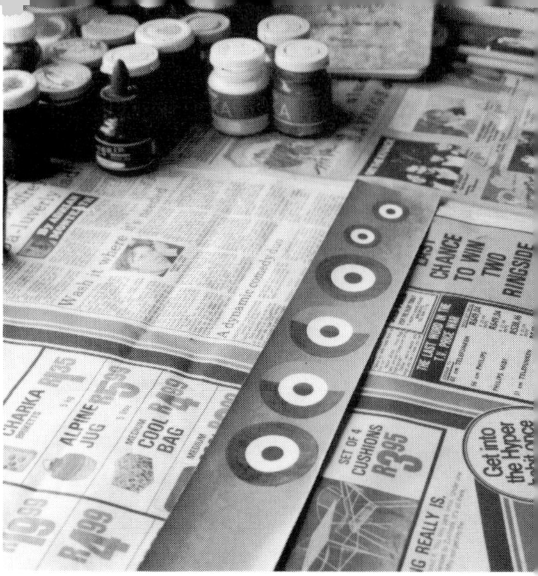

Fig 147d When everything is dry give each drawing two thin coats of clear dope and leave to dry for several hours. Note how the dope makes the colour appear wet again, and how it brings out the colour. (The two large inner roundels have been only half doped to show the effect.)

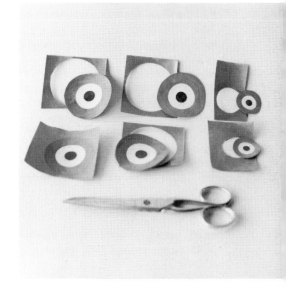

Fig 147e Cut out each roundel keeping about 1/16-in (1.5 mm) away from the edge of the design. Soak in warm water for about 5 minutes, then transfer to the model.

Fig 148 A cut out design pasted to the colour doped wing of a control line model.

Chapter 12

Where and when to fly

Where to fly

Before you rush out and spread your model over the field in separate small sticks, let us stop here for a while, and tell you one or two things about when and where to fly. There is no sense in spending so much time and energy on the model, if it only ends in failure, or worse, complete disaster.

First of all, where to fly. Now admittedly, all engine powered models sound fabulous to all of us, but the silly crowd out there, called 'the general public', think it is just an awful racket. An unbelievable attitude to you and me, but there it is. Now we do not need these people causing trouble, and having us kicked off a particular area we use to fly in, so the safest bet is to get as far away from buildings and houses as we can. That saves their complaints, and does our models a power of good, because those buildings will not bend when a model hits them, and in any case they cause turbulence in the air, which spoils flying. I am talking of free flight models with motors, but the unbending buildings will also dent a perfectly good rubber powered model, or a glider, or even a radio-controlled model just as easily. You *can* misjudge with a radio controlled model, you know!

Now your type and size of model will need an appropriately sized field. A school rugby field, or an equal sized park ground can be used for all small rubber powered models, and catapult or chuck gliders, and in some cases, for control line flying (this depends on how close the nearest houses or flats are). Free flight models should be about 20 in (50.8 cm) span, and certainly not much bigger. Here one can, if permission is first obtained from the headmaster, or park keeper, fly all sizes and types of control line models, provided of course that a silencer is used on the motor, and also that the nearest house is at least $\frac{1}{4}$ of a mile away. All free flight models, rubber, electric, glow plug, diesel, or CO_2 powered, and all towline gliders above 20 in (50.8 cm) span, will require the wide open spaces beyond the city, for real flying. Of course, all these models can be tested for gliding by hand launching, without power, or towline, in these small fields, and they are very convenient for this purpose, especially if you live in a flat. If you have a house, and the lawn is fairly large, then you can test glide small models there, and even fly electric round-the-pole models. Fly microfilm models in your lounge, or in the school hall. Flying right on your own doorstep! Always keep your eyes open for a likely test gliding, or flying spot, near your home, and really large flying fields away from the city. Radio-controlled powered models do not need a very large space to fly in, but they generally need

Above: Fig 149a *Control line flying on the local school rugby field. Club member Greg Spencer takes a few seconds longer to get that motor going at peak revs, to get the Flight Trainer, with its tiny wheels, to take off from grass . . .*

Below: Fig 149b *. . . and away she goes on another training flight. Yes, those bikes, and the rugby posts, are a bit too close for comfort! Note the absence of houses and flats nearby.*

a good spot, flat, and free from grass for take-off and landing, with any trees at least 100 yds (92 m) from this spot. Here, too, as in the case of control line models, the engine noise, even with a silencer, can be heard by people living in the vicinity of its flight area. The field, in this case, should be at least a mile or two away from any house or building, and preferably further away. For those living in, or near, hilly or mountainous areas, there is the wonderful opportunity for flying without the noise and cost of a motor. Here you can enjoy the relaxing, peaceful, radio-controlled slope soaring glider, and have the model flying effortlessly through stunts for hours on end, if you feel like it, on almost any breezy day. The only thing you need, besides your model, is the breeze. The upward flow of air, from the flat plain, will keep the model continuously buoyed up, and it can reach just about any height above or in front of you. Just be careful you do not let the model get near the back of the slope, where the downdraught turbulence occurs because, in this area, the model can be forced down with sufficient force to wreck it. Full size hang gliders, and gliders, do not fare any better, and they avoid those areas like the plague.

Below: Fig 150a *Radio-controlled models in the country, far from the city, using a specially graded area for take-off and landing. An ideal spot for free flight and control line as well. Notice the flatness of the ground, the absence of buildings, the trees in the distance, and the long grass at the sides of the cleared area, which cushions any bad landings by all types of models.*

Above: Fig 150b *Fred Wessel-Hansen with his model 'Barnstormer' (in the picture above) equipped with three functions (rudder, elevator, and motor control). An 'out-of-the-rut' model that flies perfectly.*

Below: Fig 150c *Fred taxying 'Barnstormer' out for take-off. Note the width of the runway, which allows for slight variations in the direction of the prevailing wind.*

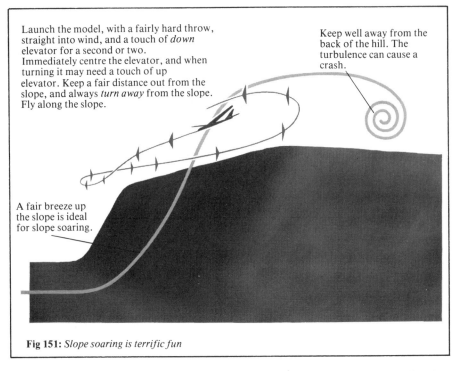

Launch the model, with a fairly hard throw, straight into wind, and a touch of *down* elevator for a second or two.
Immediately centre the elevator, and when turning it may need a touch of up elevator. Keep a fair distance out from the slope, and always *turn away* from the slope. Fly along the slope.

Keep well away from the back of the hill. The turbulence can cause a crash.

A fair breeze up the slope is ideal for slope soaring.

Fig 151: *Slope soaring is terrific fun*

So the idea is to head for the wide open spaces. If it has got rolling hills, that is not too bad, but it is also not too good; use it until you find a better place. One thing is almost a must, and that is that there should be a large area of tall grass, or very dense short grass. This is very useful for the model during its initial flights, because if it does do any wild gyrations, there is this patch of grass to absorb the bump, and so save what could be a tremendous amount of damage. No, you do not have to fret, it is not all crashes! At first your model may do a wild swing, and hit the ground rather hard, but if there is that grass, you have very little to worry about. It does give you the chance to find and rectify the fault, and have another go, without having to go straight back home for a fair size repair.

Let us have a look at the particular spot you need in this area you have found. The best way to pick the spot you want is to know how to find the wind direction first. Sticking your finger in your mouth, and trying to feel the wind by the cold side of your finger is messy, and it is terribly inaccurate. The only method to use, and it is infallible for detecting a slight change in the wind direction, is to learn to turn your head, and feel, both on your cheeks and ears, an exactly equal pressure, which means you are facing dead into wind. If you look straight ahead of you, you can point to an object from which the wind appears to be coming. Having learnt that, the rest is easy. Simply walk straight in to the wind until you are within about 50 yds (46 m) of the end of the field. Any trees, to either side of you, should be not less than about a mile away. Ideally, there should be no trees facing into the wind. Certainly they should be very far away. One thing you should avoid, at all costs, is overhead power lines. These run across country, and have a tremendously high voltage. You will soon learn

Above: Fig 152 *Dense short grass or long grass takes the shock out of an unfortunate nosedive, so saving the model from extensive damage.*

that all models, yours, mine, and anyone else's, will very often glide down right into the only tree for miles around, or hit the lone cow, or crash into that fence, or try to make a dent in those power cables. Going near those cables, or masts, has proved fatal in a number of cases, as reported in a recent overseas modelling magazine. So keep those cables as far away as you can, even if there is a wonderful field next door to them. You never know whether or not your model will land or fly near them.

When to fly

Make sure the weather is absolutely dead calm for your first flights with *any* model, no matter what type it is; that is what all the experts do.

Absolutely no wind, or dead calm, usually occurs in the early morning, up to about 8.30 am, or in the evening as the sun gets quite low. These conditions occur just about every day of the year. Instead of having to go outside to 'see what the weather is like', all you have to do is to look out of your window for a couple of minutes. Observe the tops of the trees, and bushes, in your own garden. Then look carefully at the tops of the trees in the distance. Keep looking at both for a few minutes—they will tell you exactly what the wind is doing. The tops of all these trees are dead still in calm weather. If the tops, and some leaves lower down, move very slightly, or sluggishly, then this would be 'practically calm'. Calm or practically calm, are the ideal conditions to test your brand new model in.

The clouds, too, if there are any, can be helpful. Cumulus clouds moving noticeably, usually in summer time, mean that it may rain later in the day. This is when the wind can spring up very suddenly. These clouds can, and do, quite often, build up to huge proportions on the horizon, and then quietly, without most people being aware of it, loom up right over the top of you, and the sun is still blazing hot. Suddenly the wind turns wild, and the rain starts pitter-pattering on taut coverings; everybody runs around frantically, trying to get all their stuff out of the downpour. When all are safely under cover, there is poor old what's-his-name, drenched, trying desperately to get his model down, and it is being blown all over the sky. Poor old what's-his-name, never knows what is happening, never looks at the sky, and always forgets to bring his own propellers, or fuel, or whatever.

Sometimes there is the peculiar period when the sky is completely overcast and grey. Nothing moves. Every leaf hangs absolutely still. This can go on for a few days. What fabulous flying weather this is, the air is warm without thermals, and models tend to 'float' in the air. It is the type of weather modellers dream about. It can appear at any time of the year, and it never rains.

Winter time here in the southern hemisphere where I live is mostly ideal for flying—it is completely calm, warm, almost summery sometimes, and while thermals exist, these will only take the model well up, and then it drifts out again to land a short distance away. This weather gives all control line flyers a good chance really to polish up their flying. Beginners, too, can hardly miss out with any new model, and their first flights. We always have to be on the alert though, for that dreadful, icy, south wind that can suddenly spring up, steadily increasing to a howling wind. Fortunately, this only lasts for about three days, then, just as suddenly, starts to die down and the calm is back again.

Summer time here is very hot in December and January, and thermals are big and powerful. If the day is calm to begin with, then by about 2 or 3 pm it can really be pouring with rain. Sometimes this is just a local thing, and clears within a short time. At other times it can set in, and last for about a week. This is difficult weather to predict, but the weather reports can be very useful in helping you to judge your chances for some flying in the afternoon.

That is, generally, how our weather here around my home town behaves. No matter what part of the country you live in, or what part of the world for that matter, you should get to know what you can expect at any given time of the year. The three things to remember are: listen to the weather report for the day before you want to go flying, then, on that day, watch the clouds (cumulus), and the tops of the near and far away trees.

What models have to be tested only in calm weather? All new or repaired models that fly outdoors, free flight of all types and sizes, radio-controlled models, and control line of all sorts and sizes. Some of these, such as control line trainers (with a beginner), rubber powered free flight or towline gliders, of very light construction (in the hands of an expert) and radio controlled trainers (and their very new pilots), should be flown only in calm weather. Any breeze will only make things very difficult to cope with, especially for someone without experience.

Now, go to the window again, and see if the same conditions exist. What are the trees doing now? Are the clouds still in the same place, and of the same size? Check up like this every ten minutes or so, you may be surprised. This is a very useful habit to get into; it also saves you from missing a good day.

Centre of gravity

The CG, or Centre of Gravity mark (a symbol of some sort like this ⬤) on the plan, means that the model must balance, absolutely perfectly, *at that point, and not just near it.* It is a good idea actually to mark that position on the fuselage, and the wings, with a ballpen. Make the props shown from pine, or any other wood, and glue and nail them for permanence. They can be used for all future models. You can stand them on books for any model with a long under-carriage, as this must be clear of the board while testing. When suspending the model, be careful to get the nails equidistant from the leading edge—this is very important! Carefully place the model on them, so that the nails are exactly at the ballpen marks, and then release the model, being very careful that it does not slip off. It should hang there with the fuselage absolutely level. Most models, no matter how well made, will not be exact. If it hangs with the nose very slightly down, then leave it. If it hangs with the tail down, no matter how

Below: Fig 154 *The Centre of Gravity mark should be accurately located and the prop under each wing should be carefully placed to cover the mark. NOTE that this mark is placed close to the fuselage so as not to strain the wing. It is not clever to support the wing at the tips, especially in the case of large models.*

Above: Fig 155 *Carefully check the nose-up or nose-down attitude of the model's centreline, or thrustline, in relation to the edge of the table. This model shows a very slightly nose-up attitude. (See text.)*

slightly, then you must add weight to the nose, until it does hang there absolutely level, or very slightly nose down. The usual 'weight' is a piece of Plasticine, and this should be worked to fit into, or on, the nose at the furthest point to the front, and preferably underneath. If you find that you have to use a piece of Plasticine that is far too big and clumsy, then place a small piece in position, and push lead pellets into it until the balance is right. Be sure that the Plasticine is pressed very firmly in place, and that it will not shift, or come off the model, should it land with a bump. Later, when the model is flying properly, this weight should be covered over with paper, or silk, to hold it permanently in place. This takes care of the longitudinal balance. Lateral balance is checked by suspending the model by its nose and tail, on two cereal boxes. Here you may have to suspend the model upside down, by the nose and tailskid, but this makes no difference; the main thing is that it must hang with the wings dead level. If one wing hangs low, simply give the opposite wingtip an extra coat of dope, not too much, and recheck when it is dry. Dope it again if necessary, it must hang absolutely level.

It is still fairly common, even today, to find that no CG is marked on the plan. The diagrams can only be used as a very general guide, to help you to find the approximate CG position. If your model has a large tailplane, with a lifting section, then use the larger percentage of the chord. If your model has a small tailplane area, and a non-lifting section, then use the smaller percentage of the chord. Anything in between will have to be a 'guesstimate' on your part, between the two extremes of the percentage of the chord. Then mark in this CG position as above, and balance the model. This is the best we can do at this stage, but it is better than no estimate at all. Just remember to be a bit cautious with your first few test glides, and powered flights.

Above: Fig 156 *Lateral balance is also vital to successful flying. Books make very good supports for this job, but be careful that the rudder does not rub against them and give you a wrong impression. Check the mainplane against the edge of the table to see which wingtip is the heavier of the two.*

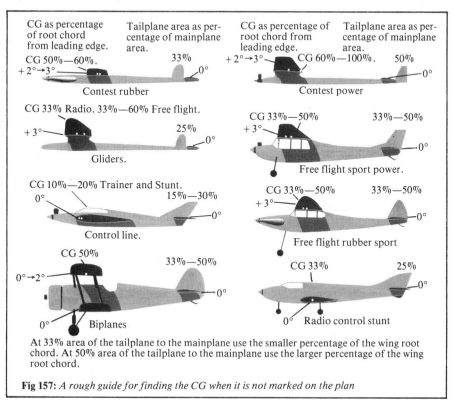

CG as percentage of root chord from leading edge.
Tailplane area as percentage of mainplane area.
CG 50%—60%.
+2°→3°.
33%
0°
Contest rubber

CG as percentage of root chord from leading edge.
Tailplane area as percentage of mainplane area.
+2°→3° CG 60%—100%.
50%
0°
Contest power

CG 33% Radio. 33%—60% Free flight.
+3°
25%
0°
Gliders.

CG 33%—50%
+3°
33%—50%
0°
Free flight sport power.

CG 10%—20% Trainer and Stunt.
0°
15%—30%
0°
Control line.

CG 33%—50%
+3°
33%—50%
0°
Free flight rubber sport

CG 50%
0°→2°
33%—50%
0°
0°
Biplanes

CG 33%
25%
0°
0°
Radio control stunt

At 33% area of the tailplane to the mainplane use the smaller percentage of the wing root chord. At 50% area of the tailplane to the mainplane use the larger percentage of the wing root chord.

Fig 157: *A rough guide for finding the CG when it is not marked on the plan*

Chapter 13

First flights

We are going to change our tactics slightly from the small all-sheet balsa glider, where the wing and tailplane are glued to the fuselage, and their angles and the mainplane position are fixed. There, we were forced to get the CG into correct position by adding weight to the nose until the model balanced at the right point—only then would it fly. That added weight represents a large proportion of the total weight of the model. Now nearly all built-up free flight models have their wings and tailplanes arranged to separate from the fuselage, and this means that the angle of incidence of the mainplane, and tailplane, can be slightly altered, together with the position of the mainplane, to get any model to fly, without having to add a lot of weight. (The mainplane position shown on the plan, should not be altered too much! About $\frac{1}{4}$ in (6 mm) should be enough for large models, and $\frac{1}{8}$ in (3 mm) for small models.) The effective angle between the mainplane and the tailplane on any free flight model, should never be less than 2 degrees, and not more than 5 degrees. All these factors are bound up with the CG on every model, and so the combinations possible are enormous, but your plan has these angles, and the CG position, and you will find that, provided you built the model reasonably well, and have it properly balanced, you should have very little trouble getting it to fly. Control line and radio models are no different—stick to the plan and what it tells you. The same applies to gliders, free flight, radio slope and thermal soarers. So all this means that the majority of models need a few slight adjustments to get them to fly reasonably well and, as you get more experience, so you will refine your adjustments to get the model to fly better and better.

Gliders

These should be treated as any other model, in that they should balance at the CG mark and, when suspended from the nose and tail, the wings should hang absolutely level. The tailplane and rudder should be free from all warps, but the mainplane can have a slight amount of washout at both wingtips, and the remainder should be true. Check that the wing is centred on the fuselage, and square to it. The same applies to the tailplane. The day has to be very calm, no breeze at all! Do your test gliding over long grass.

Learn to throw the model very gently at first, and slowly increase the power of your throw, until the model is flying and not stalling. Naturally, if it stalls with a hard throw, then you have to throw it more gently. Also, if you throw it gently, and it stalls, then you have to add a bit of weight until it does glide well.

Note: Check that the CG position is correct, and there are no warps. Start any adjustments at the tailplane. If an excessive amount of adjustment is required and the model fails to respond properly then only should you readjust the mainplane angle (see Fig 161).

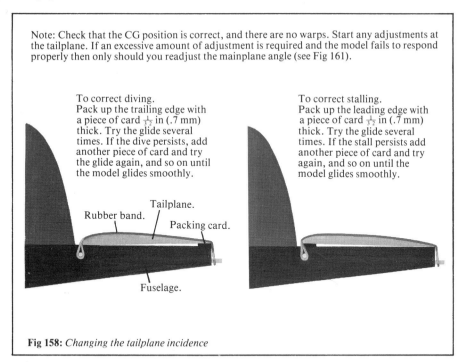

To correct diving.
Pack up the trailing edge with a piece of card $\frac{1}{32}$ in (.7 mm) thick. Try the glide several times. If the dive persists, add another piece of card and try the glide again, and so on until the model glides smoothly.

To correct stalling.
Pack up the leading edge with a piece of card $\frac{1}{32}$ in (.7 mm) thick. Try the glide several times. If the stall persists add another piece of card and try again, and so on until the model glides smoothly.

Tailplane.
Rubber band.
Packing card.
Fuselage.

Fig 158: *Changing the tailplane incidence*

The point is that *you* have to get your 'throw power' right, as well as the model's balance. Remember too, that you always point the model's nose slightly down whenever you throw it. This is most important, and cannot be overemphasised!

The balance was obtained when you put the weights in the nose to get the model to balance exactly at the centre of gravity point. Now, the extra weights your model may need, to get it to glide smoothly, should be lead pellets (preferably the ball type), as used in pellet guns. You should only add one pellet, and try the glide several times, before adding another pellet. If you have to add about half a dozen pellets to get the smooth glide on a model of about 40 in (101.6 cm) span, that is not too bad. If the model is still stalling (with six extra pellets), then stop adding them, and pack up the leading edge of the tailplane with a piece of thin card, and try the glide several times again. Be careful you do not get the angular difference between the mainplane and the tailplane down to less than 2 degrees as this causes the model to take a long time to pull out of a dive, if it should stall. You have to keep at this sort of thing until you get the model to fly in a long, 'floating', glide, without stalling. It should also *not* turn too much to one side. If it does, then check that you have the rudder absolutely straight. (You may have been testing the model with the rudder slightly out of line, or the wing may have moved very slightly out of square to the fuselage, when it landed). Before each flight, you should ensure that the wings (mainplane and tailplane) are really square to the fuselage, and sight down the nose, to be absolutely certain the rudder is still straight. You will simply be wasting your time if you do not! This test gliding process can take up quite a bit of your time, so do not be in any hurry to finish it before the model is flying properly. I have sometimes spent hours getting a model just right.

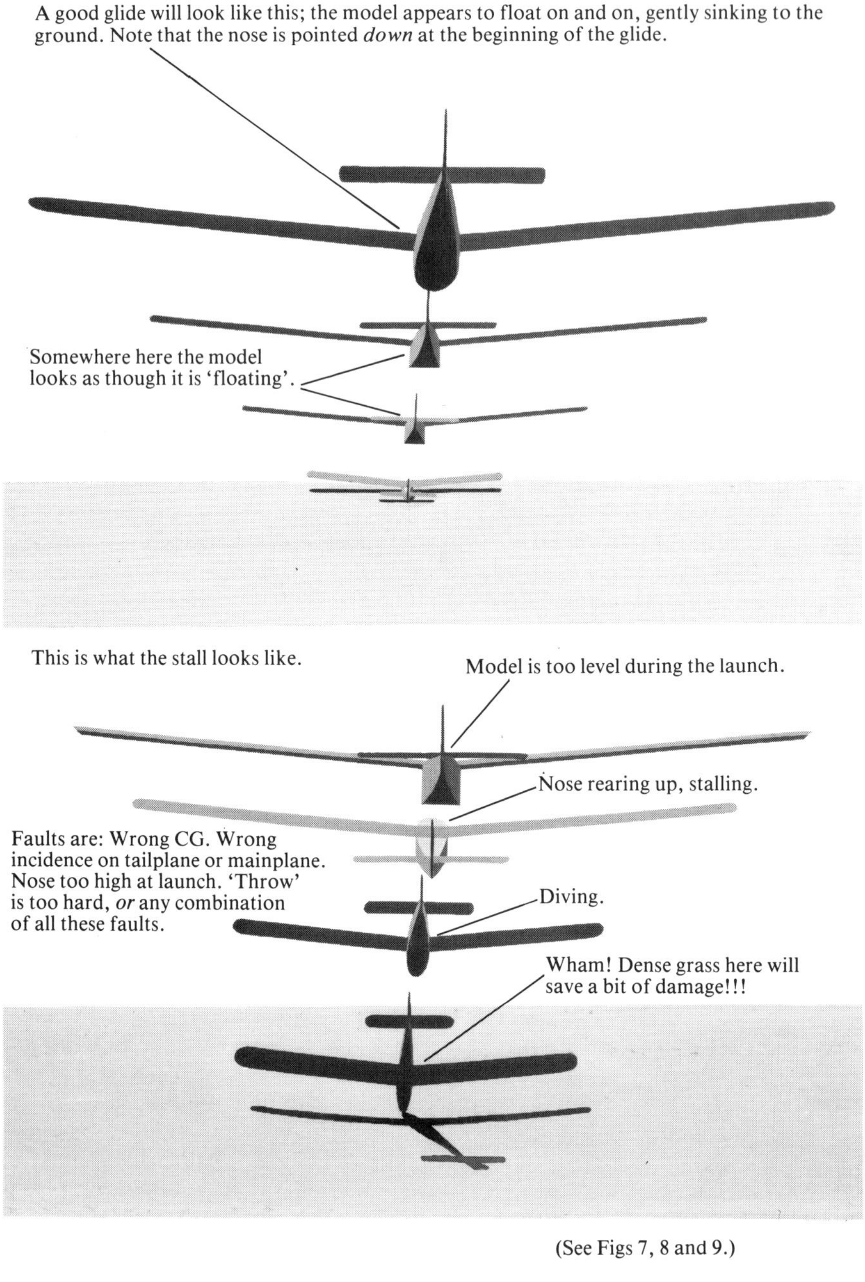

A good glide will look like this; the model appears to float on and on, gently sinking to the ground. Note that the nose is pointed *down* at the beginning of the glide.

Somewhere here the model looks as though it is 'floating'.

This is what the stall looks like.

Model is too level during the launch.

Nose rearing up, stalling.

Faults are: Wrong CG. Wrong incidence on tailplane or mainplane. Nose too high at launch. 'Throw' is too hard, *or* any combination of all these faults.

Diving.

Wham! Dense grass here will save a bit of damage!!!

(See Figs 7, 8 and 9.)

Fig 159: *How to recognise good and bad gliding*

If the plan is not marked with a CG position, then assume it is at the half-way position, and balance the model at that point by adding weight (lead pellets) to the nose ballast box. Now if the model stalls, add a little more weight to the ballast box until the model glides smoothly. Check the new balance point, which should not be more forward than one third of the chord. If it is more forward, then remove weight until the model does balance at a point one third of the way along. If the model now stalls do not add weight. Glue a strip of thin card, about $\frac{1}{32}$ in (0.7 mm) thick, under the leading edge of the tailplane, and try several glides. If stalling persists, glue on another card strip, and try the glide several times again. Continue adding strips of card until the glide is such that, when launched from shoulder height, the model glides smoothly and in a straight line, to about 10 or 12 paces from the launch point in dead calm. If you have overdone the strips of card, and the model dives, then sand the stack of cards down, until the model does fly properly.

Incidentally, if your model is a towline glider, then the balance point should not be behind the half-way point. If the plan specifies that it should be behind the half-way position, then do so. If it is not specified, then stick to the range indicated here, otherwise you may have towing problems. Do not attempt to tow the model on the line until you have the glide straight and smooth.

Most gliders these days are towline types and so, having reached the point where the model is flying properly in hand glides, the next step is to use the towline. This is a reel of nylon fishing line, of a strength sufficient for the size of glider. Attach a curtain ring to the end of the line, and tie a short length of brightly coloured cloth about 12 in (30.48 cm) from the ring, or if you can make a small parachute in bright cloth, this is preferable to the rag. This not only keeps the line better supported in the air, it also helps in finding the tow ring after the launch. It is a good idea to have some method of rewinding the line after use, such as a hand drill, fishing reel, or, best of all, an electric winch. The latter is excellent for towing the model to height, as well as rewinding the line after use.

Whichever method you use to tow the model, you will need the help of a friend. First pull out about 20 ft (609.6 cm) of line, and lay it in the direction of the wind. Attach the ring to the tow-hook, and ask your friend to hold the glider, in line with the tow-line and with a very light finger pressure. Pick up the reel and check that you are in line with the wind. Get the tow-line very slightly taut, then you and your friend begin to move forward slowly together. He must match your speed of movement exactly, otherwise the ring will fall off, or the line will jerk, and possibly break something. As soon as he feels the slightest upwards pull from the model, he should gently release his grip, and the model will float up. *He must not throw it!* You keep moving, while watching where you are going and watching the model, until it climbs straight overhead, or nearly so. At this point you stop, and the model will go on, and the ring will drop off. (You may have to 'wiggle' the line to help it off.) Watch the flight very carefully—if there is a faint stall, and the model tends to fly in a straight line, then simply add just a touch (about $\frac{1}{32}$ in 0.7 mm) of the rudder offset, to make it turn into a wide circle. This is usually sufficient to cure the stall. If, during the tow, the model weaves from side to side, stop towing, and wait for the model to release itself. To cure the weaving, move the towhook back, or add more weight, not too much, and raise the trailing edge of the tailplane slightly so that the model glides smoothly with the new weight. Test with hand launched glides.

Above: Fig 160a *Learning to tow the glider. John on his first towing flight with Steven holding the model lightly between his fingers. Note the tight line, with the rag attached about 1 ft (30.48 cm) ahead of the tow hook.*

Below: Fig 160b *The second tow was a bit too fast at the beginning, and, being slightly skew to the wind, the model veered to one side. John instantly slowed down, and the model recovered from a nasty position, released, and landed safely.*

Above: Fig 160c *The third tow was straight into the wind with a slower start. The model was climbing straight into the slight breeze, and John speeded up his towing which ended with a good short flight.*

Below: Fig 160d *The fourth tow using 30 ft (914.4 cm) of line. Note that the wind changed slightly in direction, and so they had changed their launching direction. John got the model to the overhead position before releasing it. Note that he was moving at a slow trot, and the model was climbing very fast above Steven's head.*

If the model turned to one side during the tow, then move the rudder trim tab very slightly over to counter the turn, or move the tow-hook forward by a very small amount. If the model refuses to climb (it should go up quite steeply), then move the tow-hook back a small amount. All these adjustments should be done with no more than about 20 ft (609.6 cm) of line, after you have tested the glide by hand launch, whenever an adjustment became necessary.

If you ever have a model that is very difficult to trim out, by adding the card strips to the leading edge or trailing edge of the tailplane, then you must resort to using the card strips under the leading edge, or trailing edge, of the mainplane. This has a more drastic effect on the model's flight, and quickly brings it under control. You should be careful to use this method only under difficult circumstances, and as a last resort. It is far better to use the strips under the tailplane, because the effect is easier to control. However, if you use the strips under the mainplane to get the model to glide in a more satisfactory way, then return to the use of the card strips under the tailplane, to trim out the flight path to perfection.

One last word, before we leave the gliders and move on. The methods used here for gliders, also apply to all rubber powered, and engine powered, free flight models, because when the power ceases in their flights, they then become gliders. So learn to trim their glide paths in exactly the same way as you trim gliders.

Scale rubber-powered models

These models, generally, appear to be tail heavy, and that is exactly what most of them are. When you have one under construction, try to keep every bit of construction behind the wing, as light as possible, using the lighter and softer grades of wood, and keep the amount of glue on the joints to the very minimum. All construction, under the wing to the nose, can be usually quite heavy by comparison. The whole idea behind all this, is to get the CG where it should be; much further forward than it turns out on most scale models. Rather have this extra weight made up in stronger construction, than have to add a ton of weight in the form of Plasticine, when the model is finished, and has a light weak nose. This is especially true on biplane models of the First World War, like the Sopwith Camel, and others with very short noses, more than adequate mainplane area, and very small tailplane area. In fact, the Sopwith Camel is a very difficult model to get to fly, even reasonably well, by anyone, including the experts. Try it later, when you really know quite a bit about models; it is a fascinatingly complex subject, and will really tax your ability. On high wing, or low wing monoplanes, the usual angle of incidence is about 3 degrees on the mainplane, and the tailplane is at 0 degrees. Biplanes have the tailplane and the lower mainplane set at 0 degrees, and the upper mainplane set at 1 or 2 degrees positive. The centre of gravity, generally, can be at the midpoint of the upper mainplane. Think of the biplane as a 'load' carrier, the extra wing being capable of 'carrying' an extra 'nose' or forward portion of the fuselage, together with the extra undercarriage, so we 'tame' the lift from that wing by setting it at 0 degrees, and even then one has to add quite a bit of extra weight to the nose of the biplane, to 'use up' the extra lift. The reason that a biplane does not fly nearly as well as a monoplane is mainly due to the extra drag from the extra wing and struts. (See Chapter 1).

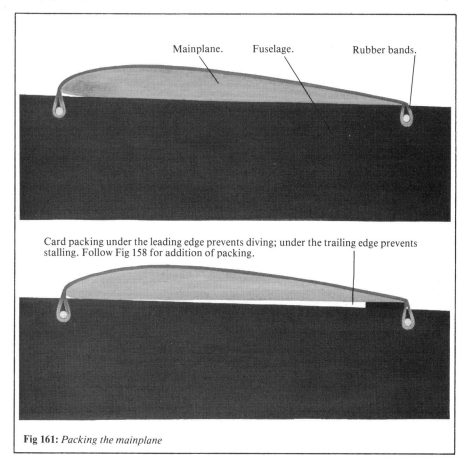

Mainplane. Fuselage. Rubber bands.

Card packing under the leading edge prevents diving; under the trailing edge prevents stalling. Follow Fig 158 for addition of packing.

Fig 161: *Packing the mainplane*

Rubber-powered models with fixed mainplane and tailplane

Usually these models have their mainplanes and tailplanes glued permanently to the fuselage, and in this case your test gliding should be carried out over fairly long, dense grass. Your first throw should be gauged to get the model to travel about 5 or 6 yds, with the nose pointed down to the spot you pick; at the same time be sure you are facing straight into a very slight breeze. Dead calm is the very best time to do any testing, about evening time if you can manage it. Have at least six throws, noting each time what the model does, *and* what your throw is like. (The grass does soften the bumps, doesn't it?) Adjust your 'throw power' first, so that you can get the feel of how much 'throw' the model needs to fly. Once you have that sorted out, you can really appreciate what the model is doing. If it climbs up, stops, and dives to the ground, it is stalling. The nose is too light, so add a small piece of Plasticine, about the size of half a pea, to the nose, stick it down tight, and try the glide again. Add a bit more Plasticine if it is still stalling a bit, and continue gliding, and adding small bits of Plasticine, until the model glides smoothly down to the point about 5 or 6 yds (4.6 or 5.5 m) away. If, at this point, the model turns very hard, and dives, then first recheck for any slight warps in the mainplanes, especially at the tips, and if there are

Alternatively, use straight castor oil or glycerine as a lubricant, *never* use car oil, Vaseline, etc.

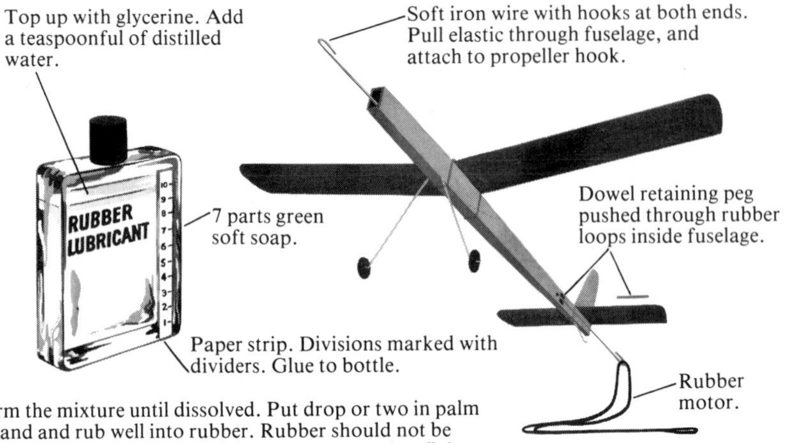

Top up with glycerine. Add
a teaspoonful of distilled
water.

Soft iron wire with hooks at both ends.
Pull elastic through fuselage, and
attach to propeller hook.

7 parts green
soft soap.

Dowel retaining peg
pushed through rubber
loops inside fuselage.

Paper strip. Divisions marked with
dividers. Glue to bottle.

Rubber
motor.

Warm the mixture until dissolved. Put drop or two in palm
of hand and rub well into rubber. Rubber should not be
too dry nor too wet. Insert rubber in fuselage. After flying
wash rubber with soap and water. Dry very thoroughly.
Pack rubber away in tin of unscented talc powder. Close tin tightly.

Fig 162: *Rubber lubricant and inserting rubber motor*

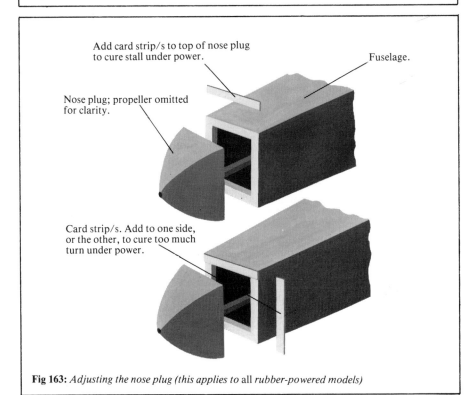

Add card strip/s to top of nose plug
to cure stall under power.

Fuselage.

Nose plug; propeller omitted
for clarity.

Card strip/s. Add to one side,
or the other, to cure too much
turn under power.

Fig 163: *Adjusting the nose plug (this applies to* all *rubber-powered models)*

warps, remove them before going on. (See under 'Warps'). Assuming there aren't any, then correct the turn by carefully bending the rudder, very slightly, for an opposite turn, and try the glide again, and if the model still turns and dives, increase the amount of turn to the rudder. Try the glide again. If the model still dives, then remove a bit of the weight. Continue all these adjustments, until the model does glide properly. Only now can you wind it up, but no more than about 30 or 40 turns, then launch the model again into the wind, with the nose pointing level to the ground, or very slightly up, releasing the propeller a fraction of a second before *gently* throwing the model. If it climbs, stops, and dives (stalling) then do not add weight, but put a small strip of card, about $\frac{1}{32}$ in (.7 mm) thick, between the nose plug and the fuselage, on top of the nose plug, and try another flight. If it stalls again, add another strip of card to the first, in the same position. Continue to add card after each flight, until the stall is cured, all the while using only 30 or 40 turns on the motor. Only after the stall under power is rectified, can you give the motor about 80 winds, and try again. This time, launch it with the nose pointing up about 20 degrees. If the model turns too steeply, while the propeller is turning, then add a strip of card on the side of the nose plug, so that the propeller will be pulling the model in the opposite direction to the turn. (You must leave the pieces of card on top of the nose plug in position while you do this.) The model will now be flying with the top, and side pieces, in place. Continue to adjust the nose plug marginally (only if the model continues to stall, or turn) until it climbs slightly with only a wide turn, or straight ahead. There will most likely be no glide to speak of, as these models do not usually get up high enough to enable them to glide. Glue the card pieces in place.

Rubber-powered models with movable planes
NB See under 'gliders' for mainplane and tailplane settings.
Here we find that the mainplanes are held on with rubber bands, and this allows us to adjust the position and incidence, and so eliminate having to use quite a bit of weight to get the glide right. When it comes to the test glide, follow the same method as set out above, except that instead of adding weight to the nose, shift the mainplane back about $\frac{1}{16}$ in (1.5 mm) at a time, or pack up the leading edge of the tailplane with a thin piece of card, about $\frac{1}{32}$ in (.7 mm), or both, if the model stalls during the test glide. It is very unlikely that the model will prove to be nose heavy but, if it is, then pack up the leading edge of the mainplane, one piece of card at a time, until the model glides properly. In any case, where the mainplane is altered in its incidence setting, be careful not to get the wing down to less than 2 degrees positive incidence and, when you reach that stage, stop. If the model is still stalling, then only, should you add weight to cure the stall. Once the glide is right, leave the wing setting alone. Now try the model with a few hand winds and follow the procedure given above, for setting the nose plug, so that the thrustline is altered to stop the model stalling, and turning too steeply, with the propeller turning. Once you get the model flying well on low turns, then only should you increase the number of turns you put into the motor for each subsequent flight, increasing that number by about 40 turns, provided that the model is still flying well. Remember that the flight, during the time the propeller is turning, is governed mainly by the angles of the nose plug, and the subsequent glide by the angles of incidence of the mainplane and tailplane. You will, sooner

or later, come to the stage where you may readjust slightly for the glide, and when you do this, be careful to readjust the nose plug slightly to compensate. You should also restart the winding procedure, starting again with very low turns and gradually increasing the number of turns after each good flight. When you have the model properly adjusted, the hand winding should be stopped. In place of this, the rubber motor is stretched out to as far as it will go, and then the hand drill, with a hook in the chuck, is engaged with the propeller, or the rubber motor, and the rubber is wound to about half of its capacity, while slowly moving in towards the model. Disengage the drill hook, replace the nose plug, check the wing for correct seating and position, check the rudder setting, and then launch as before. Once you have the model going well, always check it for any warps that may develop, because the garage or wherever you store your models, always has a change of temperature and humidity, which can easily warp a wing or rudder over, say, a week. So always check it over carefully before you go out for a day's flying, and let the first flights be gentle. Treated this way, the model will last for years.

Below: Fig 165a *Winding the rubber motor using the drill. Note how the model is held, especially the left hand over the nose. Try to keep the motor from rubbing against the side of the hole. Commence winding and counting when the rubber is fully stretched. Slowly move back towards the model while winding.*

Engine-powered models

The sports model, and the semi-scale model, can benefit by fitting the *smallest* engine specified on the plan, and this may need ballasting, or weight in the nose, to bring the CG to the point on the plan. The use of this smaller motor 'tames' the model, so that it is far easier for you to manage, and its flight is still very much up to standard. The larger motor can give you a rough time unless you are quite experienced. The same advice is true for the contest model, but if you, by some chance, have any one of these models, together with the more powerful motor, I would advise you to proceed with plenty of caution when it comes to using the motor. In all these cases start by ensuring that there are no warps that should not be there. The contest type will have all the relevant information as to what warps should be present. Stick to that religiously, you simply cannot afford to take any chances with this bird. Then get the balance exactly right, also using the props as detailed above. The test gliding is exactly the same procedure as above for gliders, as are the adjustments to obtain a good smooth glide, and having achieved this, the settings of the mainplane and tailplane should not be altered. The procedure for running your particular motor is dealt with in the leaflet enclosed with the motor, and you must stick to what they tell

Below: Fig 165b *Try to gauge the winding and moving so that you end up at the model while putting in the last few turns. (Note washout on both wingtips. Also thrust button (Fig 110) and propeller (Fig 125).)*

you. There is no other way. Get to know your motor thoroughly, by running it on a proper stand, in a well ventilated room or garage, or better still, out in the open if you can. Learn to get the lowest rev setting you can, without the engine cutting out, as well as the highest revs, and here you should remember to always set the motor a fraction *below* the highest revs, because it will speed up once it is in the model and flying. Try to find the medium revs setting as well. Some motors like those with reed valves, Babe Bee, etc, are not too happy at medium revs. (That is what we have found, maybe it is the altitude, 6,000 ft above sea level). Once you are sure of your handling of the motor, (very quick starts, like three flips of the prop only, and instant high, medium, or low revs), then install it in the model, and proceed with the test gliding. Here again, be patient, and wait for a calm day or evening. Check that the model has not developed warps, collect a friend or two, repair kit, fuel, battery, spare propeller or two, its spanner, and head for the flying field. Find the wind direction, and test glide again to be dead sure it is still perfect. Now start the motor, and once it is running smoothly, throttle it down to low revs, and set the motor cut-out timer to about 5 seconds, and launch at gliding speed, level to the ground, and straight into the slight breeze if any. Now at low revs, there is very little power, and so the model should do nothing more than have a prolonged glide, level to the ground, and maybe circling gently. If it circles tightly and comes down with the motor still running, then stop. Should the model turn to the left, then if the turn is gentle, there is no need to worry about it, as this is usually brought about by the torque reaction from the propeller, and the model will not dive in on that side. If the model turns to the right, then we have several possibilities. Most powered models, of the scale or semi-scale and sport type, cannot turn to the right under power, without diving at the same time. A few contest duration models can do the right turn under power, without diving, but they are very few. This right turn and dive, is brought about by the gyroscopic effect of the propeller, and should be avoided.

Take the two bolts, holding the motor, out on the side to which it turned, and place a washer between the motor and the firewall, on each bolt. Replace the bolts, tighten, and try the flight again, using the same throttle setting. If the motor is a beam-mounted type, then simply loosen all screws, and reset the motor so that the motor is pointing very slightly in the opposite direction to the turn. Tighten all the nuts, and try the flight again. If the model stalled, then place a washer on each of the top bolts, between the motor and the firewall. On beam-mounted motors, place the washers between the motor and the beams on the two back bolts. The purpose in both cases is to tilt the motor to point slightly down, to cure the stall under power. When tightening the nuts be very sure you tighten them only sufficiently to ensure a firm hold. Do not tighten them so much that the wood is crushed. Now try the flight again with low revs. If the stall is still there, add another washer to the top bolts, or the two rear ones. On beam-mounted motors, if you could not get a slight bias on the motor, then you should drill the mounting holes slightly larger, fuelproof them, remount the motor, and try again. Once over this initial hurdle, things go a bit more easily. Now get the motor set at half revs, and leave the timer set at 5 seconds. Do any trimming necessary, only at the motor mount, until you get the flight climb straight or in a slight, gentle, curve to the left, without stalling. All the adjustments should be carried out as above. Let me say at this point, that if you have a model that flies well on only medium revs, all you need do for the moment is leave the motor at

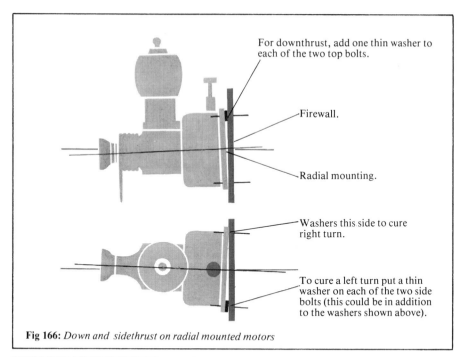

For downthrust, add one thin washer to each of the two top bolts.

Firewall.

Radial mounting.

Washers this side to cure right turn.

To cure a left turn put a thin washer on each of the two side bolts (this could be in addition to the washers shown above).

Fig 166: *Down and sidethrust on radial mounted motors*

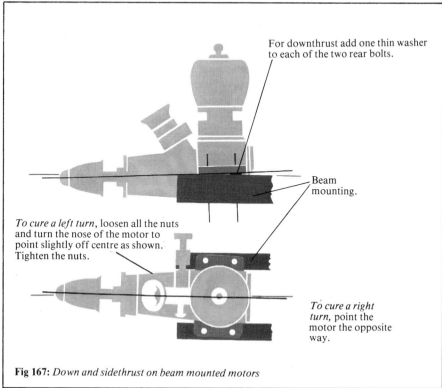

For downthrust add one thin washer to each of the two rear bolts.

Beam mounting.

To cure a left turn, loosen all the nuts and turn the nose of the motor to point slightly off centre as shown. Tighten the nuts.

To cure a right turn, point the motor the opposite way.

Fig 167: *Down and sidethrust on beam mounted motors*

medium revs, and reset the timer to say 10 or 20 secs, but do this with a bit of thought. 20 secs, when your model is flying well, can get it fairly high, and, if it is a hot day with thermals, it could go a very long way. Rather, under these conditions, try 10 secs. In winter time of course, there are usually no thermals, or only very weak ones, and you can give it about half a minute, if your model flies in circles. Also, if you have the motor adjusted for down or side thrust, or any combination thereof, and you think the glide could be better, then you know by now what adjustments to make to cure the glide faults, and you should go ahead and make them. But be careful! Make only very slight adjustments, and test fly with short flights, after which you should then also be prepared to adjust the engine thrust line, and here too, the adjustments must be very fine.

Now, if your model barely flew with medium revs, it will very definitely fly on full revs. All that has been said above applies equally well here. The whole point, of course, is that you should never, never, go straight to full revs after· getting the test glides over. Every free flight, with an engine, should be taken through the low revs tests, then the medium revs tests, and lastly the full revs test flights of 5 secs. The change, from one set of tests to the next, can some-times be such a big jump and, because of the increase in power from one to the next, the slight fault, say at low revs, can be quite pronounced with medium revs. If you missed the medium revs test, you could have a really spectacular crash by going from low revs straight to high revs. Just be patient, and a little cautious, and when you have the model sailing beautifully around the sky, the kick you get out of your success is the most fabulous reward for all your time and care. Keep it that way every time you go out, by giving the model a quick check the night before you go out. By the time you reach this stage, you will not have to wait for calm days, and can take the model out even on quite breezy days.

Control line models

Here you have exactly the same aerodynamic effects that have been explained at the beginning of this book. Fortunately, though, we do not have to worry about things like dihedral, weight, colour schemes (coloured dope) and smaller engines. The motor size to use is the one specified on the plan, or an equivalent. Because these models are about half the size, or smaller, of the equivalent model in free flight, for the same size engine, they have plenty of power. We find that they are usually fairly robustly constructed, and therefore do not usually develop warps (unless you built one in on the frame). Being more compact, they are easier to transport and store. Flying is far easier to accomplish than in free flight, and the flying site is more readily come by. The only snag is the noise, not to us, but to the general public as mentioned earlier. Here the use of a muffler helps, but it is, generally, still better to get away from built up areas as far as possible. (That motor can still be very irritating, even with a muffler.)

Small models, about 18 in (45.7 cm) wingspan, should preferably have a hard sand, or tarmac surface, for take-off and landing. If you have to fly from grass, then use wheels of at least $1\frac{1}{2}$ in (38.1 mm) with fairly thick tyres. Larger models can cope with grass, or lawn, for take-off and landing, but here, too, things are easier and smoother with a sand or tarmac area. Again, as with free flight, it is a must to know which way the wind is blowing and, as you are a beginner, you will have more success if you start flying in calm, or very slight breeze, conditions. In a good breeze, a beginner is in trouble and will invariably crash,

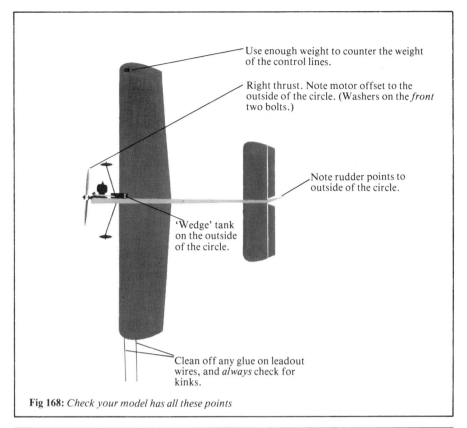

Use enough weight to counter the weight of the control lines.

Right thrust. Note motor offset to the outside of the circle. (Washers on the *front* two bolts.)

Note rudder points to outside of the circle.

'Wedge' tank on the outside of the circle.

Clean off any glue on leadout wires, and *always* check for kinks.

Fig 168: *Check your model has all these points*

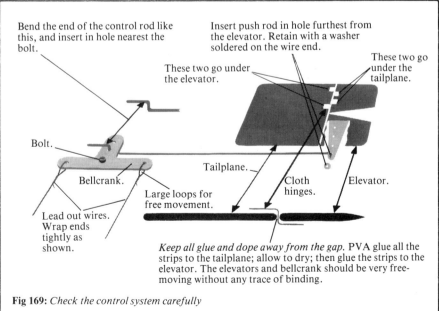

Bend the end of the control rod like this, and insert in hole nearest the bolt.

Insert push rod in hole furthest from the elevator. Retain with a washer soldered on the wire end.

These two go under the tailplane.

These two go under the elevator.

Bolt.

Bellcrank.

Tailplane.

Cloth hinges.

Elevator.

Large loops for free movement.

Lead out wires. Wrap ends tightly as shown.

Keep all glue and dope away from the gap. PVA glue all the strips to the tailplane; allow to dry; then glue the strips to the elevator. The elevators and bellcrank should be very free-moving without any trace of binding.

Fig 169: *Check the control system carefully*

so avoid this for a while, until you've had a bit of experience. While you are building your model, you will find you need a break on occasion, and if you do this, take the opportunity to practise turning round and round on one spot, holding your fist (right or left hand) stuck out at right angles from the shoulder. Do this outdoors, not indoors.

You just cannot get too much practice at this before you finish your model because, if you have never done any fast turning around like this, and you suddenly do it with a brand new model (even with no breeze), you do not have a chance. You are going to get very giddy, and then, I can promise you, you are going to bring back a model that is practically junk. Even those tough, come-apart-in-a-crash-and-nothing-is-broken, prefabricated plastic models, can get very bent on occasion, and what fun is there in breaking it? It is far more fun to fly! So practise getting over the giddy whirling! It will not hurt, I promise! But do it gently at first, until you are used to it a bit, then try more turns. Before you install the motor in your model, make sure you know how to get it going, on about the third or fourth flip of the propeller, and how to get low, medium, and high revs, without it cutting out. Also, teach your friend how to do it, so that when you go flying he can do it for you. Then make sure you can do all that with the motor installed. Learn to put in only enough fuel to run the motor for about 30 seconds. You can use up windy, no-flying days on this sort of thing, so that when that lovely calm day arrives, you will not have waited in vain. Several things have to be checked before you take your model out. First and foremost is that it balances on the exact spot marked on the plan, and if there is right thrust on the plan, (assuming you are going to fly with the right hand, and in an anti-clockwise direction), you have it on your model, and that the rudder is set for a right hand turn. Also check that the pushrod is in the hole nearest the outer edge of the elevator horn, and, if possible, the inner hole on the bellcrank, and that the leadout wires work the elevator, very, very easily, but without a sloppy action. Then grab the spares box, fuel, starter battery, propellers, model, and friend, and head for the flying field.

First find the centre of the field, if it is a small one; check the wind, slight as it

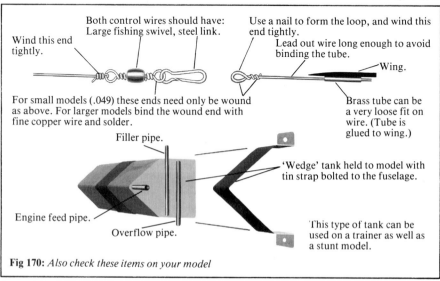

Both control wires should have: Large fishing swivel, steel link.

Use a nail to form the loop, and wind this end tightly.

Wind this end tightly.

Lead out wire long enough to avoid binding the tube.

Wing.

For small models (.049) these ends need only be wound as above. For larger models bind the wound end with fine copper wire and solder.

Brass tube can be a very loose fit on wire. (Tube is glued to wing.)

Filler pipe.

'Wedge' tank held to model with tin strap bolted to the fuselage.

Engine feed pipe.

Overflow pipe.

This type of tank can be used on a trainer as well as a stunt model.

Fig 170: *Also check these items on your model*

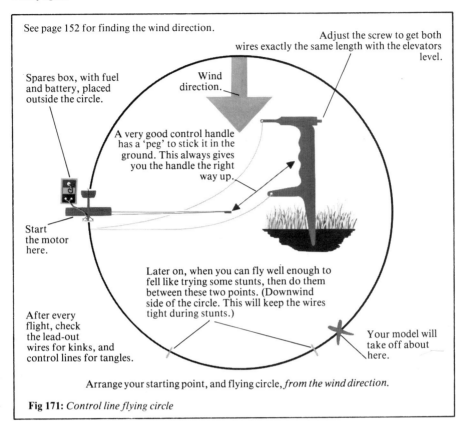

See page 152 for finding the wind direction.

Adjust the screw to get both wires exactly the same length with the elevators level.

Spares box, with fuel and battery, placed outside the circle.

Wind direction.

A very good control handle has a 'peg' to stick it in the ground. This always gives you the handle the right way up.

Start the motor here.

Later on, when you can fly well enough to fell like trying some stunts, then do them between these two points. (Downwind side of the circle. This will keep the wires tight during stunts.)

After every flight, check the lead-out wires for kinks, and control lines for tangles.

Your model will take off about here.

Arrange your starting point, and flying circle, *from the wind direction.*

Fig 171: *Control line flying circle*

is (See Chapter 12). I know it is only a faint breeze, and why bother about its direction? Well, when you have the model up, and going well, you may find the lines going slack, or, in other words, the model may move in towards you, and you will not know what is happening, or what to do about it. It is quite simple. The wind will have sprung up, and a gust will be pushing the model towards you. All you will have to do is to nip back quickly, and this will keep the lines taut. In practice this means you move backwards, away from the model, the whole time. This is because it is very difficult, the first few times out flying, to tell exactly where things are happening in the blur of trees and buildings, as you turn around with the model. I have had to describe all this, as you have not seen it yet. When you have done it you will realise what I mean. All you must remember when you are out there alone with your giddiness, and the model that never seems to want to come down, is that as soon as the model appears to come towards you, you move backwards, and around, at the same time, and do it all the time the model is up, and quickly, you simply cannot quit! You did practise going around with your fist stuck out? Remember?

So you have checked the wind and you know where it is coming from. Now place the model on the downwind side of the circle, pick up the control lines and let them pass through your fingers, to check that they are not twisted or tangled, and stand on the centre spot. Now, holding your arm out in front of you, do not move your wrist. Simply point your entire arm up slightly from horizontal, and your friend should point up, meaning of course, that the elevators are pointing up. Similarly, when you point your arm down, that means elevators down. With your arm pointing at the model, the elevators are horizontal. Of course, if he points down, when your arm is up, it means you must turn the handle over 180 degrees. Then go through the drill again, to be sure the handle is the right way up in your hand. This simple drill is a must. Now let your friend get the motor running to full revs and, as soon as he has it going, you signal, by pointing, with your left hand straight out to your side. This means 'let her go'. Now you should have just a touch of up elevator, as the model accelerates along the ground, and watch the model carefully, to see when it leaves the ground, because, any second from now, you have to level it out, with the control handle giving very slight 'down'. This you must judge for yourself as the model flies, and must not be so much as to dig the nose back in the ground. You have to watch the model, and judge this bit, to try to keep the model level, and simply go around with it, until the motor stops (only 30 seconds' fuel, remember?). If you can keep your arm from jerking up or down, you will have a much better chance. Make all your movements smooth. Notice that when you point up, the model will go up, and when you point down, the model goes down, meaning that where you point, the model will go. That is all you should remember, once the model is off the ground. To land, simply keep your arm following the model, as it slowly sinks after the motor has stopped and, when it is just above the ground, slowly add up elevator, more and more, so that the model stalls on to the ground for a 'three pointer'; keeping the up elevator, until it stops running. While it is still calm, keep right on practising until you feel you can handle the model.

Below: Fig 172 *Take off with a bit of 'up' elevator.* **1** *Up elevator.* **2** *Handle back. (Arm up.)* **3** *Neutral.*

Above: Fig 173 *Flying level* **1** *Neutral elevator. As soon as the model leaves the ground, give a touch of* 'down', *and instantly neutralise.* **2** *Handle neutral.* **3** *Neutral.*

Below: Fig 174 *Landing. When the motor cuts, and the model nears the ground, give a little 'up' elevator, and slowly increase the 'up' so that the model stalls on to the ground. Hold 'up', until it stops running.* **1** *Up elevator.* **2** *Handle back. (Arm up.)* **3** *Neutral.*

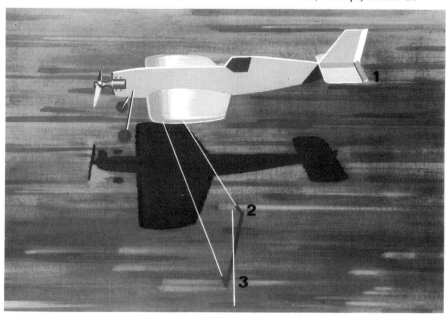

One or two things to watch for. When flying, if the model does not respond, and feels 'light on the wires', you may be using wires that are too thick and heavy, the rudder may need more offset, the motor may need more offset, or more weight may be needed on the outer wingtip. If the model is over-sensitive, and will not fly straight and level, add more weight to the nose, to bring the CG forward, and desensitise the elevator by moving the control rod to the outer hole on the elevator horn, and the inner hole on the bellcrank. Small models also should be kept straight and level in a high wind, as any climb will cause them to be blown high, the wires go slack, you lose control, and *wham*!

Learn to fly the model level first, and keep it that way for a couple of days, until you really know what you are doing. After a while, you will during this time, experiment with the little 'jiggles' at the control handle; you will find that the model undulates slightly, and on occasion you will stick the nose in the ground. This is why you have a 'trainer'; it is tough enough to take it a couple of times. Only when you can stop sticking the nose in, and bring the model down to a fair landing, should you try a gentle climb and bring it down to level again, all at the downwind side of the circle. This will involve just a little 'up' elevator, and almost at once a little 'down' elevator, and then a very slight 'up' movement, to bring the model out of the 'down', to level it. Get this right before you do anything else. Now, when you can do that with your eyes shut, so to speak, move the pushrod on the bellcrank to the outer hole (not the elevator yet) and do the whole flying schedule, above, again. Note that the model will be more sensitive than before. When you have that right, then move the pushrod to the inner hole on the elevator, and try again. All OK? Right, now you can do the climb, and dive, and level out, all at the downwind side, and bring the model down in one piece. The whole idea is to know yourself, and the model, and the whole 'feel' of this new experience, before moving into the next stage, which is quite fantastic.

Aerobatics

The trainer you have been learning to fly with is usually not up to much when it comes to stunts, because it is too heavy, has the wrong angle of incidence, and the wrong aerofoil for aerobatics. Some of these trainers can be made to perform loops, and after that, nothing. Then if you want to go on and learn stunts, purchase a good stunt model, and find out from your dealer if your existing motor will fit the new model. Generally you may also need a hotter fuel, and definitely a change of propeller—one that is designed for stunts. So it is up to you to sort out with your dealer exactly what you will need. As your trainer may be capable of loops, especially if you can use a hotter fuel, and change the propeller, then try it out for loops. Better still, if you know a modeller who is good at stunts, ask him to try your model out for you. That way you will at least know if your model is capable of loops. Then it is up to you to do the same.

Up to now you have had the motor running either well, or indifferently, and, sometimes, it has cut out for no apparent reason. Now you just have to have it running perfectly. You cannot afford to have it cut out, or running with a splutter, no matter how slight. I am going to assume that you are using a motor that is in good condition, and that you have learnt from experience, exactly how to get what you want from it, except the last bit of power.

When you have the motor running at peak revs, and if you try to get that tiny bit more, it starts to fade (this is while running on the ground, before you fly the model), then bring it back to peak revs, and let it settle there for a moment. Now turn the needle valve slightly more open (richer). This may be an eighth of a turn, or slightly more, or slightly less, depending on your particular motor. The idea is to have it running very slightly richer than it does at peak revs while still on the ground. (The motor will lean out, by itself, when you fly the model.) Take careful note of exactly how much you turned the needle valve; and fly the model. Listen to the motor, and note if it is running smoothly. When the flight is over, do the same thing again, trying to set the needle valve, by opening or closing it, a few degrees more than the last time. If the motor runs, while flying, better than it did on the first flight, then obviously this last setting is better than the first. So you keep trying, after each flight, and noting the exact position of the needle valve, to get the motor to always give a very smooth run at full revs, and without any splutter, no matter how slight. You now have the motor doing its best.

Take off as usual, and be careful to note the wind direction. All aerobatics are done downwind. Get the model up to about 12 ft to 15 ft (3.6 m to 4.6 m) for a few laps, and then, when downwind, give full 'up' elevator. Keep your arm pointing at the model the whole time. It will go right around the loop by itself. When it is at the bottom of the loop, level out, as you did with the trainer after a dive. Go around for a couple of laps until your nerves settle down, and then try it again. Do not get over ambitious and try to keep on looping. The lines will get twisted up and you can lose control. You must untwist the lines after each flight, and always check the leadout wires for kinks.

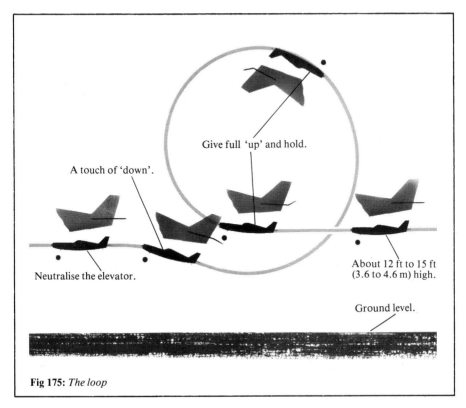

Fig 175: *The loop*

Now, when you get a calm day again, try the next trick, which is inverted flight. First you do a half loop, and, when the model is upside down, immediately give a touch of down.

Now think that all you have to do is to hold the model in the inverted position, once it is on its back. So this means giving less than full 'down', and holding it like that, so that the model is now flying inverted. (It is also flying in the opposite direction to its take-off.) Continue upside down, giving very little corrections, and all these are 'down' or slightly less 'down', to keep the model flying. To recover: give full 'down'. The model will do half an outside loop, coming out on its original flight path, and fairly high up.

The next one to learn, is the follow-up to this one, and is known as the 'horizontal eight'. Essentially it is the same half loop to start with, but allow the model to get into the inverted position in a shallow dive, then give full 'down'

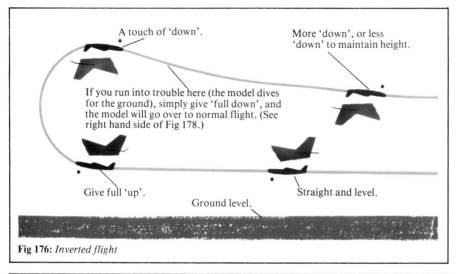

A touch of 'down'.

More 'down', or less 'down' to maintain height.

If you run into trouble here (the model dives for the ground), simply give 'full down', and the model will go over to normal flight. (See right hand side of Fig 178.)

Give full 'up'.   Straight and level.

Ground level.

Fig 176: *Inverted flight*

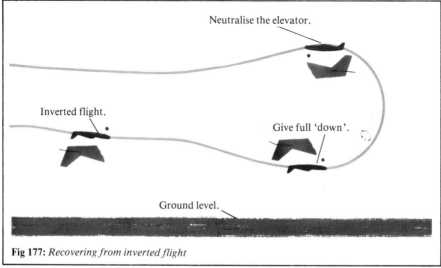

Neutralise the elevator.

Inverted flight.

Give full 'down'.

Ground level.

Fig 177: *Recovering from inverted flight*

elevator, and the model will go right around up the other side, to complete the second half of the 'eight'. Level out, and go around in straight and level laps, to sort yourself out. Practise this for a while, before trying the next stage. When you can do the first stage properly, instead of levelling out, allow the model to go into another shallow dive, and then give full 'up' elevator, to start the half loop again, and so on. Watch your altitude! Always be prepared to continue straight and level, if the model gets near the ground—either right side up, or inverted.

The bunt, or outside loop, is brought about by holding full 'down' elevator, when the model is flying at a good height above the ground. Allow the model to complete the entire loop, and find through practice just how high the model should be, at the beginning of the bunt, so that it will clear the ground, and, also, not be too high at the top of the manoeuvre.

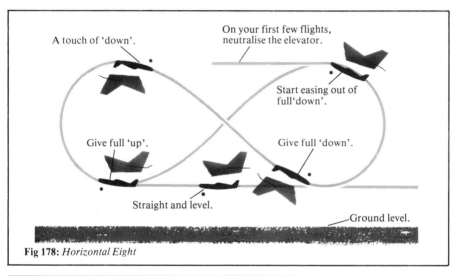

Fig 178: *Horizontal Eight*

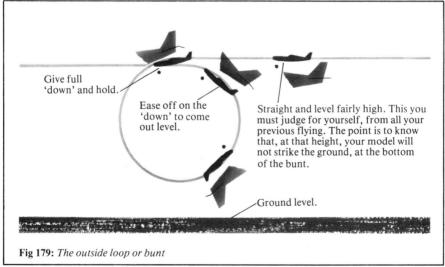

Fig 179: *The outside loop or bunt*

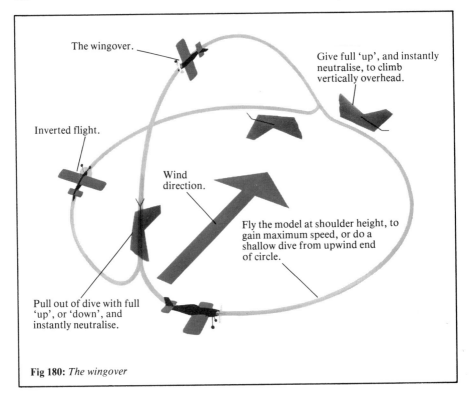

The wingover.

Give full 'up', and instantly neutralise, to climb vertically overhead.

Inverted flight.

Wind direction.

Fly the model at shoulder height, to gain maximum speed, or do a shallow dive from upwind end of circle.

Pull out of dive with full 'up', or 'down', and instantly neutralise.

Fig 180: *The wingover*

A wingover is started by climbing, in a gentle curve up from level flight, at the very bottom, downwind end, of the circle, straight over the top, into the wind, pulling out at the top end of the circle, into either inverted, or upright, level flight. This is done to keep the wind pressure on the rudder, holding the tail down, the nose up, while going over the top, and so holding the lines tight over the top. The big thing to remember, in any manoeuvre, is to keep the flight curves wide, to avoid a loss of speed during the manoeuvre. A sudden jerk on the control handle is to be avoided at all costs, as this will cause loss of speed, consequent line slackness, and therefore loss of control.

If you have bent a model at any stage, then try to reconstruct what you did, and what the model did, so that you do not suffer from the same mistake again. Just about any manoeuvre can be worked out from what you now know, so do not be afraid to try out what you want.

Speed

For this, the model simply *must* be highly streamlined, and the motor needs just enough space to 'breathe' properly, to enable it to work efficiently. No under-carriage is fixed to the model, it takes off from a 'dolly', and lands by skidding on the belly. Only one line is used for control, called monoline, which imparts its action to the bellcrank by twisting along its length. The motor and its tuning, the design of the propeller, and the make-up of the fuel, are the main factors in the struggle for ever more speed. International class speed models are restricted in the fuel though, to either 80 per cent methyl alcohol and 20 per cent castor oil, or to 75 per cent methyl alcohol and 25 per cent castor oil for glow plug motors, but diesel motors can use anything the modeller chooses for the fuel. Because monoline is only one line, and the method of working is different, the modeller must learn to fly all over again, but the reduction in drag of the single wire is well worth the extra trouble. To prevent the 'whipping' of the model to increase speed, the modeller is obliged to rest his wrist on a special pylon, and to learn to use wrist action only to control the flight.

Surging fuel feed is a problem that is met in different ways, and ranges from the pen bladder, where fuel is pumped into the bladder, and the pressure then eliminates the need for venting to replace the partial vacuum in the tank, to the sealed pressure tank, filled with fuel and sealed. A tube leads air, under pressure from the motor crankcase, to the tank. The air replaces the used fuel, and applies pressure on the surface of the fuel. The 'chicken hopper' tank has a small and large tank in one. The large tank feeds the smaller tank through the balance of air in a ventilating pipe; and the small tank, which feeds the motor, is not affected by gravity, or centrifugal force, while the motor is running, thus allowing a smooth flow of fuel. The standard propeller must be modified to have thin smooth blades of very true aerofoil section that are slightly flexible, and this area seems to offer just as much scope for inventiveness, as any other, in this fascinating aspect of aeromodelling. The course is over one kilometre, doing so many laps at a set radius. The minimum wing area is 80 sq in (516 sq cm) for a 2.5 cc motor. The larger motors have slightly larger models.

Chapter 14

Radio control

Channels or functions

You have a choice between radio control units with one, two, four, five or six channels or functions. Each channel or function operates one control—for example, just the elevators or just the ailerons. Buy an inexpensive two- or four-channel radio to start with; more than that will be too complicated and expensive.

Proportional control

Moving the stick partly to the right moves the rudder a proportionate amount to the right; more stick gives slightly more right rudder. Similarly, moving the stick partly towards neutral again moves the rudder back a little. This is called proportional control. All modern radios use this principle for each function.

Two-channel system

Each stick performs *one* function so you can operate the rudder and elevators, or rudder and motor control. A ratchet-controlled trim lever next to each stick allows for a fine adjustment to correct any fault in flight, but return the trim lever to neutral

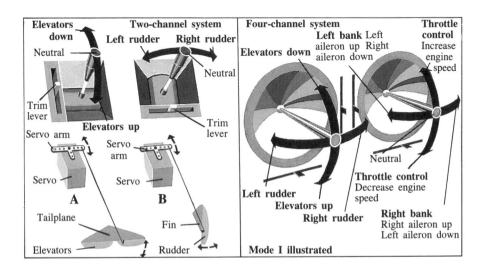

Fig 180a *Two- and four-channel radio control systems.*

after landing and before curing the fault. (*Note*: A single-channel radio operates the rudder the same way as the stick in drawing B, Fig 180a.)

Four-channel system

Each stick performs *two* functions. These are the rudder, elevators, ailerons, and motor control. Visit your hobby shop to decide which mode suits you best.

Mode 1		Mode 2	
Left stick	**Right stick**	**Left Stick**	**Right stick**
Elevators	Throttle (motor)	Throttle (motor)	Elevators
Rudder	Ailerons	Rudder	Ailerons

(Figs 184 and 185 highlight control sticks and trim levers. Go back to figs 24 and 25 to see the controls and how they operate.)

Before installing the radio equipment in the model, it is best to connect everything while it is still in the foam container. Carefully place the batteries the right way round in the battery box and transmitter. Tape a piece of paper to each servo lead, plug them into the receiver sockets marked CHL 1, CHL 2, etc, and mark the number on each paper. Plug the battery lead into the socket marked BATT, and the other end, via the switch, to the battery box plug. Always switch the transmitter on before the receiver.

Now, depending on whether you have a two- or four-channel system, refer to the diagrams above. Move the left stick in the direction of the arrows in the diagram. With the two-channel radio only one servo will operate, so mark it 'elevator'. In the four-channel radio, one servo operates the rudder, the other the elevators. Again, mark the servos clearly according to the arrows in the diagram, then do the same with the right-hand stick and the other two servos.

Model types

Having built and flown a few different types of model successfully, there is now every reason to progress to radio control and, with a knowledge of gliders and powered models behind you, there is every chance of success. There are several ways to go when you start. As in control line, it is always better to start with a trainer, or a fairly docile model, until you get the feel of things. There are gliders and powered models. Gliders are thermal soarers and slope soarers, and these latter models are capable of quite a few more stunts than the thermal soarers. Here there is quite a saving, too, in that neither type has the expense of the motor, fuel, propellers, etc, and the whole flight is silent and peaceful, even when there are other flyers around. There is nothing, or very little, to worry about in the form of collision with another model. Powered models are broken down mainly into scale, stunt, and racing models, and then, as in free flight, there are the 'fun' models. These can be just about anything that will fly— modern, old-timer, hybrid, seaplane, scale, semi-scale, or anything else, in fact.

Free flight to radio control

You can rush out and buy a new model trainer, motor to suit, radio that goes with it all, etc, or you can take one of your free flight models, check that it is large enough to take the weight of the radio, and has enough space for it, and can take the added weight of reinforcement to the fuselage and mainplane. This model will only become a trainer, and therefore will not be capable of more than a few stunts when you are good enough (this applies to gliders as well as powered models) but will always be used as a fun model. To alter it, you will need to remove most, if not all, of the covering, in most cases, once you have made up your mind that it can be converted.

As you are new to this aspect of modelling, you will find it far easier, and less expensive, to start with a model you already know and can alter very simply. It also means that the flight characteristics are not new to you, and the addition of radio control will help you, rather than hinder you, by giving you the control over the model that you do not have at the moment. It is marvellous to be able to stop a stall, or unwanted turn, that can sometimes be very hairy in free flight, and do something about it before it gets out of control, and so save the model by getting it down in one piece. You then have the opportunity to do any corrections, and have another go. Then, when it is properly adjusted, you have endless fun! And this trainer will be part of your life for a long time to come. Even when you graduate to a fully-fledged stunt model, you will, on more than one occasion, come back to this model for a bit of sheer fun and relaxation. The stunt model is quite a handful, and can get a bit tiring with all the concentration needed to do the stunts, and it has got to be nursed like a baby if you want to get the most out of it. It is not a model you can teach yourself to fly on, as it requires practice and skill to fly it, and since you do not possess these yet, it is out of the question. The trainer does not need much skill to fly it, in fact, if you are good at getting your free flight models to work, you can simply let the model with the radio in it free flight for the first few seconds until it is well up, before you touch the controls. That way you can avoid getting into trouble if you do not feel too sure of yourself with the radio. Under these circumstances allow the model to get really high, before you try out the radio, but keep it up, and do not be afraid to try. If the model gets out of control, simply centre the stick and wait—it will

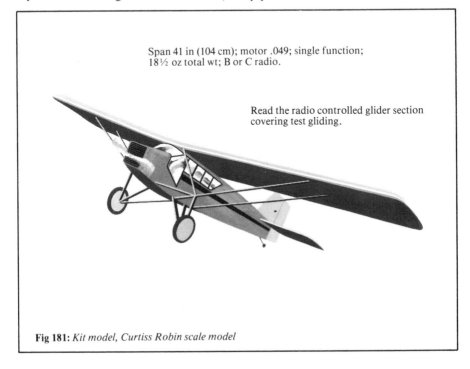

Span 41 in (104 cm); motor .049; single function;
18½ oz total wt; B or C radio.

Read the radio controlled glider section covering test gliding.

Fig 181: *Kit model, Curtiss Robin scale model*

recover by itself—then try again.

There are all sorts of ways you can work out which radio, and how many functions, to install. You can work this out from the wing area, flying weight with and without radio, number of controls and their weight, etc, but the easiest and quickest method is to ballast the model, and then check the amount of weight it has carried. Keep the total weight of the radio to well below the amount of weight your model can carry. This way you will not overload your model and engine, and the stability will not be too heavily taxed which, in turn, gives you a much better chance of success.

Slit the covering on three sides of a bay on one side of the fuselage, directly under the CG, and insert a bit of weight like Plasticine, between foam styrene, and PVA to the floor of the fuselage, checking that it is under the CG by balancing at the correct point. Test glide and test with the motor, after taping the covering back in place. Continue to add Plasticine, or lead pellets to the Plasticine, until you get the model to fly with full power in a climb of about 10 degrees, and the glide should not be affected too much. It will, of course, be a bit faster, but should not be plummeting. The whole idea is to see if the model can carry a weight of about 3 to 10 oz, or more, depending on the size of the model and its weight before you started. Do these tests in calm weather only, so that the wing is not overstrained. You may find that you will have to increase the incidence of the mainplane with one or two pieces of card packing under the leading edge, but be careful you do not overdo this. Just be slightly cautious, and you will be surprised at what your model can carry. Remove the weight after you think the model has reached its limit, and measure it. Now this weight represents the weight of alterations, additions, receiver, servos, batteries, tank, control rods, hinges, and maybe a stronger undercarriage, if the present one

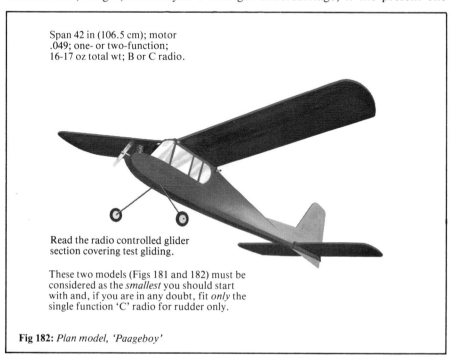

Span 42 in (106.5 cm); motor
.049; one- or two-function;
16-17 oz total wt; B or C radio.

Read the radio controlled glider
section covering test gliding.

These two models (Figs 181 and 182) must be
considered as the *smallest* you should start
with and, if you are in any doubt, fit *only* the
single function 'C' radio for rudder only.

Fig 182: *Plan model, 'Paageboy'*

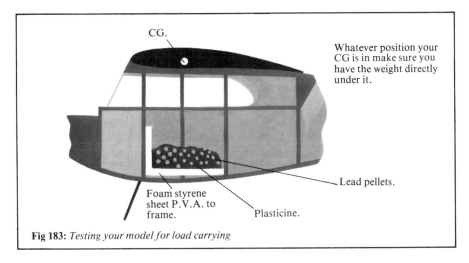

CG.

Whatever position your
CG is in make sure you
have the weight directly
under it.

Lead pellets.

Foam styrene
sheet P.V.A. to
frame.   Plasticine.

Fig 183: *Testing your model for load carrying*

showed signs of distress when the model landed. The main weight is taken up by
the receiver (about 2 oz), batteries (6 oz), and servos (1.5 oz each), and you
should also add about 0.25 oz for each control rod. Add all these weights up for
your model, subtract this from your Plasticine weight and this gives you roughly
what you can allow for the alterations and additions. Do not try to cram a lot of
radio into this model, rather put in one servo less than the model can comfortably carry, otherwise it will be too heavy and this will make it tricky for you to fly.

Radio types
Average or large radio (A)
At the moment there are three types of radio. The first is the average digital
proportional outfit, that can be seen on the large radio controlled models, and
this weighs about 13 oz, when fully installed, with 4 servos (4 functions).
Average weights are: receiver 2 oz, size 1.9 cm W, 4.4 cm H, 6.3 cm L; servo
1.5 oz, 1.8 cm W, 3.9 cm H, 3.7 cm L. Battery weights vary according to the
radio and should be checked with your hobby shop. Allow roughly 3-5 oz for
this. Padding, in the form of foam rubber for the receiver, will be roughly
0.5 oz, and about 0.25 oz for each pushrod. The on/off switch is about 0.25 oz.
(*Note:* 1 oz = 28.349 gm, 1 in = 2.54 cm.)

Mini radio (B)
The new mini-proportional systems, designed especially for smaller models,
from 0.010 to 1.0 power, is currently available in two, three and four functions.
As this is a low power system, it must *not* be used in the larger models. Weights
are: receiver 1 oz, servo 0.75 oz, battery 100 mah, 1.5 oz. Here, too, the rubber
foam for the receiver, pushrods, and on/off switch, must be added to the radio
weight. Use the figures above for this. These radio outfits, together with the
sub-miniature type, will one day be found to appeal to a greater proportion of
modellers than the larger type, simply because more small and medium size
models appeal, cost-wise, to the majority of modellers. Not all modellers can
afford the larger outfits, and therefore larger models.

Sub-miniature radio (C)
This is the smallest, and lightest radio outfit, which comes in four types, each

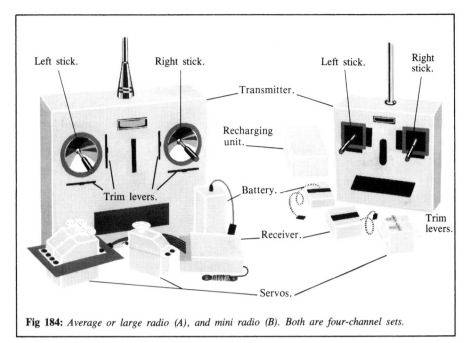

Fig 184: *Average or large radio (A), and mini radio (B). Both are four-channel sets.*

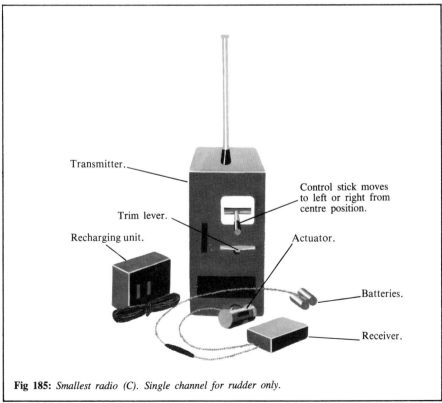

Fig 185: *Smallest radio (C). Single channel for rudder only.*

for a specific size of model. It is a pulse proportional type, and is suitable only for rudder only models, or single function. The *Baby* weighs 2.1 oz (Airborne weight) for 0.010 and *Pee Wee* 0.020 powered models up to 36 in (91.4 cm) span. *Baby Twin* weighs 2.3 oz for 0.020 power and slow flying 0.049 powered models up to 40 in (101.6 cm) span. *Standard* weighs 3.1 oz for *Babe Bee* and slow flying TD 0.049 powered models up to 42 in (106.6 cm) span. *Stomper* weighs 3.5 oz for hot (fast) 0.049 power to slow flying 0.15 powered models. All these have ni-cad batteries in the model, and a 9 v battery in the transmitter.

Models below 40 in span are tricky subjects for your first radio control attempts and are not recommended. Later, when you know more about flying, and setting up a model with radio, you can try them as a challenge to your skills. Here are a few examples for you to see what is possible with models of various sizes.

	Wingspan	Wing area	Flying weight	Radio	Functions	Motor
A	41 in (104 cm)	240 sq in (1,548.3 sq cm)	18 oz (510.28 g)	C	1	0.049
B	42 in (106.6 cm)	246 sq in (1,587.0 sq cm)	16 oz (453.58 g)	B-C	1-2	0.049
C	48 in (121.9 cm)	430 sq in (2,774.1 sq cm)	40 oz (1,133.9 g)	A	1-3	0.099

The best way to appreciate what we are looking at in the above figures is to convert them into oz per sq ft of wing loading. In 'A' above, the wing area of 240 sq in is divided by 144 (the number of sq in per sq ft): 240 ÷ 144 = 1.6 sq ft. Now take the weight (or mass) of 18 oz and divide this by the sq ft, thus 18 ÷ 1.6 = 11.25 oz per sq ft. So the wing loading in 'A' is expressed as 11.25 oz per sq ft. In 'B' it is 246 ÷ 144 = 1.7 sq ft and 16 oz ÷ 1.7 = 9.4 oz per sq ft, whilst in 'C' it is 430 ÷ 144 = 2.9 and 40 ÷ 2.9 = 13.7 oz per sq ft. You can now see clearly that the model in 'B' has the lightest wing loading and will therefore be far easier to fly than the model in either 'A' or 'C' (all other factors, such as design, and quality of building, being equal of course). Generally though, the larger model will be found to be the easiest to fly, even though the wing loading is higher. *Do not exceed this loading of 13 oz per sq ft*; keep it less if you can manage it. Always go for the lightest wing loading in any model, especially in your first radio attempt, because the higher the wing loading becomes, the more difficult the model gets to fly.

Notice that all three models can be flown with just one function, and in the case of 'C', two or three.

Alterations to free flight models for radio control
Wing alterations
All free flight models should have their main spars strengthened by the addition of an extra spar (or spars), plus the $\frac{1}{16}$th in (1.5 mm) sheet web with grain vertical, as illustrated, and an additional ply brace. As all models are different, you must decide for yourself how best to alter your wing. (See the illustrations, as a general guide, as to what should be done.)

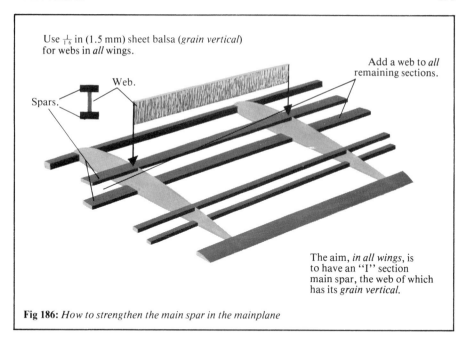

Use $\frac{1}{16}$ in (1.5 mm) sheet balsa (*grain vertical*) for webs in *all* wings.

Web.

Spars.

Add a web to *all* remaining sections.

The aim, *in all wings*, is to have an "I" section main spar, the web of which has its *grain vertical*.

Fig 186: *How to strengthen the main spar in the mainplane*

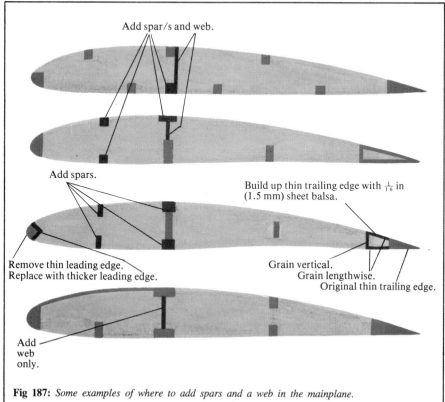

Add spar/s and web.

Add spars.

Build up thin trailing edge with $\frac{1}{16}$ in (1.5 mm) sheet balsa.

Remove thin leading edge.
Replace with thicker leading edge.

Grain vertical.
Grain lengthwise.
Original thin trailing edge.

Add web only.

Fig 187: *Some examples of where to add spars and a web in the mainplane.*

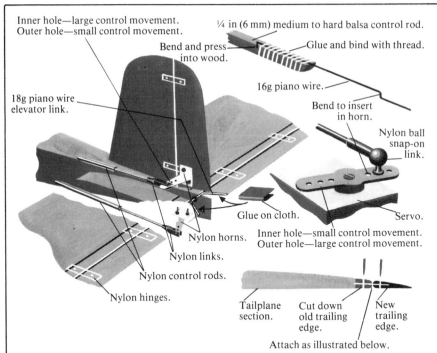

Inner hole—large control movement.
Outer hole—small control movement.

¼ in (6 mm) medium to hard balsa control rod.

Bend and press into wood.

Glue and bind with thread.

16g piano wire.

18g piano wire elevator link.

Bend to insert in horn.

Nylon ball snap-on link.

Glue on cloth.

Servo.

Nylon horns.

Inner hole—small control movement.
Outer hole—large control movement.

Nylon links.

Nylon control rods.

Nylon hinges.

Tailplane section.

Cut down old trailing edge.

New trailing edge.

Attach as illustrated below.

Fig 188a: *Tailplane and rudder alterations for small models*

In all models, because the speed with the motor working is high, the pressure exerted by the controls is high. Therefore, for your first flights, have the rudder or elevator move only about ⅛ in from the neutral position (the model will react too violently if you have more movement on the rudder or elevator), until you have learnt to control the model.

Remove covering entirely, carefully cut through frame, and add two medium to hard spars. *Cover, and fuelproof,* then add hinges.

Use control links and horns as in illustrations above.

Toothpicks.

Nylon hinges from hobby shop.

Section through tailplane.

Slit spars for hinge. Insert hinge. Pierce spar and hinge. Push in ends of toothpicks, and cut off flush. Coat with fuelproofer *on toothpicks only.*

Do the rudder the same way as the tailplane.

Note *Do not* get dope or fuelproofer in the gap *after* installing hinges.

Note 'V' cuts to avoid tailplane and rudder interference.

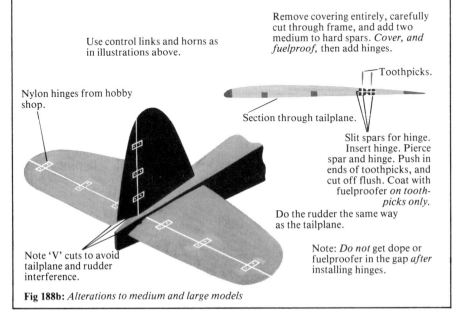

Fig 188b: *Alterations to medium and large models*

Small models: elevator and rudder

The tailplane needs a small elevator on small models (30-40 in span) (76.2 cm-101.6 cm). The trailing edge should be cut down to about half its width, and the elevator is a new trailing edge attached with either cloth hinges, as in control line models, or with hinges that can be bought from your shop. These latter should be attached as shown, as also the control horns, nylon links, and the pushrods. When making up the control rods, and connecting them to the servo and to the control surface, be sure you *do not* have metal to metal pushrods and horns, and that a metal part is not rubbed by a metal pushrod end, especially if you decide to make these small parts yourself. If you keep this kind of thing to a metal pushrod end working in a plastic (nylon) control horn, that is fine, but never metal to metal. Do the same for the rudder.

Medium and large models and scale models: elevator and rudder

On medium and large models, the size of the elevator should be about $\frac{1}{3}$rd of the chord from the trailing edge, and the rudder in line with the elevator line, if possible. If not, then make the rudder about the same proportion as one elevator half. Remember that either the elevator must have a cut-out for the rudder, or the rudder must have a cut-out for the elevator. In either case it will mean that two spars must be fitted along these cuts and the hinges attached. On scale models of any size, these controls can be as on the full size aircraft, that is, you should use the same elevator line, and the same rudder line, as the full size aircraft used.

Fuselage

The fuselage is next. On small models the cabin sides, from the nose to the wing

Mark in a straight line down the side of the fuselage, where the control rods will fit. From the centre line of each former, work out, on each former, how far from the centre line the control rod will be. (All this can be drawn in on the plan, using the side and top view.) Connect this mark with the mark on the fuselage side. Drill the holes for the rods at these points of intersection. Test fit the rods. (*Do not* glue them yet.) Fit receiver, batteries, servos as Fig 191.Mount the servos on the hardwood rails, connect the rods to the servos, rudder, elevator, and motor (where used).Test the servos and control surfaces for *smooooth* action. Make all adjustments to this whole set-up until smooth action is obtained, then glue the outer cases of the rods to the formers.

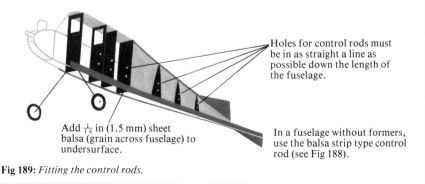

Holes for control rods must be in as straight a line as possible down the length of the fuselage.

Add $\frac{1}{16}$ in (1.5 mm) sheet balsa (grain across fuselage) to undersurface.

In a fuselage without formers, use the balsa strip type control rod (see Fig 188).

Fig 189: *Fitting the control rods.*

trailing edge, should be covered with $\frac{1}{16}$th in (1.5 mm) soft sheet balsa. Medium to large models should use $\frac{1}{8}$ in (3 mm) sheet for the same addition. As the top front surface of the fuselage is usually covered, leave this, and cover the under-surface of the fuselage with sheet balsa, $\frac{1}{16}$ in (1.5 mm) for small models, $\frac{1}{8}$ in (3 mm) for medium and large models, from the tip of the nose to the tip of the tail, and should have the grain of the wood running across the length of the fuselage. If you can arrange it, leave the top of the fuselage open to get at the receiver, batteries, and servos. If this is too awkward, then cut a hatch in either the undersurface, or one side, for the same purpose, and ensure that the hatch can be securely closed with screws. The charging jack point and the on/off switch should be placed on the opposite side of the exhaust outlet. Do not cover

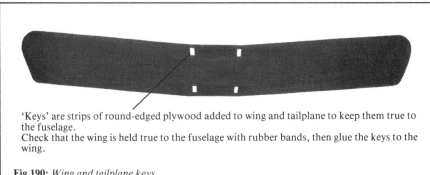

'Keys' are strips of round-edged plywood added to wing and tailplane to keep them true to the fuselage.
Check that the wing is held true to the fuselage with rubber bands, then glue the keys to the wing.

Fig 190: *Wing and tailplane keys*

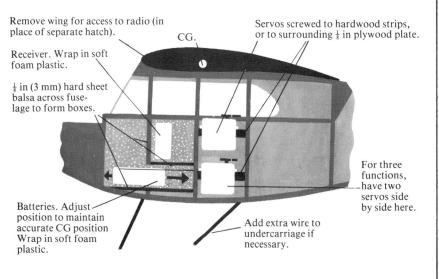

Remove wing for access to radio (in place of separate hatch).

CG.

Servos screwed to hardwood strips, or to surrounding $\frac{1}{8}$ in plywood plate.

Receiver. Wrap in soft foam plastic.

$\frac{1}{8}$ in (3 mm) hard sheet balsa across fuse-lage to form boxes.

For three functions, have two servos side by side here.

Batteries. Adjust position to maintain accurate CG position Wrap in soft foam plastic.

Add extra wire to undercarriage if necessary.

This is a guide only as all models are different. The main idea is to have all the weight centred around the CG, the batteries being movable until the CG is right, then pad them into position.

Fig 191: *Where and how to install the radio*

the fuselage until after the radio has been installed, together with the servos and links to the elevator and rudder, and all have been tested for perfect working.

Controls

Make sure the controls work very freely, but are not sloppy. They must be perfect. On small models, the amount of movement of the surfaces can be small, about $\frac{1}{8}$ in (3 mm), either side of neutral is sufficient to start with. Medium and large models can use about $\frac{1}{4}$ in (6.3 mm) movement to start with, and on all models the fin and tailplane should, ideally, be glued to the fuselage. If not, then be very sure to 'key' them, so that they always have the same settings, and the bands holding them in position should hold very firmly, they should not budge when in position. The wing too, should not move, even slightly, from its proper position, and here too, it should be 'keyed' to the fuselage, to keep the wing dead square to the fuselage. Add in a platform for the receiver, allowing extra space for soft plastic foam to wrap around the receiver, and a compartment for the batteries. A firm platform should also be made for the servos, and allowance should be made for a 'clunk' tank to be fitted if you have a fairly large model. This saves having to land, every few minutes, to 'fill her up'.

Radio installation

Install the radio as indicated in the diagrams (ask your dealer to explain it if you are in any doubt) and, after testing that the installation works perfectly, fix the aerial down the fuselage, or out to one wingtip. Cover the sides of the fuselage, on medium and large models, with soft $\frac{1}{8}$ in (3 mm) sheet balsa. Small models can have the paper, silk, solarfilm (or similar), or soft $\frac{1}{16}$ in (1.5 mm) balsa sheet covering, if the model is anything up to about 40 in (101.6 cm). Be careful to keep all the wiring neat, and, above all, make sure it does not flop about; tape it in place using double sided tape (from your hobby shop). Nobody can afford to have the wiring broken through vibration, or a slight change in the CG position on any model. Use electrolube on the switch, and on plugs and sockets, to extend their life and cut down on 'electrical noise'.

Downthrust and sidethrust

As the wing is now operating at, or near, its maximum lift, it is a good idea to take out a little of the downthrust you needed for free flight (when it was not carrying the extra load of the radio). If, by some chance, you had no downthrust for free flight, even with the motor at full revs, then do not worry about it, just leave it as it is. If you had the thrustline set for a slight turn, then you must guess how much to take out, so that the model will fly straight under full power. This will be a very slight adjustment, and can be done with the string to propeller tips and tailskid, or rear of rudder, measurement. Set the motor over, so that the out-of-square measure is cut in half. You may have to do this again, after the first flight, to get it absolutely right, as it is impossible for me to foretell what exactly will happen to your model. However we will be pretty close with this adjustment.

Propeller balance

The propeller needs to be thoroughly balanced if you have not done it before, because with the motor running flat out most of the time, any slight imbalance will cause a continuous vibration which will soon break the wiring, loosen joints, and wear out the motor very quickly. Altogether not worth it! Your hobby shop has the special shaft for balancing the propeller size you are using on this model.

Carburettor
Some motors can, and some cannot be fitted with the special carburettor for motor control. It is not really necessary, as you can fly without motor control, but it is a lot more fun if you can fit one. Discuss this with your hobby shop as motors are all different, and you should know what can, and what cannot, be done with your particular motor. These people are very helpful, and will give you any amount of advice for your motor, and its link-up with the radio.

Starter spring
If you are using a motor with a starter spring, do not remove the spring for starting, you will always need it, as not all separate electrical starters will get the motor to start, but the spring works 100 per cent if your motor is clean, the fuel has always been filtered, and you know your needle valve settings. If the fuel is dirty, then even a good starter will not get it to work. Nothing will, until you clean it, and the tank, out properly. Naturally, if your battery is flat, or the plug is dead, or the cylinder head is loose, you will not get the motor to start. First rectify these before blaming the 'wretched' motor. The spring will start the motor, on the first or second flip of the propeller, every time.

CG and warps
The rest is very simple. Before you go out to try it, there are a few things to do. Back to base one, and that means check that there are no warps, anywhere, except for equal slight 'washout' at the tips, and that the CG is exactly where it was before.

Chapter 15

Flying by radio control

Control practice

Run the motor, and check that, if you have motor control, the motor responds to the radio correctly, that flat out the motor does not misfire, especially when you raise the nose to point up to about 90 degrees, return it to horizontal, and the motor can hold low revs again without misfiring. Next test the control of the rudder, it must come back to neutral when you centre the stick; the same applies to the elevator, and also check that the deflection of the rudder is the same to both sides. The elevator can have slightly more 'up' than 'down' movement, but not the other way around. Now tether the model by its tail, and weight the tail down, otherwise it may tip on to its nose, and practise the controls on the ground with the motor running, to get used to the noise, and the amount of movement of the stick that is necessary to give a very slight movement to the controlled surface. If you have elevator control, leave this control alone, and concentrate on the rudder only. The whole idea, of course, is to practise as far as possible on the ground, before doing anything wild in the air. When practising the rudder on the ground, be sure to start by standing behind the model, practising the thought of left turn, right turn, and then do the same thing standing in front of the model. Yes! You will have to be on your toes, as this is the difficult part, knowing when to put the stick over in the same direction as the turn, and when to put the stick over in the opposite direction to the turn. Do not think you can do this any old time, and rush off to get the model up in the sky! Just practise it for a couple of minutes, and then stop. Switch off the motor and the radio. Pack it all away. Leave the batteries on trickle charge. Then set it all up again in the afternoon and see if you can get it right without a mistake. If you cannot, and, usually you will not, it only means that you need more practice, until you can get it right without a mistake. In the air you simply cannot make mistakes, your first mistake is your last. OK? Right, then practise until your eyes fall out. You can now, at this stage, practise an occasional up elevator and down elevator, but notice that it makes no difference where you stand. The same applies to motor control. See the point of it all now? It is simply to make all your mistakes, and learn to rectify them, before flying.

Rudder only control

Assume now that you are over that bit, and you have the model all checked, and the radio all checked, and you are out on the field ready to go. This is a calm, windless day. The first thing to do is test glide the model as usual, making any adjustments to get the glide straight this time, there must be no turn at all, and no tendency to stall or dive, perfect in fact. What you have here is a free flight model with one control. This is a lot better than no control. It means that you can bring the model, more or less, to where you want it in the sky, and you can bring it in to land very near to where you stand, and you can even do a stunt or two with it. When you have had no control before, that is a huge extra to be thankful for. One thing all these models can do, which the hot stunt model could never even dream of doing, is to make use of thermals for soaring flight. All you have to do is get the model up very high, and learn to search for, find, and stay in the thermal for real fun. Now this model can be hand launched or, if you have a smooth flat space, you can let it take off. OK. Let's start it up (if there is a slight breeze face the model directly into it), let your friend hold the tail for take off, get the motor up to full revs, and then, very slightly close the throttle, to just below full revs. Stand directly behind the model, check that it is facing directly into the breeze, and give the rudder a last check, of left, right, and back to neutral. Leave the stick centralised, set your mind on the rudder, and signal 'let her go'. Your friend must just let go of the tail, he must not push it. So off it goes, and all you have to do is watch very carefully, and not use the rudder unless the model begins to veer off to one side. Then your control must be used, and this is entirely up to you. Keep the model straight into the wind, until it has climbed up to a good height. If it shows any tendency to rear up and

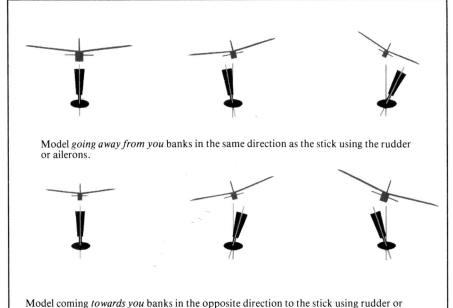

Model *going away from you* banks in the same direction as the stick using the rudder or ailerons.

Model coming *towards you* banks in the opposite direction to the stick using rudder or ailerons. (To recover from the bank illustrated, push the stick towards the 'down' wing.) Learn to use slight movements for power models, and towline gliders on the tow, as the speed is high, and a slight movement is all you need at first.

Fig 192: *Learn the rudder and stick movements thoroughly (See under gliders).*

stall, then kill that stall with a bit of rudder, put in, and returned to neutral, put in, and returned to neutral, to ease the model into a slight turn. If your model 'kicks' sideways, when you give it a touch of rudder, then try moving the stick only half the distance, and hold the position a little longer. Try to keep the movement of the stick smooth and even, rather than a quick jerk, sort of squeeze it over, and back to neutral. Now do the same thing again, but for the opposite turn. This will have the model climbing in S turns, into the wind. *Never*, on your first flights, hold the rudder over to one side, or the other, for too long, as the model may turn too quickly, and if you try to rectify this with opposite rudder, the model may start to swing, from left to right, too rapidly for you, and the result can be disastrous. Let it go right on climbing, until it is well up, but keep it, with those 'quick blips' of rudder, upwind from your position. When it is well up, let it do what it wants to for a couple of seconds, and study its flight, to see if it needs a bit of downthrust to kill a stall, or sidethrust to stop any circling. If you have trim on your transmitter, then use it to get the model flying as straight as possible. Now, instead of letting it wander about the sky in an aimless way, try to steer the model in a large square to your left, with the one side of the square coming straight towards your position. This last section will be the landing approach after a 'circuit'. A few times around will be all you will manage, before the motor cuts, so keep the square about 50 yds, or metres, on all sides. When the motor cuts, and the model is still high up, then try to do this

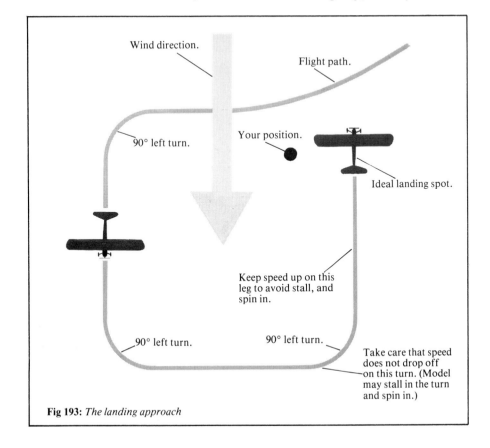

Fig 193: *The landing approach*

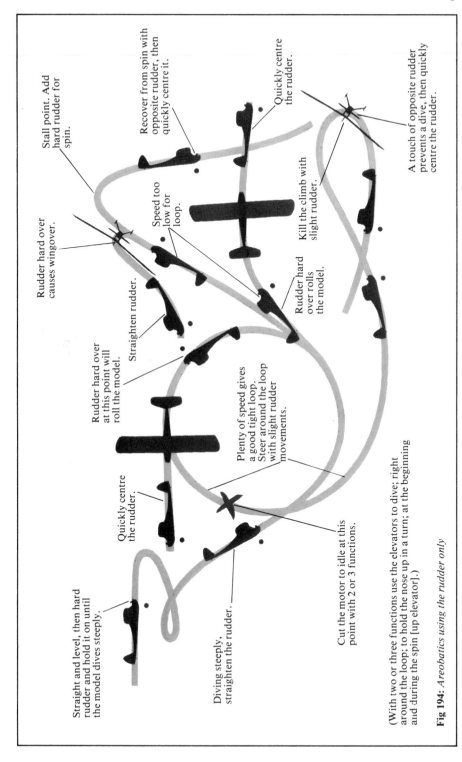

Stall point. Add hard rudder for spin.

Recover from spin with opposite rudder, then quickly centre it.

Quickly centre the rudder.

A touch of opposite rudder prevents a dive, then quickly centre the rudder.

Rudder hard over causes wingover.

Speed too low for loop.

Kill the climb with slight rudder.

Straighten rudder.

Rudder hard over rolls the model.

Rudder hard over at this point will roll the model.

Plenty of speed gives a good tight loop. Steer around the loop with slight rudder movements.

Quickly centre the rudder.

Straight and level, then hard rudder and hold it on until the model dives steeply.

Diving steeply, straighten the rudder.

Cut the motor to idle at this point with 2 or 3 functions.

(With two or three functions use the elevators to dive; right around the loop; to hold the nose up in a turn; at the beginning and during the spin [up elevator].)

Fig 194: *Areobatics using the rudder only*

square circuit, so that, on the last section, the model is gliding straight towards you (into the wind), keeping it in a straight glide until it lands. Simple, and very relaxing, once you get the hang of it, and always fun. Stunts are a bit limited, in that all inverted flight is not possible, and on some models rolls are also difficult, if not impossible. This is the case when a model has very pronounced dihedral; the less dihedral it has, the easier it is to do a roll.

Two functions (rudder and throttle)

Here, you have virtually the same as above, except that you can, at take-off, leave the model at your feet with the motor on idle, and take off entirely by yourself. Just open the throttle, and off she goes. When it is up to height, you can throttle back to cruise, or glide in a gentle dive (with idle, which is a little faster than power-off glide), and then open up to flat out to get the model to pick up speed in the dive, and build up excess speed, to go up and over in a loop. Cut the power to idle as the model begins to descend. You may have to help it a bit for the dive, by adding a touch of rudder, as for rudder-only control. It depends on the power the motor has for that particular model. The other lovely bit is when you throttle back to idle, and let the model glide down. At a certain point in the glide, you ease the throttle open a touch, and the model slowly levels, but is still sinking down until the wheels touch, and the model is running along the ground with the tail up, then add power for an exciting 'touch-and-go'. Tricky, but a lot of fun. You can also land from this glide, but the power should be above the idle, so that the model is in a very shallow glide, and the approach is from quite far out. Another thing you can do with this approach, when about 2 or 3 ft (60.9 cm or 91.4 cm) from the ground, is to add a touch of throttle so that the model maintains height, and you can then indulge in some exciting low flying. Be very careful though, that you do not fly smack into someone, or something, or snag a wingtip on the ground in a turn. *Never* do this anywhere near people, as some spectators have been killed; do it in the wide open spaces where all you can lose is the model.

Two functions (rudder and elevator)

In this case, of course, you have no throttle control, but elevator instead. This means that for take-off, you can use a touch of up elevator to get off more quickly, and hold this on until the model is well up, then return it to neutral. Steep dives should not be prolonged, because you have the motor going flat out, and so the speed builds up very quickly, and on the pull out the wings can fold up. The same thing can happen from the top of the loop, where the model enters the dive with full power. When it reaches the pull out at the bottom of the loop the speed is excessive, and the wings can give way.

Turns are easier than they are with two functions of rudder and motor control, because you can give a touch of up elevator on the turn to hold the nose up. Landings too, are a real joy, as you can level the model out just above the ground, and then slowly ease the stick back, so that it does the old fashioned three-point landing.

Three functions (rudder, elevator, and throttle)

All of the above and more. At take-off you can use a touch of up elevator to get off more quickly, and hold this until you reach a good height, then ease forward to neutral, and ease back on the throttle. The elevator adds easy climb and dive when you want it, and also when doing a turn you can keep the nose up with a touch of up elevator. Some models bank over more than others, and if yours does this, and you want a steep bank, then, as you give more up elevator (this will tighten the turn), you should, at the same time, turn the rudder in the opposite direction very quickly. This 'top rudder', as it is called, will now be holding the nose up! Your motor should be flat-out. To recover from this: at the same time, stick forward, and opposite rudder, then reduce the throttle. You have to watch this very carefully, as the recovery can look very sloppy if you get the timing wrong. With elevator too, the loop and some other manoeuvres become a lot simpler, because the initial dive is done directly with the elevator, and so the model does not lose a lot of altitude to gain speed for the stunt. The landing approach should be straight into the slight breeze, if any, nose down in the glide until just above the ground. This last bit, you will find, has to be done with quite large movements of the stick, because flying speed is reduced in the glide. At about 3 ft above the ground, start easing the stick back, so that the model is level with the ground, and hold it with the elevator in that attitude, and it will simply sink gently down, down, until the wheels are running on the ground. Make any adjustments to the thrustline to cure any faults of the power on flight. These adjustments must be very slight. If you had to add a bit of down trim to the transmitter when the model was flying on full power, then add a very little downthrust, and remove the downtrim. The same method should be used for any turn that had to be trimmed out. Simply reset the side thrust slightly. What we are aiming for, is that the model must fly straight and level with full power and the stick in the dead centre, or neutral position; only then is it fully trimmed.

Four functions (rudder, elevator, ailerons, and motor)

When you reach this stage, then the best thing to do is to build a model designed specifically for four functions. But a word of warning—if you have skipped the above two, or three function stages, then you are asking for trouble, unless you

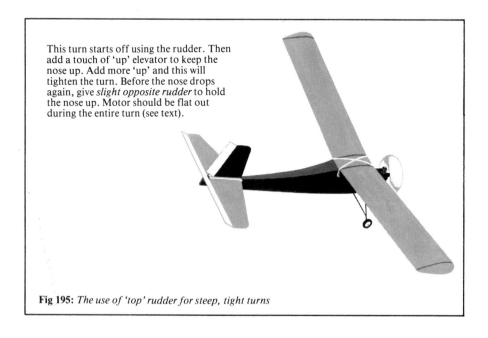

This turn starts off using the rudder. Then add a touch of 'up' elevator to keep the nose up. Add more 'up' and this will tighten the turn. Before the nose drops again, give *slight opposite rudder* to hold the nose up. Motor should be flat out during the entire turn (see text).

Fig 195: *The use of 'top' rudder for steep, tight turns*

have a very competent flyer of radio models to help you (although even they can come unstuck on occasion, like we all do), and a novice by himself is doomed to failure.

This new model is quite a bit different from what you have had until now. It is more powerful for its size and weight, and therefore it will fly and react to the controls faster than your previous model. It will not glide as far as the other model, nor as slowly, and it will stall quickly if you let the speed drop too much; this usually happens somewhere on the landing approach. So keep your speed up when landing, and *never* try to 'stretch' the glide, either, when landing. It will nearly always do a snap roll, and dive, right before your eyes, if you do. It is better to look silly, and let it land a hundred yards from you, than try to 'get it in' to the landing area. This nearly always happens if your motor cuts out unexpectedly, and you are forced to glide in 'dead stick'.

This model with its lack, or near lack, of dihedral will bank very easily, and so you have to be on your toes from the moment it leaves the ground until it is well up. You have to fly the model the whole time it is in the air, unlike the other, more stable, converted free flight models you have been flying up to now. So I must assume that you have trained yourself to this stage and you are ready for this last bit, then the addition of ailerons is simple to cope with. Let us start at the take-off. You have checked the controls, the motor does not cut with the model held at 90 degrees at full revs, and it will come down to a good idle. Set it to face the slight breeze, and with full throttle, concentrate on the rudder only to keep it straight on the run. As it gets to flying speed give it a touch of up elevator, and hold that while it climbs, using small touches of aileron to keep the wings level. (Where you used the rudder, on a rudder only model, you are now using the ailerons.) Get the model well up, and then neutralise the elevator, for level flight. Now try a turn. Where you used the rudder before, to control a turn, you now do it with the ailerons. Ease the ailerons over gently for a left bank, only a little bit, and almost at the same time ease the stick back a bit, to keep the nose up. Just hold it all like that, until the model is facing back towards you, let everything back to netural, then give a slight squeeze to the opposite aileron to get the wings level again. Let it go over the top of you and away a bit, and try that turn again. Now try the 'landing pattern' as you did for single function, and try throttling back slightly but keeping a good height, passing directly over-head into the wind. Throttle back to about half, and make a 90-degree left turn across wind, and put in a touch of down trim. Do another 90-degree left turn, letting down to about 50 ft (15.3 metres), followed by another 90-degree left turn across wind at a height of about 20 ft (6.1 metres), taking care the speed does not drop off in the last 90-degree turn, to face in to the wind and heading straight towards you. Get the speed up a bit if it wobbles, open the throttle slightly and keep it moving, and keep the wings level. When it is about 2 or 3 ft (0.6 or 0.9 metres) from the ground, be ready for any gusts, and start easing in a bit of up elevator, slowly at first, and then gradually faster as the model begins to settle. Try to hold the model from rearing up at the point where you apply the elevator, by holding the stick steady for a second, and then progressively faster back on the stick, until it lands, and keep the stick like that to the end of the run. Steer the run on the ground with the rudder. The landing is always the part where you should be very watchful, and with your throttle ready to give full power to help you out of any tricky situation that may develop. Try to judge the last part of the approach, so that the model is gliding with its nose well down. If you cannot do that for any reason, then be sure to 'come in' with a bit of power and speed, to avoid a stall. You can cut back to idle just before you apply up elevator, and the model begins to sink.

Aerobatics

Now you can take the model up to a good height, and try a few aerobatics. First, a stall. Get the model in front of you, into wind, and ease the throttle back to idle, gently easing the stick back, in one slow continuous movement. Watch the model, and gauge the stick movement, from it. Get the model to about 45 degrees, and wait until it begins to 'mush' forwards, using the rudder to keep the wings level. To recover: at the same time, down elevator, and open the throttle wide. If, at this stage, the model falls into a spin, cut the throttle to idle, centralise the elevator and wait a second, to see if it will recover by itself. If not, then apply full opposite rudder, and as soon as the spin stops, centralise the rudder quickly. Pull out of the dive gently, with up elevator, and ease up in a long curving climb, giving full throttle at the beginning of the climb to regain altitude.

Spins are brought about by doing a stall, with motor throttled back to idle, and holding full up elevator. Wait until the model is vertical, then hold it like that, with the elevator central, and keep the wings level with the rudder. Just before the model stops moving, give full rudder, left or right, and hold the rudder, together with full up elevator, and hold this too. Recover as above, but centralise the elevator first.

Loops are straight and level into wind with full throttle, and you should give up elevator. Steer the model straight with the rudder all the way around the loop. Cut the throttle to idle when the model is at the top of the loop. When it is level again, quickly return the stick to neutral, and open the throttle for a dead level recovery.

To do a roll: get the model dead into wind, straight and level, then raise the nose very slightly, return elevator to neutral, and put the aileron stick hard over to the left or right. Give a touch of down elevator, when the model is upside-down, and instantly return to neutral. When the wings are level again, instantly return the ailerons to neutral. Use full throttle for the entire stunt. If the model gained height, or veered to one side, you gave too much down elevator (gained height), or it was too late, or early (veered to one side).

Inverted flight is the same roll and elevator timing, but you should centralise the ailerons when the model is inverted. Hold the nose up with a touch of down elevator. To recover: add more down elevator to raise the nose, centralise, and hard over on the ailerons to right side up and level. Quickly return the ailerons to neutral.

There are quite a few other stunts to be learned and they are worked around these basics. All you ever need, when working out a new one, is plenty of height, and the knowledge, and practice, of all of the above stunts.

Gliders

Thermal soarers are lightly constructed, so that they can easily be lifted by weak thermals. Their main ability is to circle tightly in a thermal, in order to utilise the lift available from small or weak thermals. They therefore have quite a bit of dihedral and high lift aerofoils, and the wing, which is set at a positive angle of incidence, is about twice the length of the fuselage, and has a high aspect ratio. Aerobatic slope soarers have very little dihedral, if any, and usually a symmetrical aerofoil section set at 0 degrees angle of incidence, to allow easy inverted flight. These models have ailerons, and are capable of more aerobatics and higher speeds than thermal soarers.

Gliders need only one or two functions for thermal soaring, or slope soaring, if stunts are not the main aim. In this case, stunts being the object, I would recommend you go for the slope soarer. Learn to fly with one or two functions first, using only the rudder and elevators, which are quite simple to learn even though you are new to it all. As under 'Control Practice', practise with the model on the ground, using the rudder and elevator, until you have the hang of it, then try the model in the air. Also, if you are converting a free flight model, do the same test using the Plasticine weight to determine the weight of the radio the model will carry comfortably, and strengthen the wing and fuselage in exactly the same way. Then, as above, go through the whole test flight schedule before towing the model up.

The test gliding is extended by learning to use the radio at the same time. Switch on the transmitter, and then the receiver in the model. Holding the transmitter in your left hand, launch the model by hand, as you have just been doing. Now, while the model is still gliding, try a very gentle left or right turn, just ease the stick over very slightly, and then instantly over to the other side, and back to neutral. That is about all you can do in one hand-launched glide. Keep right on practising this shallow flight, with turns done very gently. As the model is going away from you, and you are only using the rudder, you should have no trouble at all in learning. You may find that your model tends to swoop up (when you give it too much rudder it will turn, dive, pick up speed, and swoop up). When this happens, give it a touch of down elevator while it is swooping and, as soon as the nose is down just below level, put the elevator back to neutral. Let the model settle down to a steady glide, before you use the controls again. (You are doing all this over long grass aren't you? It does save your model from getting bent). OK, just keep right on practising—it will take a bit of time to get the hang of it. Then practise it all again tomorrow, and the next day, and so on, until you can do it, and get the model to do exactly what you want, and can bring it to earth really gently, and not stick its nose in the ground, or stall it. Now you can throw the model slightly up, with quite a bit of energy, at about a 10 degree angle, and while it is going up, give first a touch of down elevator, to level the model high up (about 10 ft (2 or 3 m) above your head height). Learn to fly it down, either straight ahead, or in slight gentle turns, until you can do it well. Learn to do fairly steep turns (not too much at the beginning), until you have it taped. If you have been practising all this with a friend, and he has learnt to glide the model as well, and learnt how to throw it properly, then it is a good idea to get him to launch the model towards you now. Let him make the first few glides gently, because you will be practising how to push the rudder stick towards the 'down' wing to correct a turn now. (When the model is going away from you, you correct the turn by pushing the stick towards the 'up' wing). Yes, this is the tricky bit. Think about it! Then do it, and practise until you can fly the model well either way. (That static ground practice did help didn't it?) Also, remember that down elevator is down, no matter which way you face; it is the rudder that has to be thoroughly learnt.

If you have only single function (rudder only), on your first tow try not to use the rudder until the model is well up. If you are forced to use it, to correct a strong turn, then remember to use very slight amounts of rudder movement because the high speed of the launch makes that large rudder very effective, and you can quite easily over-control, and have the model swinging wildly from left to right, or worse, it can swing right around and *wham*!

The same applies to two or more functions on towline gliders. With elevator control on a model though, you should put in a touch of up elevator when the model is about to be launched, and hold this on until the model is at the top of its climb, when you give a touch of down elevator to get it off the hook quickly and cleanly. Of course, the same advice for the rudder holds true here as well as for single function.

Your first tow should be fairly slow, with the model up to only about 50 ft (15.3 m), because it is quite difficult, on your first flight, to get it down in one piece. If you get the model too high you will find it disorientating when the model starts to move rapidly in all directions, whilst you are trying to keep track of which control to use, and how. The best way is to keep the model in front of you, and heading straight into wind, for the entire flight. When it is near the ground, *ease* in a bit of up elevator, to get the model nearly level to the ground, and hold it in that attitude, until it sinks to the ground. Keep right on practising, with this short tow, and the model kept straight into the wind. When you have this well and truly mastered, and the short tow as well, then give the full length of line for the tow, to get the model high; bring it around behind you, then keep it into wind, so that it again lands upwind from where you are. Practise this for a short while, until you can really handle the model properly, and not feel that disorientation any more.

If you are using one function only, and the model shows a tendency to stall when flying free, then put it into a gentle turn, to get rid of the stall. Correct this stall, with a minute addition of weight to the nose, but the model should still have a very slight stall left in, which should disappear with the gentlest of turns. This set-up will allow it to 'float' in the weakest thermal.

Thermals are quite easy to spot, but not easy to stay in. You can see the effect of one on the model's flight because, as the model passes through one, the whole model rises bodily upwards. If one wing should pass through it, you will see the wing get 'kicked up'. The trick now, is to circle back to that spot, by turning towards the wing that was affected, and continuing to circle that area in fairly wide turns, until you spot where the thermal is, then turn the model as tightly as you can, to keep it in the thermal. Once in it, keep the model turning tightly as she goes up. Don't get too carried away, otherwise you may have trouble seeing it, to control it out of the thermal.

To get a single function model out of a terrific thermal (especially if you are beginning to lose sight of it), simply put on full rudder and hold it on, until the model is spinning or spiral diving down to a manageable height, then give full opposite rudder to stop the spiral, and instantly neutralise the rudder. As the model will tend to zoom up again, kill the climb with another spiral dive, and so on, until the model is well clear of the thermal. Just remember to keep it moving away from the thermal, in as straight a line as you can manage, and it will eventually come out.

Two function models are simply put into a straight dive, leading away from the thermal. If, when you level it out, you see it is still going up, then simply repeat the straight line dive again, until it *is* clear of the thermal. In both cases, you will see when the model is not moving upwards, and that is when you have it out of the thermal.

Chapter 16

Motors

Buying your motor

Your motor should be purchased after you have decided on the type and size of model you prefer, because the motor will be specified on the plan. If you do not like the motor called for, then be very sure you get one of equal power, and always insist on it being in an unopened box or container. *Never* accept one that has been opened, no matter what is said, or what the price may be. All motors in their unopened containers have not been fiddled with, and possibly damaged, such as having the needle valve bent, or strained, or having the motor dropped on that hard floor. Also, if the container is very crushed or dented, do not take it, it may have been dropped, or squashed under something heavy.

While you are shopping, collect the correct fuel, 'free flight' propeller, or the largest propeller for that motor, and one or two spares, fuel tank and correct size fuel tubing, battery and leads, the correct size mounting bolts and nuts plus a few spares, a small shifting spanner for the nuts and propeller nut, a screwdriver to fit the bolts, and a drill for the size of bolts. You also need a piece of plank ½ in (12.7 mm) thick, 4 in × 6 in (10 cm × 15 cm)—pine or mahogany will do. Do not use obeche or jelutong, they are not strong enough.

On opening the carton, check that all parts, backplate, cylinder head, plug, and carburettor, are tight. If you do find something loose, do not tighten it too much, just make sure it is firmly held in position. Use the shifting spanner for this, never a pair of pliers. These can slip very easily and burr a part, which will then be even more difficult to tighten in the future. *Keep the carton and the instruction leaflet.*

Mounting the motor

Cut the plank for beam mounting, and drill the holes, being careful to ensure the drill is vertical. Bolt the motor to the plank, and mount the plank in a vice. If you are using a separate tank, be sure to have its mean level in line with the needle valve, and as close to the back of the motor as possible. Double check that you have the correct fuel, and fill the tank. Double check your propeller size, then fit it to the crankshaft. Turn the crankshaft anticlockwise to the beginning of compression, and turn the propeller until one blade is at '2 o'clock', then tighten the nut firmly (not too tightly). Place newspapers behind, to protect the wall from oil splatters. Exhaust fumes are extremely bad for you, so open the window and door very wide.

Top: Fig 196 *Mount the motor on a plank (cut an oblong slot in the plank end) and mount in the vice as shown. Note the angle of the propeller when tightening the nut. (See text.)*

Above: Fig 197 *One flick of the propeller starts the motor. You should practice here, at the vice, until you can do it every time you try to start the motor. It's easy if you follow the method in the text. Try it!*

Starting the motor

Before we begin, let me say that when I have seen modellers trying, and failing to start a motor, the fault has been with the modeller (usually twirling the needle valve in a haphazard way), and not with the motor! The motor is very precisely made, and when properly set up to start it does so instantly. Human beings are, generally, very sloppy in their methods, and have to learn to be very much more precise. So, when it comes to your motor, you will have to drop any sloppy habits, and learn to adjust it properly. This will involve very accurate settings of the needle valve, and in the case of the diesel, the compression lever. Then too, there are all the other things to remember, like keeping it all clean, especially the fuel and the way you transfer it to the tank, and seeing that the leads from the battery are always in good shape, etc. So, with your motor, learn to be as 'unsloppy' as you can. Besides that, you should, at the same time, learn to 'feel' what should be done at any stage, using your instincts to help you—it is half the fun!

What does a diesel, or glowplug motor, need to make it run? The simplest possible answer is that they only need fuel, air (oxygen), and a heat source. If you provide these in the right amounts, your engine will run. In both cases, the carburettor supplies the fuel and air in the right proportions (if you adjust the needle valve correctly). The glowplug motor must have the plug and battery to supply the heat, to burn the fuel. The diesel motor has to have its compression adjusted correctly (by you), to supply the heat to burn the fuel.

Now, whether you know all about motors, or not, *you must read the pamphlet, or back of the carton, that comes with the motor.* It tells you all you have to know about the motor—the correct fuel to use, the right size and pitch of propeller for the various applications, the correct setting of the needle valve (you cannot do this by guessing), and in the case of the diesel, just how to set the compression lever (you cannot guess this one either). So, if the instructions tell you to open the needle valve, say $2\frac{1}{2}$ turns, it means exactly that, not 3 or 4, or

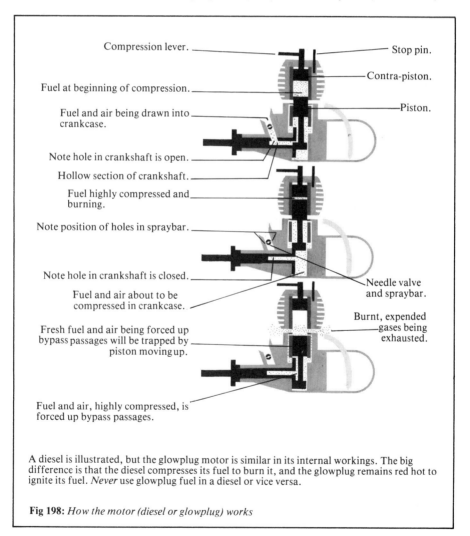

Compression lever.

Stop pin.

Contra-piston.

Fuel at beginning of compression.

Fuel and air being drawn into crankcase.

Piston.

Note hole in crankshaft is open.

Hollow section of crankshaft.

Fuel highly compressed and burning.

Note position of holes in spraybar.

Note hole in crankshaft is closed.

Fuel and air about to be compressed in crankcase.

Needle valve and spraybar.

Fresh fuel and air being forced up bypass passages will be trapped by piston moving up.

Burnt, expended gases being exhausted.

Fuel and air, highly compressed, is forced up bypass passages.

A diesel is illustrated, but the glowplug motor is similar in its internal workings. The big difference is that the diesel compresses its fuel to burn it, and the glowplug remains red hot to ignite its fuel. *Never* use glowplug fuel in a diesel or vice versa.

Fig 198: *How the motor (diesel or glowplug) works*

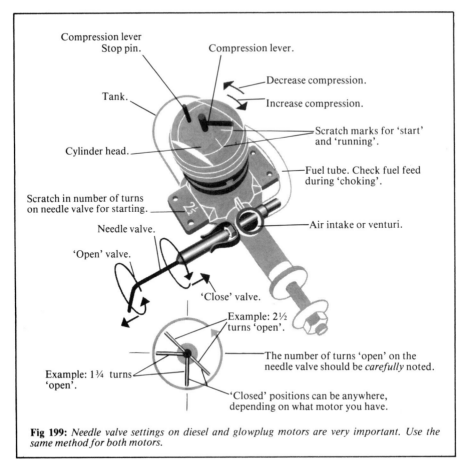

Compression lever
Stop pin.

Compression lever.

Decrease compression.

Tank.

Increase compression.

Scratch marks for 'start'
and 'running'.

Cylinder head.

Fuel tube. Check fuel feed
during 'choking'.

Scratch in number of turns
on needle valve for starting.

Needle valve.

Air intake or venturi.

'Open' valve.

'Close' valve.

Example: 2½
turns 'open'.

The number of turns 'open' on the
needle valve should be *carefully* noted.

Example: 1¾ turns
'open'.

'Closed' positions can be anywhere,
depending on what motor you have.

Fig 199: *Needle valve settings on diesel and glowplug motors are very important. Use the same method for both motors.*

any other guess, but $2\frac{1}{2}$. If you use fuel that is not mentioned, or a size of propeller that is not mentioned, then you are on your own, and good luck to you. So to begin with, stick religiously to what it tells you, and you will not go far wrong. Some pamphlets also include a section on curing faults which is well worth reading and remembering.

The carburettor

This, in both the diesel and the glowplug motor, serves the same purpose, and that is to draw in fuel and air, and mix these in the right proportion for that motor. To do this means that the fuel is varied in proportion to the air, by the needle valve setting. This is a very precise measure, and so the manufacturer has worked out exactly what this must be for the motor you have—hence the need to set that needle valve properly to start with. Turn the needle valve right in (not too tight), and note its position carefully. Now turn it anticlockwise (to open it), noting exactly how many turns you give it from its original position when it was closed. If you are in doubt, as to how many turns you have given it, then wind it in again, and start over. You *must* get it right!

To 'choke' the motor means that you place one finger over the air intake tube, and then turn the propeller over compression. Be careful here that you do not leave your finger on the tube after going 'over compression', as the piston can force air and fuel back into the fuel line in the form of bubbles, and you can mistake this for a leaking fuel line. This choking action draws fuel through the tube from the tank, into the carb, and then into the crankcase. While doing this you should note the fuel flow in the tube. There may be one or two small bubbles in the tube but there must not be a continuous row of them, as this means that there is a leak somewhere, and air is getting into the fuel at this stage. This will only cause you untold frustration, so remove the tube when this happens, and replace it with a new one.

To 'prime' the motor means that you put a drop of fuel into either the venturi (air intake tube), or the exhaust port. (Some motors do use both, and they will tell you when to do this). Then start the motor straight away, because the longer you leave the prime, or choked fuel, the more some of the ingredients will evaporate, and starting becomes difficult. You should never have to keep on priming or choking the motor to get it started. When this happens, you should look for some fault, either on the motor, the fuel, battery, or in your starting technique.

All the above applies to the diesel and the glowplug motors, but, from here on we will separate the two.

Diesel motors

In this type of motor, the compression lever lowers, or raises, a contra piston in the cylinder head, which varies the compression, and this varies the combustion space, which has to be correct to cause the fuel to burn. If the lever is wound clockwise, the compression is increased, and anticlockwise it is decreased. In a new motor you will find, generally, that the lever has been set at the factory for starting, so make a note of exactly where that lever is pointing, and do not move it! At this point, let me say that if you have to increase the compression at any stage, before the motor is started, be careful that you do not flood the cylinder at the same time, as this can cause an 'hydraulic lock' (the propeller cannot be turned easily, and feels as if it is jammed.) If you force it to turn, you will probably bend the conrod. In this situation, decrease the compression by about $\frac{1}{2}$ a turn, blow hard at the exhaust ports to clear the excess fuel, and then try to turn the propeller gently. Proceed cautiously until the motor fires, or the 'lock' decreases. Do not be alarmed if you hear a sharp 'click' at this point, it is just the contra piston being pushed up.

Follow the advice on the pamphlet exactly for the prime, or the number of turns on the propeller, for the choke. Set the needle valve exactly, and with the compression lever in the right place, proceed to flip the propeller, or use the starter spring. If the motor runs and dies out, it is starving, so open the needle valve about $\frac{1}{8}$ of a turn, and try again. If it vibrated heavily and stopped with a shudder, it was slightly over-compressed, so release compression by about ¼ of a turn, but leave the needle valve alone. Before restarting, note if the exhaust is wet with fuel. Turn the piston up until it is level with the exhaust port, and blow hard to clear the excess fuel. Try to start it again. As soon as it fires, slowly raise the compression again if the motor is running in spurts, (a sort of 'brrrrp, brrrrp, brrrrp'), until it runs smoothly. Now turn the needle valve in slowly, until the motor runs fast and smoothly. *Note how many turns the needle valve was opened to start the motor, and where it is now.* You may find that you had to turn it in, say $\frac{1}{2}$ a turn, to its present position. Make a note of this, and when you run the motor again, check this, as it is the vital information you need to be able to start, and run, your motor very quickly at any time.

If you keep on trying to start, and the motor does not even 'pop', then check that there is fuel in the line, and in the tank. (Starting can, on occasion, use up a lot of fuel). Check the needle valve setting (do it again if the motor refuses to start), compression setting, backplate, and cylinder head for looseness. (Never overtighten these, they should be just tight enough not to be easily moved). All OK? and it still refuses to start? Then increase compression by about $\frac{1}{8}$ of a turn, and try again. If, after a number of tries, the motor still refuses to fire, then increase compression by another $\frac{1}{8}$ of a turn, and so on, until it does fire. But be very careful that the motor is getting sufficient fuel during all this, and keep an eye open for the 'hydraulic lock'.

If fuel is not being drawn into the cylinder (with the needle valve open to the correct setting, and you are choking it correctly), then there is probably a blocked jet. Remove the tubing from the carb, unscrew the needle valve right out, and carefully unscrew the nut on the spraybar, and remove it. Clear the tube, and the holes, using a piece of very fine control line wire, or better still, a piece of stiff nylon fishing line. Check the fuel is clean (filter it through a clean stocking if you are in doubt about its cleanliness), the tank is clean, and the fuel tube is clean. Reassemble the spraybar, keeping the holes horizontal, and gently tighten the nut (not too tight), and replace the tube and the needle.

When the motor fires, and the propeller goes backwards and forwards, it is getting a fraction too much fuel, and the compression is too high. Back off the compression lever, about $\frac{1}{3}$rd of a turn, until the motor either runs properly, or stops. Check the needle valve setting if it stops. Blow out the excess from the exhaust, and try again.

When you have the motor running properly, then continue to turn the needle valve in (noting the number of turns), until the motor begins to cut out, or cuts out completely. That is as far as the needle valve can be turned in. Take a note of the number of turns this takes, because you will want to avoid this particular point in the future.

When you go out flying, first let the motor warm up a bit, especially in cold weather, then adjust it to peak revs, using first the needle valve, and then the compression, then readjust the compression to a fraction below this point (less compression), and open the needle valve very slightly (richer). This is done because the motor will lean out, very slightly, when the model is flying. If you do not do this, and you try to fly with the motor set at peak revs only, you may find that the motor cuts out as you launch the model.

Glowplug motors

Here too, you will find the information, as to how much you have to open the needle valve, and how much prime, or choke, the motor needs, in the pamphlet. In the case of some motors that are packed in transparent blister packs, you will find the information on the back of the card. As this is vital information, do not throw the card away; you should keep it, as you never know how long you may leave the motor between times of using it.

So set the needle valve properly, prime or choke the motor, then connect the battery to the top of the plug (if you are using a 2v accumulator then make sure the lead is long enough to drop the voltage so that the plug glows red, not white or yellow), and straight away engage the starter spring, or flip the propeller over very smartly. Do not over-wind that spring, you will only weaken it, and it works extremely well if you do it properly.

If the motor does not fire after a few tries, then disconnect the battery first. (It goes flat far more quickly if you do not, and anyway it does not help to leave it on). These are the usual faults that occur: the fuel is not feeding through (check the tube and needle valve setting); the tank is in the wrong place; the plug is loose or damaged; the cylinder head is loose; the crankcase back cover is loose; there is too much fuel (blow out the excess from the exhaust) or there is too little fuel (needle setting is too lean); the fuel is dirty (bits of grit or grass caught on the tank filler); the battery is flat or the leads are broken or loose fitting; or the fuel has gone flat because the cap has been left off the fuel can.

Only connect the battery to test the plug. Check this by turning the propeller over until the piston is in line with the lower lip of the exhaust port, and see if there is a red glow on the piston when the battery is connected. Check the battery is not flat if the plug does not glow.

Should the motor run, and then die out, open the needle valve $\frac{1}{8}$ of a turn and try again. After several tries, and the motor continues to die out, then open the valve again by $\frac{1}{8}$ of a turn and try again several times. Continue this treatment until it does keep running. Note the position of the needle valve, then slowly turn it in until the motor runs smoothly. Restart it on this new setting to check that it is correct.

If the motor has a very wet exhaust, and will not start, then close the needle valve $\frac{1}{8}$ of a turn, and blow out the excess fuel from the exhaust. Try again several times, and if it still has a wet exhaust, and will not start, repeat the process. When it does start, and continues running, note the position of the needle valve, then slowly turn it in until the motor runs smoothly. Restart it on this new setting to check that it is correct.

If you have to run the motor in for a certain period, then be sure you are doing that with the correct fuel and propeller. Once you are over that bit, then learn to throttle the motor down to low and medium revs, so that you *know* how to handle it for various applications. At the same time, practise starting it for really quick starts, like about two or three flicks of the propeller from a cold motor. Learn also to start quickly when the motor is still hot, again taking only a flick or two of the propeller to get it going. This ability to get it running quickly is very important if you are thinking of going in for competitions, but it is also important if you do not, because there is nothing that can frustrate you more than getting to the flying field and then sitting there for hours, flicking the propeller, with absolutely no joy from the motor at all. Practice running it while it is in the model, not on the bench. Once in the model the motor sometimes seems to have a will of its own, and you just have to get to know it all over again.

Well that's the story of aeromodelling, but let me repeat what I said at the beginning of the book. Model aircraft are *not toys*, as you will by now appreciate, and also what I have given you is just the beginning, although it is sufficient to enable you to fly your model. If you find that you are stuck at any time, why not simply go back and find the answer somewhere in the book.

See you on the flying field!

Index

Other PSL books for modellers...

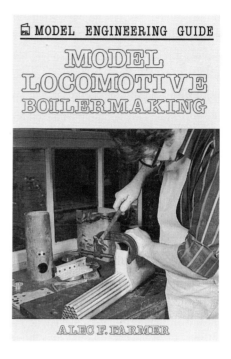

Modelling Ships in Bottles

Jack Needham. Constructing model ships in bottles is an art that has intrigued the 'non-initiate' for centuries. In this delightful book Jack Needham shows, with the aid of many clear photographs and diagrams, that the principles are in fact very straightforward and that no 'cheating' is necessary. In addition to basic information on masts, rigging, hulls, researching etc. he also includes fascinating novelty projects—such as putting a mermaid in a bottle! He demonstrates that beyond a few simple tools and materials all the successful modeller requires is care, patience and a steady hand. Now, with the aid of this book, *you too* can become a 'master shipbuilder'.

Model Locomotive Boilermaking

Alec Farmer. In well-illustrated, step-by-step instructions the author explains the process of constructing a model coal-fired locomotive boiler, from the selection of tools and materials, through the working of the metal, to the testing of the finished job. As well as being a satisfying project in itself, boilermaking also provides plenty of opportunities for improving general model engineering skills. Alec Farmer draws on his many years of practical experience to create an invaluable guide to this absorbing craft, highlighting the pleasures yet at the same time warning where the problems may arise and advising how they can be avoided.

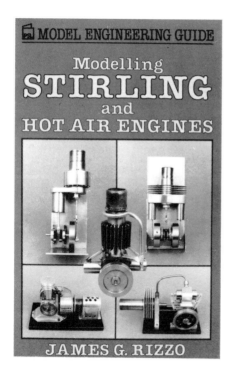

Modelling Stirling and Hot Air Engines

James G Rizzo. This book, the second of PSL's series of Model Engineering Guides, describes not only the components of a typical hot air engine but also explains how model engines of varying degrees of complexity may be constructed from essentially scrap materials. The evolution of these engines from the early machines of the Rev Stirling is described, and concepts such as pressurisation and the measurement of engine parameters introduced. Model engineers of all levels will find this well illustrated book is valuable not only for its individual projects but also for its thorough analysis of these often under-rated but attractive and practical engines.

Introducing Benchwork

Stan Bray, prize-winning modeller and former associate editor of 'Model Engineer', describes in detail the tools required and all the processes likely to be involved in any benchwork project. Includes: the bench itself; interpretation of drawings; cutting and filing metal; bending and threading; adhesives and fillers. With his many years of model engineering experience, Stan Bray has many a wrinkle to pass on to beginner and old hand alike. Over 200 photographs and diagrams.